IN BLACK AND WHITE

The Publications of the Southern Texts Society

IN BLACK AND WHITE

An Interpretation of the South

BY LILY HARDY HAMMOND

edited, with an introduction, by Elna C. Green

The University of Georgia Press

Athens and London

Publication of this book was made possible in part by a grant
from the Watson-Brown Foundation.

© 2008 by the University of Georgia Press
Athens, Georgia 30602
All rights reserved
Set in Minion by Bookcomp, Inc.
Printed and bound by Thomson-Shore
The paper in this book meets the guidelines for
permanence and durability of the Committee on
Production Guidelines for Book Longevity of the
Council on Library Resources.
Printed in the United States of America

08 09 10 11 12 C 5 4 3 2 1

08 09 10 11 12 P 5 4 3 2 1

Library of Congress Cataloging-in-Publication Data
Hammond, Lily Hardy, 1859–1925.
In black and white : an interpretation of the South / by Lily Hardy
Hammond ; edited, with an introduction, by Elna C. Green.
p. cm. — (The publications of the Southern Texts Society)
Originally published: New York : Fleming H. Revell Co., c1914.
Includes bibliographical references and index.
ISBN-13: 978-0-8203-2982-6 (hardcover : alk. paper)
ISBN-10: 0-8203-2982-7 (hardcover : alk. paper)
ISBN-13: 978-0-8203-3062-4 (pbk. : alk. paper)
ISBN-10: 0-8203-3062-0 (pbk. : alk. paper)
1. African Americans—History—1877–1964. 2. African Americans—Southern
States—Social conditions—20th century. 3. Southern States—Social
conditions—1865–1945. 4. Social movements—Southern States—History—20th
century. 5. Women, White—Southern States—Political activity—History—20th century.
6. Social gospel—Southern States—History—20th century. 7. Liberalism—Southern
States—History—20th century. 8. Progressivism (United States politics)—History—20th
century. 9. Southern States—Race relations—History—20th century. 10. United
States—Race relations—History—20th century. I. Green, Elna C. II. Title.
E185.61.H22 2008
973'.0496073—dc22   2007031018
British Library Cataloging-in-Publication Data available

Contents

Introduction to This Edition

ELNA C. GREEN

My first encounter with Lily Hammond's *In Black and White* was through Anne Scott's pioneering book *The Southern Lady*. Scott, who later noted her "accidental discovery" of *In Black and White*, placed Hammond in the foreground of southern white women of "advanced thinking" at the turn of the century. Recognizing the subversive nature of Hammond's work, Scott imagined the impact it had on Lily's southern white neighbors.[1] A few years later, while still in graduate school, I ran across Lily Hammond once again, in John Patrick McDowell's book on Southern Methodist women and the social gospel.[2] That book served to ground Hammond firmly in the women's missions movement in the New South. She stood at the confluence of the early-twentieth-century movements called "progressivism" and the "social gospel," reform efforts that scholars often treat separately but in which Hammond and other Southern Methodist activists engaged jointly. I thumbed through *In Black and White* and read another of Hammond's published essays, but thought little more about her at the time.

Then, more recently, I stumbled onto Lily Hammond once more, this time through her engagement with the Southern Sociological Congress. My research had by then turned toward southern social welfare history, which had led me to the annual reports of this organization. I was intrigued to discover here yet another side of Hammond. Not only was she a racial liberal and an adherent of the social gospel, but she was also an expert in social welfare issues. I reread *In Black and White*, seeing in it far more than I had twenty years earlier. It was, as much as anything, a wide-lens plan for improving the South through a social welfare agenda, but one that refused to ignore racial inequality as did most contemporary southern welfare proposals. Now thoroughly excited about this multifaceted woman, I went looking for a biography of her, but came up empty-handed. Somehow Lily Hammond had not found a biographer, and the more I learned about her, the more this fact perplexed me.

Many of Hammond's colleagues and coworkers have received scholarly attention as the field of southern women's history has blossomed in the last two decades. We now know much more about women's lives in the South, regardless of their race or class. We have learned a great deal about rural women, and even more about urban women. We have probably learned the most about women's organizations. But despite the outpouring of research on southern women, Lily Hammond has receded into brief footnotes, usually by scholars who have read *In Black and White*. This invisibility is mystifying, since Lily Hammond once stood as the intellectual center of the southern women's social reform and social gospel movements. The author of ten books and dozens of articles in regional and national venues, active in both regional and national organizations, Hammond was among the most respected leaders of her generation of southern women, yet today she is virtually unknown.

In the pages that follow, I have reconstructed Hammond's life and career from the limited sources available, placing her in the historical context of the New South, the social gospel, progressivism, and women's activism. I have also reproduced several of Hammond's shorter essays, which give some sense of the development of her thinking over time. The remainder of this volume is devoted to a new edition of *In Black and White*, originally published in 1914. My hope is that this project will help revive interest in Lily Hammond and reclaim a place for her in the inner circle of the South's white civil rights pioneers.

In one of southern history's many rich ironies, Lily Hardy Hammond—the South's most prolific female writer on "the race question"—was born in New Jersey and died in New York.[3] Despite these northern demographic bookends, Lily's genealogy gave her solidly southern credentials, which she would lean upon heavily in her reform work. Her parents, Henry G. and Huldah Hardy, were both originally from slaveholding families in North Carolina.[4] Born September 24, 1859, Lily was the fifth of their seven children, but the first born outside the South. (Her older siblings had been born in Virginia or North Carolina.) As an adult, Lily clearly identified herself as a southerner, and occasionally exaggerated her relationship to slavery. For example, she once wrote, "Memory holds in tender keeping many ebony faces and loving ministrations of those who never seemed slaves—only friends and playmates."[5] Yet Hammond would never have actually played with children who were then enslaved, having been born in New Jersey on the cusp of emancipation. This tendency to stress her ties to the Old South was undoubtedly an attempt to shore up any doubts about her "southernness," since southern whites were notoriously suspicious of so-called outside agitators. As she openly challenged southern racial conventions, she needed the protection afforded by the label "true southern womanhood" and worked hard to shore up that identification.[6]

Why her family had moved north on the eve of the Civil War remains a mystery. But whatever brought them north had, by 1870, situated them in Clarkstown, New York, some twenty-five miles north of New York City, where her father worked as a "broker."[7] Little information on Lily's childhood has surfaced, other than the fact that she was educated at the Packer Institute, a prestigious girls' school in Brooklyn. (Coincidentally, Mary White Ovington, one of the cofounders of the NAACP, also attended Packer, graduating several years after Lily.) Lily's education, of a quality far higher than that available to most southern women of her generation, influenced her in many ways, including giving her perspective later on the quality of the educational system in the South.

One very problematic source on Lily's early years is a peculiar memoir she published in 1916. Titled *In the Garden of Delight*, it purports to be a diary of a year she spent recovering from an unnamed but debilitating illness, filling her time by watching the birds in the garden. (Lily did indeed suffer from a serious health problem, as discussed below.) The surnames of individuals making appearances in the memoir were turned into birds as well: her husband was identified as John Bird, her cousin as William Wrenn, another cousin as Chad Grackle, a neighbor as Bob White, and so on. The account is frustratingly vague on details that would help confirm the events in the text, but in it she offers a narrative of her childhood.

In the Garden of Delight begins when Lily was a small girl, living with two maiden great-aunts, Letitia and Virginia, somewhere near the fictional village of Chatterton, Tennessee. Her parents never appear in the text; the reader assumes that they were deceased and that Lily had been taken in by relatives. Lily insisted that she disliked the pet names ("Lydia" and "Lyddie") family members used for her.[8] A fire destroyed the aunts' home when Lily was sixteen, and Virginia died shortly thereafter. Letitia decided to move them both to "the city" (never named, with a population of "tens of thousands"). There, she believed, her niece Lily would receive a better education and would benefit from the "progressive" urban climate.[9]

In the Garden of Delight does not mention a date for Lily's marriage to John "Bird," but it does relate that John's orphaned nephew, David, lived with the couple, as did great-aunt Letitia. Without David, she wrote, she and her husband would have been childless and would have grown old alone. Completing the household was elderly and devoted "Uncle Milton," a live-in servant formerly employed by Lily's great-aunts. Few other details of Lily's life emerge from the memoir, much of which was devoted to discussing the impending marriages of the next generation of her family.

The memoir is problematic. Information found in census reports and other reliable records contradicts many of its details. For example, from her birth until at least the 1870 census, Lily lived with her parents in New York, not with any great-aunts in Tennessee. The family had live-in domestic servants, but none of them was elderly like "Uncle Milton." By the 1880 census, Lily's mother had died, but her father was still living. After Lily married, she and her husband had three children. None of these facts seem to match the story in the memoir, so the "memoir" appears to be largely fictive, one of several pieces of fiction Hammond published in her lifetime.

Bits of information gleaned from other sources help reconstruct Lily's life story. In her book *In Black and White*, for example, Hammond describes how she first visited New York tenement houses and worked in an urban mission as a teenager (until her disapproving family put a stop to it). Her volunteer work in New York exposed her to urban ills and to urban reformers many years before most southern women of her generation. This background gave Lily an unusual combination of identities that would serve her reform career well: she held those much-emphasized southern credentials, including her family's past slaveholding, but she also was thoroughly familiar with urban life and the most advanced northern reform movements. She could speak with authority to audiences in both regions. Lily's experience in northern slums and the social welfare literature she read voraciously also prepared her to see social problems as the product of class-based poverty rather than race-based inferiority, a conviction about which she would write passionately for many years.

Another bit of biographical information comes from an article Hammond wrote for the journal *Outlook*, published in 1903. In the introduction to Hammond's essay, "A Southern View of the Negro," the editor noted that Lily had spent "twenty-eight of her forty-three years" in the South.[10] Thus, she had to have left New York when she was about age fifteen or sixteen (a chronology that does fit with the fictive narrative of her childhood in "Chatterton"). Extant records give no accounting of where she lived or what she was doing from then until her marriage at age twenty. In these years she might have gone to college or normal school, but, despite her substantial literary skills, no mention of any higher education appears in any of her writings. The four-year gap in her biography remains.

For southern women of Lily's generation, higher education would have been exceedingly rare. Southern states lagged far behind those in the Northeast in both the quantity and the quality of higher-education opportunities for women. As late as 1903, only two women's colleges in the South offered a full four-year degree, the rest being normal schools or "seminaries."[11] Southern families who desired the highest-quality education for their daughters had to be willing to send them north; a small but steady stream of southern women matriculated to Smith, Wellesley, and other northern schools. Families in the New South's emerging urban and industrial leadership, attempting to establish themselves as arbiters of the region's values, saw improved education for their daughters as one of the attainments that defined their class.

Lily Hardy came of age at a time when the New South's urban middle classes were competing with older planter interests to define the region's future. Industrial development, centered especially on cotton manufacturing, complicated class dynamics in the South as businessmen and manufacturers struggled to gain control over the region's political and economic institutions. Urban middle-class leaders, as part of their program of reshaping the South in their own image, rejected the violent racial politics of Reconstruction and called for an updated version of paternalism. The "better classes," as they called themselves, would take care of "the Negro question" without having to use violence. With the occasional cooperation of the "better classes" of blacks, these middle-class city dwellers would practice a modern noblesse oblige, which they believed would keep both the black and the white working classes under control without having to resort to the violence and illegal activity of the previous generation.[12]

An example of this cooperation between the better classes of both races was the temperance movement of the 1880s. In communities across the South, white reformers reached out to black reformers to work on local and state prohibition referenda. Needing the votes of still-enfranchised African American men to pass any prohibition proposals, white temperance leaders saw black women as a tool to garner those votes. Women served as the connection point between the two middle-class communities. The movement to abolish alcohol by referendum in Atlanta in the 1880s was remarkably interracial. One historian, writing in 1970, noted that the "campaigns of those years witnessed a degree of integration and free association which has rarely been equaled since." On election day in 1885 (the first of several attempts to restrict alcohol in the city), the Women's

Christian Temperance Union (WCTU) set up lunch stations near polling places, serving milk donated by Clark University students, with "substantial help from scores of Negro women."[13] In a subsequent election in 1887, the WCTU again set up a lunchroom near one of the polls, and "a bevy of dames of white and colored complexion served lunches to white and colored voters who wore the blue" symbol of support for Prohibition.[14]

A similar series of events transpired in Charlotte, another leading New South city. Beginning with a campaign in 1881, black and white prohibitionists joined forces. The men created an interracial organization, the Prohibition Association, and ran dry candidates for local office. The women organized separately, creating the Ladies Prohibitory Society for whites and the Colored Ladies Prohibition Association for blacks. Each worked separately for the same cause. A second referendum, in 1886, continued the biracial efforts, this time led by segregated chapters of the WCTU that had been established in the interim. While maintaining the separate organizational structure, black and white women met together more frequently in this second campaign.[15]

After yet another failed election, the city's prohibition movement began to disintegrate, but Charlotte's women continued their interracial efforts. Following the model of cooperation from the prohibition campaign, middle-class women of both races worked together to build hospitals for African Americans in the city. As Glenda Gilmore has noted, these agreements to work across racial lines did not imply a commitment to civil rights, to racial equality, or even to working together with civility. Nevertheless, this generation of middle-class women had launched a small-scale interracial cooperation movement long before men gave it a label and turned it into a regional organization.[16]

For many years, women's historians believed that black and white middle-class women's groups had operated so separately from one another that they were literally unaware of the others' efforts. But as the foregoing account of temperance campaigns from the 1880s makes clear, historians have since uncovered much evidence of women's interracial activities. Black and white women worked together in both religious and secular settlement houses, in efforts to build orphanages and reformatories, and in campaigns to establish free kindergartens and day nurseries. Although African American women might have had a different vision of these social welfare activities, their interracial nature was nevertheless quite real. Mary Frederickson has argued persuasively that these interracial activities were originally misinterpreted by scholars. Reading quite literally the contemporary accounts (mostly produced by white women), historians concluded that white women took the initiative in these encounters, reaching out paternalistically to help their unfortunate sisters. White women condescended to their black counterparts, who said nothing in order to continue the flow of resources that white women controlled. But Frederickson depicts this silence as a form of dissemblance rather than deference. "Black women took the position of endorsing an agenda created by white women . . . allowing white women to take credit for drawing up innovative agendas and progressive interracial programs." The ideas, however, often came first from black women, who approached white women's groups for help in implementing them.[17]

Thanks in large part to her marriage, Lily Hammond gained access to this quiet world of southern women's interracial activism just as it was germinating. In 1879, Lily married a Methodist minister, John Dennis Hammond. Born May 12, 1850, in Franklin, Georgia, John was the son of Dennis F. and Adeline Hammond. The elder Hammond was an attorney and slaveholder who moved his family to Atlanta around 1860, where John finished his secondary schooling. John graduated from the University of Georgia in 1870 and had just taken his first pulpit in Roswell, Georgia, when he was awarded a scholarship to attend Drew Theological Seminary in New Jersey. He graduated from Drew in 1875.[18] The first student from Georgia ever to attend Drew, John received there training far more liberal than he would have obtained at any southern institution, or for that matter at a large number of northern seminaries.[19]

How or where John and Lily met is not clear, but attending Drew put John close enough to New York that the meeting may have occurred during the years of his seminary training. After graduating, Hammond returned to Georgia and was assigned to several different pastorates over the next several years. At the time of their marriage in 1879, John served in Athens's Oconee Street Methodist Church.[20]

Being a minister's wife gave Lily an automatic position of leadership among local women in any community where they lived. Not all ministers' wives desired that role, but Lily clearly embraced it. Well-educated, extremely well read, articulate, and ambitious, Lily would use her opportunities to their fullest.[21] John's ministerial career may also have offered some impediments to Lily's ambitions. They moved so frequently that Lily sometimes had difficulty maintaining her positions of leadership in Methodist women's circles. In the first decade of their marriage, for example, they moved five times.[22] Lily frequently had to reestablish herself in the local women's organizations and work her way back up the ranks of leadership. Still, the itinerant life of a Methodist minister meant that the Hammonds would come to know leaders in communities across the South and would be able to use those ties in building their respective reform careers.

In 1886, the Hammonds were sent to Missouri, where John was initially assigned to pastor the First Methodist Church of St. Louis. Two years later, he was elected president of Central College, a Methodist institution in Fayette, Missouri[23] (the first of three separate college presidencies that John held during his career). Their children, Henry, Katherine, and Frances, were born in 1887, 1889, and 1893, respectively, during their tenure in Missouri. Remarkably, given the demands of household duties in a young and growing family, Lily launched herself into women's missions work and published her first essays on social reform and the social gospel during these years in Fayette.[24]

These early essays apparently caught the attention of the regional leadership of the Southern Methodist women's home missions organization. By 1895 Lily was appointed to the Leaflets and Education committee of the regional organization.[25] Lily's first publication, titled "The Parsonage and Home Mission Reading Course," was written on behalf of the committee assigned to create a reading course for Southern Methodist women. Lily explained the purpose of the course: "We want to know of everything that is being done in all the world to uplift the fallen, to better the condition of the poor, to bring the classes together, to make straight paths for stumbling feet, whether the work be for the physical, mental, or spiritual betterment of those who need it." She recommended (and probably had selected) two books for the initial readings: *Our Country*, by Josiah Strong, and *Applied Christianity*, by Washington Gladden.[26] Both writers were prominent within the social gospel movement.

The social gospel had been slower to penetrate south of the Mason-Dixon line, where evangelicalism held such powerful sway. Evangelical Protestantism focused on the salvation of the soul and the rewards of the afterlife and had rejected the role of good works in achieving personal salvation. As Lily Hammond herself noted, "I know the feeling is very strong in the South against any attempt at regeneration by man-made law instead of by spiritual processes" (60). But "socialized" churches—or "institutional" churches, as they were often called—had adopted the philosophies of writers such as Strong, Gladden, and Walter Rauschenbusch. One of the most important American theorists of the social gospel, Rauschenbusch argued that Christians had a duty to extend the kingdom of God to those on earth. Rather than individual salvation, the social gospel urged Christians to work for the salvation of society as a whole as a way to hurry to arrival of the kingdom of God.[27]

The social gospel encouraged Christians to focus on religious experience rather than revealed theology, an emphasis that appealed to many evangelicals.[28] Though few southerners stood in the vanguard of the national social gospel movement, still many in the region embraced the ideals of civic righteousness. And while Methodists held no monopoly on the social gospel in the South, they were "easily the most receptive" to the message of "liberal Christianity" in the South.[29]

Historians initially tended to underestimate the strength of the social gospel movement in the South, partly because they had focused too exclusively on men's activities. Ministers and theological writers left the most visible historical footprints, and when scholars looked for evidence of the social gospel in the South, they more easily found publications by ministers such as Edgar Gardner Murphy and Alexander J. McKelway.[30] The small number of southern churchmen to write such texts suggested a minimal acceptance of the social gospel in the region. But women were less likely to write theological tracts or serve as ordained ministers in this era, and therefore left fewer published—and easily recoverable—sources. Instead, evidence of women's social gospel commitments appear in more obscure sources: annual reports of women's missionary societies, minutes of women's temperance organizations, unpublished accounts from social workers, and other women's activities. As Mary Agnes Dougherty noted, the "essence of social Christianity" involved carrying out the gospel, not theorizing about it, and women were more likely to be activists.[31] We have only recently begun to recover and rethink this rich history.

Scholars also initially underestimated the influence of the social gospel in the South because of their unexamined assumption that the movement was restricted to the region's white churches. Parallel activities by African Americans seemed inspired by a desire for racial equality or class distinction, not by affinity for the social gospel. Several recent historians have challenged this view and have begun connecting African Americans to the social gospel movement.[32] Although African Americans may have resisted the label "institutional church," nevertheless they added to their church work day care centers, homes for the elderly, employment bureaus, and night classes. Black ministers such as Henry Hugh Proctor of Atlanta, Sutton Griggs of Memphis, and John Milton Waldron of Jacksonville, Florida, built socially oriented congregations in their respective cities. Black churchwomen such as Lucy Craft Laney, Lugenia Burns Hope, and Nannie Helen Burroughs all carried out their commitment to a Christian society through both religious and secular organizations.[33] As a result of these two new streams of interpretation, the South's social gospel history has begun to look much denser.

Although many southern whites may have resisted the social gospel's focus on this world rather than the next, they would not have been put off by the social gospel's approach to race. The social gospel in the United States was tinged with the nativist and racist ideas of the era, particularly in the writings of Josiah Strong, who perceived Anglo-Saxons to be the chosen people and America as the location of the coming kingdom of God on Earth. The most definitive statement of the precepts of the social gospel, the Social Creed of the Churches adopted in 1908 by the Federal Council of Churches, avoided explicit comment about race. Historian Paul Harvey has noted that southern social gospel supporters did not ignore race relations, but they were never able to reach a consensus on how to handle "the negro question." Focusing their energies on helping poor whites was easier, and perhaps as a result, whites who were better educated would improve their treatment of their black neighbors.[34]

Nor would most southern whites have found the social gospel offensive because of its views on women and gender. Social gospel leaders such as Rauschenbusch held negative views on feminism and the women's rights movement. Rauschenbusch in particular focused on the family as the cornerstone of a Christian society, and perceived contemporary changes in gender roles as a threat to the survival of the family. Although welcoming women's participation in the work of the church, he believed that all people should marry and that all women should become mothers, which translated to advocacy of public policy that would encourage the strength and stability of the American family. Woman suffrage was the only plank of the 1912 Republican Party platform that Rauschenbusch did not endorse.[35] Such opposition to changing gender roles made the social gospel a more comfortable fit in the conservative South.

Several scholars have argued that the social gospel was partly a response to the nineteenth century's feminization of religion in the United States. So thoroughly had women taken over the charitable and other evangelical activities of the Protestant churches by the end of the century that contemporaries began to criticize the church for failing to inspire men to similar devotion. William James was one noted critic, writing that the church had failed to present an ideal worthy of inspiring heroic manhood. The social gospel partly met some of these needs by offering men a vigorous, activist, religious role model. Women's organizations had focused on the needs of women and children, but the social gospel created new masculine activities that helped draw men back to the churches.[36]

While this gendered interpretation of the origins of the social gospel may be accurate, the muscular Christianity practiced by men involved with the social gospel did not appear to keep women away from the movement, and reform-minded women found strength and support in the social gospel's precepts. Frances Willard's famous "Do everything" motto drew upon her belief that alcohol abuse was the result of deplorable social conditions rather than individual moral failures. Under her leadership, the WCTU engaged the full range of social gospel causes.[37] Southern women followed suit. Baptist women's leader Fannie E. S. Heck "engaged in a whirlwind of charitable, reform, and missionary society activities" in North Carolina. Under Heck's leadership, Southern Baptist women expressed their approval of state legislation to limit women's working hours, and supported education, child labor restrictions, and racial uplift measures. Virginia's Lucy Randolph Mason read Walter Rauschenbusch and other social gospel theologians, and became convinced that being a true Christian meant pursuing social change. Her career in organized labor was an expression of her religious convictions as much as of her political convictions.[38]

The social gospel clearly had much in common with its more secular contemporary, the progressive movement. Both perceived unrestrained capitalism as the source of much human misery. Both movements had great faith in the voluntary efforts of individuals but eventually came to recognize the need for government action to effect and enforce many reforms. Both countenanced (limited) roles for women activists and women's organizations, and both found ways to avoid the entanglements of race, largely by focusing on class instead and hoping that this approach would eventually solve the South's racial problems. Lily Hammond and a handful of other racial liberals, however, would eventually come to reject that approach and insist upon a more direct attack on the South's racial codes.

Most women active in the Southern Methodist home missions movement identified with progressivism and the social gospel. Large numbers of activists were participants in both secular and religious organizations that promoted social reform. The Methodist organization's periodical, *Our Homes*, regularly featured articles that could just as easily have run in national progressive journals such as *McClure's* or *Harper's*. Essays on kindergartens, child delinquency, immigrants, and child labor, and Hammond's own essay on Southern factory conditions, demonstrate the easy intertwining of progressivism and social Christianity.[39]

Lily later reported that she gave many speeches and lectures in her years in Missouri,[40] but rural Missouri did not offer the vigorous reform environment that would give Lily a platform for larger public service. Nor did Macon, Georgia, where the family lived for two years in the 1890s when John was appointed president of Wesleyan College.[41] But her husband's ministry soon took them to a more promising location. In 1898, John was appointed the secretary of the Board of Education of the Southern Methodist church, a post he would hold for the next twelve years, a luxurious period of stability for a Methodist minister. The job moved the Hammonds to Nashville, one of the vibrant centers of Southern Methodism and a hotbed of women's activism. From this post, John and Lily would begin very active reform careers, which would bring each of them into positions of leadership in their respective circles. Both were soon embedded in a dense network of reform-minded southerners that stretched across the entire region.[42]

Nashville was the home of the Methodist regional conference, and important denominational leadership resided in the city. Leaders of the Methodist women's missionary organizations were required to live in Nashville, which was also the home of the conference's periodicals, the quarterly *Methodist Review* and the weekly *Christian Advocate*. The Methodist women's periodicals—the *Women's Missionary Advocate* and *Our Homes*, which merged in 1911 to become the *Missionary Voice*—were also based in Nashville, and their editors usually resided in the city.[43]

Nashville's Methodists eagerly sponsored educational institutions in their community. For the first forty years of its existence, Vanderbilt was under the auspices of the Methodist Episcopal Church, South. Also, after 1906, Nashville was the home of the Methodist Training School for Religious Workers.[44] The city's educational landscape was dotted with non-Methodist institutions as well, for both blacks and whites. Teacher training took place at Peabody Normal College, which in 1903 became the George Peabody College for Teachers. Baptists opened Belmont College in 1890. Three institutions for African Americans had been established in 1866: Fisk University (sponsored by the American Missionary Association), Central Tennessee College, and Roger Williams University. A decade later, Meharry Medical College began training African American doctors. In 1912, Nashville became the site for the new Tennessee Agriculture and Industrial State Normal School for Negroes (later Tennessee State University.)

Thanks partly to the presence of these black colleges, Nashville's economy produced a prosperous black middle class.[45] Like their white counterparts, black middle-class women created a busy world of social work. In the nonslave states, African American women had been running charitable and mutual aid organizations since the early nineteenth century. In the slave states, black women began building orphanages, hospitals, and other charitable institutions almost immediately after emancipation. Many of these efforts grew out of women's groups within the black churches. The first such organization in Tennessee was probably the Daughters of Zion of Avery Chapel, founded in Memphis in 1867.[46]

By Lily Hammond's generation, several black clubwomen had emerged as leaders in Nashville. The most prominent was Mattie Coleman. A native of Clarksville, Tennessee, Coleman graduated from Central Tennessee College and then from Meharry Medical College in 1906. She married a Colored Methodist Episcopal (C.M.E.) Church minister, worked as a doctor and a medical examiner, and was elected president of the Women's Council of the C.M.E. in 1918.[47] Nettie Napier and Minnie Lou Crosthwaite were also important figures in Nashville's black middle class. Napier, a graduate of Howard University and Oberlin College, was married to a prominent local banker and Republican Party activist. In 1907, she organized the Day Home Club, which operated a day nursery for the children of black working mothers. Napier was also active in the National Association of Colored Women. The wife of a local physician, Minnie Lou Crosthwaite became the first black teacher in the Nashville city schools in 1879. A graduate of Fisk's normal program, she later became an instructor there and helped establish the YWCA chapter at Fisk. Crosthwaite was also active in interracial cooperation efforts.[48]

Nashville's African American clubwomen were thus pioneering the same kinds of social reforms as their white counterparts. Although white women had several antebellum reform experiments, such as the School of Industry (opened in 1837) and the Protestant Orphan Asylum (established in 1845), the flowering of the white women's reform movement came after Reconstruction. One local example was the Polk and Scott Day Home, founded in 1886 as a day nursery for white children. Local branches of national women's organizations also formed. Nashville was the home of the first local chapter of the WCTU in the state, established in 1882.[49] Through the WCTU, many women were exposed to contemporary social issues in addition to temperance. As Hammond herself later noted, "Through this body Southern women took their first steps in organized service."[50] The state's WCTU worked to raise the age of consent, to establish a girls' reformatory, and to put police matrons in city courts. Nashville also had an active chapter of the YWCA, which established a boardinghouse for working women in 1911.[51]

From within this rich culture of voluntary associations, Lily quickly emerged as a leader in the world of Southern Methodist women's missions. The women's home missions movement of the Southern Methodist Church had in fact some of its earliest roots in Nashville, with the organization of the Woman's Bible Mission in 1874. This locally oriented group raised money for the church's foreign missions but also concentrated on visiting the sick and the poor in their own community. The first major project of the Woman's Bible Mission was the establishment of a home for unwed mothers, still a tremendously controversial effort in this era.[52] In 1893, Methodist women opened a city mission in Nashville that operated a kindergarten and a sewing school, in addition to holding Bible classes and revival services. Nashville's Methodist women pioneered in the creation of settlement houses, opening the first church settlement in the South, in 1901. The women's home missions movement spread rapidly across the region, and by 1908, almost sixty thousand Southern Methodist women had joined.[53] Lily Hammond was recognized as "among the first women of the Church to rally to support" the movement.[54] In 1898, the first year of her residence in Nashville, Lily was elected first vice president of the new Woman's Board of Home Missions. The following year, when the Southern Methodist women decided to establish a Bureau of Social Service, Lily was its first superintendent.[55]

While many reformers like Lily Hammond eagerly joined secular and religious organizations, some leaders of the Methodist home missions movement worried that the secular progressive movements might dilute the Christian activism of its women. They feared losing "the well-equipped women of the church" to the secular organizations.[56] The male leadership of the church could be even more hostile, arguing that Christians should not be "so absorbed in a Christless social service" or push the church into "all sorts of pretentious programmes of 'social betterment.'"[57] The Southern Methodist church would struggle for decades with the question of women's proper role within the denomination, and much of that debate centered on the social reform activities inspired by the social gospel.[58]

While the church debated the proper role for women, Lily Hammond and other Methodist women activists pushed ahead in their work and established themselves as among the most progressive elements in southern society in their generation.[59] Their concern for the poor—especially for poor women and children—led them to the child labor movement, the settlement house movement, the temperance movement, and other progressive causes. Their determination to meet the challenges of the social gospel led them to demand laity rights within their churches and voting rights in the secular world. They did not hesitate to work in ecumenical groups, as they saw "no denominational lines in our effort to reach the fallen."[60] Nor did they see themselves as bound by the region's Jim Crow practices; their conviction that God had placed no racial limitations on their activities led them to work on behalf of and in conjunction with African Americans in the South.

By the turn of the century, Methodist women's reform activism in the South had evolved along more professional lines. Mirroring trends across the country, voluntary charitable movements were abandoning older visions of "lady visitors" who distributed mostly good cheer, and instead were adopting casework standards and were expecting professional training of their workers. The Chicago School of Civics and Philanthropy (later part of the University of Chicago) and the New York School of Philanthropy (later part of Columbia University) set the gold standard for such training. Professional training programs in the South were smaller both in number and in size, but began to appear in larger cities such as Richmond, New Orleans, and Atlanta.[61] In Nashville, Methodists established the Methodist Training School, which tried to incorporate the most current ideals from the developing fields of sociology and social work. Their settlement houses, day care centers, and other social welfare institutions were frequently run by trained professionals rather than lay volunteers.[62] (The role of the volunteers became, increasingly, fund-raising.)

Again, Lily Hammond was well prepared to lead a movement focused on social welfare. She was deeply read in the transatlantic literature on the topic, and she quickly emerged as one of the South's leading female experts on reform policies and practices. She began a period of remarkable productivity, publishing essays in regional journals like the Nashville-based *Methodist Review* and in national venues such as *Harper's* and *Outlook*. She also wrote several review essays on new publications about social welfare topics. Lily became a conduit of ideas, funneling the most current thinking on social issues from across the Atlantic world into the homes of Methodist women throughout the South.[63] Lily's publications exposed women far from the centers of southern progressivism, who would not have had daily contact with settlement houses, visiting

nurses, and day nurseries, to the ideas and the projects of the generation's reformers. She also developed an extensive network of contacts across the region,
with leaders in a variety of movements and organizations.[64]

By the early 1910s, organized Southern Methodist women had embraced the
broad range of reforms that the social gospel endorsed. Many of these causes
had moved far from traditional religious concerns and into decidedly secular-
sounding issues. The Woman's Missionary Council supported protective labor legislation for women, occupational health and safety laws, old-age pen-
sions, workmen's compensation, collective bargaining, and a minimum wage.[65]
Such causes often required legislation rather than voluntary activism, moving
activists even further into the political arena. As Methodist women spoke in
increasingly political terms, the male hierarchy of the church grew more concerned about the direction their missions work had taken. The church would
move several times to reduce the autonomy of the women's organization.[66]

Although her interests covered a vast range of reform efforts, including housing and child labor, Lily increasingly came to focus her work on race. For many
southern white women like Lily Hammond, religious and reform activities gave
them unparalleled interracial contacts with black middle-class women. African
American schoolteachers, college students, and clubwomen were among their
close coworkers in the Bethlehem centers, free kindergartens, school betterment associations, and civic organizations. Learning early, as Will Alexander
later noted, to think of African Americans as human beings, this small group
of racial liberals developed a decidedly different point of view from the reign-
ing ethos of the South's leadership.[67] Lily Hammond was convinced that the
better classes of whites in the South were the key to improved race relations.
Whites needed to be educated about the problems facing African Americans in
the South. Educated, middle-class whites would be the force to moderate the
most virulent manifestations of racism. They—and they alone—had to power
to change racially discriminatory laws. The urban middle class especially set the
tone of race relations for the region, and women were the key to reaching the
middle class.[68]

Never the shrinking violet, Lily boldly shared these ideas about race, trying to
educate other southern white women about the problems of black women and
their families. She was convinced that southern whites knew very little about
the lives of their black neighbors. In the 1899 meeting of the Woman's Home
Mission Society, she "spoke commandingly" of the movement to help "women
of the negro race."[69] In April 1901, Lily was one of the three women who led the

effort to commit white Methodist women to the support of women at Paine College, a Methodist institution for African Americans in Augusta, Georgia. The Home Mission Society agreed to build an annex for women, and continued to support it for many years. Lily was a constant advocate of Paine College, and black education in general, for the remainder of her life.[70]

Already recognized as a regional leader, Hammond now moved on to a more national stage. In 1903, Lily published her first essay on race in a national journal. "A Southern View of the Negro," published in *Outlook*, succinctly summarizes her views in this period. Directing her message to a national rather than a southern audience, Lily tried to counter the evidence of rising racial discrimination and violence in the South with hopeful recent signs of "a large and growing class of Southern whites" who held more moderate views on race. She noted the white support of black education at Paine College and its importance in "sending out men and women of good scholarship and fine character to become leaders of their race as teachers, preachers, and citizens."[71]

In a second essay directed at northern audiences, published two years later in the magazine *The World To-day*, Hammond provided another optimistic assessment of the South's recent advances in education. She emphasized the South's commitment to education and reminded her readers that the South's poverty prevented the region from providing adequate schooling for either blacks or whites. She reported that "men of the New South . . . would do justice for justice' sake . . . but they also know that the public school education of the negroes is a matter of self-interest to the whites, a necessity if the South is to be commercially developed, or to remain a safe place of habitation for the whites. No republic can safely shelter masses of ignorant people, whether they are allowed to vote or not; and ignorance is none the less dangerous for being covered with a black skin." She ended the essay: "The outlook is full of hope."[72]

If her messages to the North during these years were pleas for patience and support, Lily's writings directed to southern audiences took the form of stern lectures. Whites' "present opinion of [blacks] is formed from its unsuccessful members," she argued,

> the shiftless negroes who pretend to furnish our unskilled labor, or who tramp in maddening procession through our kitchens. We know next to nothing of the life in home or school or church of the successful negro, whether skilled laborer, teacher, or preacher; the better the negro succeeds the less visible he becomes to the eye of the white man, while his vagabond brother quite fills our field of

vision. And yet it is in this withdrawal of the better negroes, in the still greater differentiation of classes in the race, that the hope of democracy lies. . . .

The true measure of the effect of education on the negro is his ability to create and maintain a real home; and it is just at the point where he is enabled to do this that he passes beyond our ken. Yet figures speak for him to some extent. The many millions of dollars on which the ex-slaves pay taxes, their increasing ownership of their homes and farms, and the increasing number of those who are able to maintain themselves by professional services to their own race, are proof patent that the educated negro is not a failure from either the personal or the national standpoint.[73]

Hammond's work was most controversial in the South, and she faced a wall of opposition. She and other white women who shared her views met with public hostility and private ostracism. In 1905, a Tulane University professor, William Benjamin Smith, condemned those who attempted to help blacks, who he argued were mentally incapable of absorbing an education. He suggested that a tighter enforcement of segregation in the cities would help rid the South of the race problem, "for there disease and death will do their deadly work." Smith especially condemned "this vision of a higher race stooping down with arms of love and lifting up the lower to its altitude . . . The higher race may indeed stoop down . . . but never to rise again."[74] Louise Young, a white woman eager to work with Methodist missions for blacks, accepted an offer to teach at Paine College and met with shocked disapproval by her family. They considered it disgraceful and said they would rather see her in the penitentiary than at Paine.[75] Bertha Newell, a leader of the Methodist women's interracial work in the 1920s, was married to a Methodist minister who did not "wholeheartedly endorse her work." She wrote privately that running "counter to public opinion" was difficult, but "hardest of all" was the opposition of members of one's own household.[76]

Other white southerners faced more dire responses to their expressions of racial liberalism. Latin professor Andrew Sledd had been forced to resign his post at Emory College in the furor over his 1902 article in the *Atlantic Monthly* titled "The Negro, Another View." Sledd had heaped denunciation on southern whites for the barbarity of lynching and suggested it was time to abandon the principle of racial inequality. Even though Sledd was married to the daughter of Methodist Bishop Warren Candler, Sledd's teaching position was quickly terminated, and he fled to the safety of graduate school at Yale after he was burned in effigy and threatened with tar and feathering. John Hammond futilely protested the case to Bishop Candler: "It will be a reproach to us as a church if we don't get him back. We need him more than he needs us, and we can't afford to stand before the world in the attitude in which his departure from Emory has placed us."[77] Sledd stood as an example of the limits of the region's tolerance for challenges to the rapidly advancing Jim Crow state.

Even outside the South, public expressions of racial sympathy were relatively rare. At the same time that Lily was publishing essays on race relations, many national journals were reluctant to do so. The *American Journal of Sociology*, for example, did not publish a single article dealing with race until 1901, and then waited more than four years to do so again.[78]

Although most southern whites probably found Lily's ideas repugnant, in Nashville she found a small but important circle of reformers who shared her progressive views on race relations. She was a close friend and coworker of Kate Trawick. Active in many of the same organizations as Hammond, Trawick was the wife of Professor A. M. Trawick of Vanderbilt. The Trawicks were leaders in the YMCA and YWCA movements, and Kate was widely known as a leader committed to extending the Y's benefits to black women.[79]

Lily also shared liberal views and friendship with Sara Estelle Haskin. After 1909, Haskin was on the faculty of the Methodist Training School in Nashville. Editor of the Methodist youth journal *The Young Christian Worker*, Haskin would also become a powerful force for the Bethlehem settlement house movement. ("Wesley House" was the name Southern Methodist women gave to their settlements for whites; "Bethlehem House" was the name given to their settlements for blacks.) Like Lily, Haskin combined her interests in Methodist missions and the YWCA. In 1917, when the Nashville YWCA began holding meetings for black workers at a local hosiery mill, Haskin conducted the meetings.[80]

Lily remained a central figure in this circle of race rebels until her health suddenly compelled her to withdraw from the work. In 1905, Lily became gravely ill. The exact nature of her condition was never described in any public documents, although the fact that she spent a lengthy period at the Steuben Sanitarium in Hornell, New York, suggests tuberculosis. The annual meeting of the Women's Missionary Society noted her absence: "Resolved, that this body express its regret at the absence of Mrs. J. D. Hammond from this meeting, and send the following message: 'Beloved, we pray that in all things thou mayest prosper and be in health, even as thy soul prospereth.' "[81] (Despite her absence, Lily was elected to offices and committees as usual during this meeting.)

The following year, still convalescing, Lily sent a message to the annual meeting, read to the assembly by her friend and colleague Tochie MacDonell. "When the board met a year ago I was looking forward to being at this meeting, well again, and doing my share of the work I love. Now I am saying 'next year' again, and with more reason, too. I am getting well, only the road is longer than I thought." In response, her coworkers sent word that "we miss the wise counsel and inspiring presence of our beloved Second Vice President, Mrs. John D. Hammond."[82]

The next year found Lily still in the sanitarium. She again wrote to the annual meeting of the Home Mission Society: "I am almost ashamed to say a word to you. I feel like an old cripple who hobbles out every time the army marches by and shouts, 'I'll be with you the next time!' until nobody believes it. But I will, I will. . . . My doctor used to look grumpy when I said home mission work, but now he owns up that I'll be at it again. . . . And I hope before the year is out to be a high and happy private in the ranks at West End Church, Nashville."[83] The imposed respite from her activism clearly was frustrating.

The gap in her published work in these years suggests that her illness did not permit her to write, and Lily's previously energetic publication record ceased temporarily. But her ardor for "the negro question" had not faded. From her hospital bed she still urged Methodist women to continue their support of Paine College:

> Dear women, while I am still an officer among you, let me say one word for something very near my heart. Some of you know how keenly concerned I have been from the beginning in our work for the negroes. When I was too little to understand how right it is, I always had to fight for the under dog; and the more I understand the spirit of Christ and the love of God, the more I feel that the greatest debt is to the neediest. . . . It is the Christian women of the white race who more than any other class can solve and dissolve the race problem, save our dear land from dishonor, and lift helplessness and ignorance into a new and hopeful life. Stand by our school at Paine.[84]

By 1910, Lily began returning to her work, publishing essays on social issues and attending meetings. The following year, John was chosen as president of Paine College, and the family moved to Augusta. The Hammonds' brief tenure at Paine had many ramifications for Lily's reform career, taking her out of the inner circle of leadership in Nashville and perhaps contributing to her reduced stature in the women's missions movement. But perhaps most importantly, the four years at Paine seemed to influence Lily's thinking on race relations. The Hammonds' years at Paine were stormy and ended painfully, and Lily's message and approach to reform shifted in these years.

A joint effort of the M.E. Church, South, and the C.M.E. Church, Paine was opened in 1883. Although its initial faculty and staff were all white, within a decade Paine had an integrated faculty and board of directors. As secretary of the Board of Education, John had spent many years advocating for increased support of Paine College and Lane College, the two Methodist schools for African Americans.[85] His impassioned pleas usually fell on deaf ears, however, as the leadership of the Southern Methodist church preferred to concentrate its resources on white institutions. As early as 1902, John began to sound resigned to the church's neglect of its avowed commitments to black education. "It is useless to go over the old argument in favor of these noble institutions," he wrote. "There is nothing to be added. But it is of the utmost importance that, if possible, the Church be induced to do all that it has long been convinced it ought to do. These schools stand as the solitary representatives of our missionary zeal for the negroes of the South."[86]

Southern Methodist women had taken a particular interest in the female students at Paine. In 1901, partly as a product of Lily Hammond's prodding, their Board of Home Missions decided to build an annex for women there. For many years afterward, they raised considerable sums to support the institution.[87] Hence Lily and John had years of experience with the institution before John was elected president of Paine in 1911.

Some of the Hammonds' difficulties at Paine stemmed from the ongoing debate in the South over the nature of black education. Paine had been established as an institution for the training of teachers and ministers. The original curriculum was "traditional," insisting on the value of Greek and Latin for the training of ministers. But during the 1880s and 1890s, the South had been swept up by the "industrial training" philosophy most associated with Booker T. Washington and Tuskegee Institute. The idea of industrial schools appealed to white southerners, who saw them as a way of ensuring a continuing supply of manual laborers. Northern philanthropists embraced the ideal as well and poured donations into schools run on the Tuskegee model.[88] Paine, envisioned as "Emory in ebony,"[89] tried to resist the move toward industrial training. Bishop Charles Galloway, a prominent Methodist supporter of black education, articulated it most clearly: "the rudiments of an education for all, industrial training for the many, and a collegiate training for the few who are to be the teachers and leaders of their people."[90] Despite the presence of such committed supporters, Paine found it difficult to resist the seductive call of industrial education. In the 1890s, under president George Walker, it added a cobbler shop, where the students learned a trade while repairing their own shoes. Other industrial programs followed.[91]

By the time the Hammonds arrived, the majority of students at Paine were in either the industrial program or the high school program. In 1912, only 9 of the 337 students were taking the full college curriculum (and even they were required to take courses in the Industrial Department.)[92] John Hammond was determined, however, to protect the programs of higher education intended to prepare black ministers, teachers, and other leaders. "We recognize," he wrote, "the need of the race for its own preachers, teachers, and literary men, as well as for its own public servants in the various professions. While we admit the great value of industrial training for the negro, we at the same time believe that the higher college and university training is of still greater value in the present state of his development, because his advancement cannot be secured without competent leadership from his own midst."[93] He did not attempt to dismantle the industrial program, but he refused to give in to further attempts to undermine the "liberal course."[94]

The Hammonds' residence at Paine meant that Lily now joined a select sisterhood of white women whose lives were tied to (and changed by) the region's black colleges. Mary DeBardeleben, who first worked at the Bethlehem House in Augusta, became a teacher at Paine College. Her contact there with "the better class of Negroes" was a life-changing event, pushing her to view her mission in new terms. Rather than trying to uplift African Americans, DeBardeleben came to believe that she needed to interpret "the new Negro" for white southern youth.[95] Louise Young, educated at Vanderbilt, Wisconsin, and Bryn Mawr, became dean of women at Paine College in 1919. She found herself "literally living in a Negro world" and felt transformed by it. (She later moved to Scarritt College, where she taught one of the earliest black history courses offered in a southern white college.)[96] Another example was North Carolina's Rosa Steele, whose life closely paralleled Lily Hammond's. Steele was the wife of the white president of Bennett College in Greensboro. A Methodist and a native New Englander, she lived in the college community surrounding Bennett, where the Steeles regularly dined with black friends.[97] Such white women, who lived with, worked with, taught, and socialized with middle-class African Americans, could not be accused of ignorance of the social work of these black women or of conditions in the black community. These women became the white leaders of the budding interracial cooperation movement.

From her new residence in Augusta and with renewed health, Lily now threw herself back into the work she loved. She renewed her home missions work at the local level and was promptly elected to the standing committee on social service of the Women's Missionary Society of the North Georgia Conference.[98] In 1913, she addressed the annual conference on the subject "Some of the Problems of the South." Describing Lily as "a veritable dynamic of power and inspiration," the annual report noted that her subject was "not always a popular one"; nevertheless, Hammond "moved upon the hearts of the vast audience as perhaps no other speaker."[99]

Lily and John continued to participate in the larger world of social gospel activism. They embraced, for example, the Southern Sociological Congress, organized in 1912. Religious and secular organizations sent delegates to its meetings, which brought together reformers from North and South to discuss social problems and their solutions. The most prominent figures in southern welfare and reform circles were members of the congress. Its historian has acknowledged that the long-term impact of the congress is unclear, since measuring changes in public opinion is difficult. But at a minimum the congress can be credited for promoting modern social welfare thinking, the organization of state boards of charities, and organized charities in the South.[100] At meetings of the congress, many southerners had the opportunity to hear for the first time leading regional and national reformers such as Florence Kelley of the National Consumers League, Julia Lathrop of the federal Children's Bureau, Hastings Hart of the juvenile court movement, and Alexander McElway of the child labor movement. As Ronald White has noted, the Congress "consistently included blacks within its program to a degree unprecedented in the South."[101]

The Southern Sociological Congress intertwined progressivism, racial liberalism, and the social gospel more clearly than any other organization. Social gospel advocates such as Walter Rauschenbusch and Charles Macfarland addressed its meetings. The SSC's statement of purpose echoed the "Social Creed" of the Federal Council of Churches.[102] It is no wonder that the Hammonds felt drawn to this organization. In its very first year of operation, John Hammond was on the Congress's standing committee on "Negro Problems." The next year, the meeting focused its entire program on race relations. Between three hundred and four hundred people attended the meeting in Atlanta, where Lily was one of the featured speakers.[103] Given the year before she published *In Black and White*, her speech, "The Test of Civilization," was something of a dress rehearsal for the ideas of the forthcoming book. "Our problem is not racial," she argued, "but human and economic. The coincidence to so great extent in the South of the poverty line and the color line has confused our thoughts; we hold the negro racially responsible for conditions common to all races on his economic plane."[104]

From their posts at Paine College, Lily and John now received wide recognition as experts on race relations and were invited to speak at numerous conferences and meetings. John was a speaker at the Negro Student Christian Conference held in Atlanta in 1914. This interracial conference, organized by A. M. Trawick, included speeches by Booker T. Washington, Robert Moton, Lugenia Burns Hope, and James McCullough. The conference, which published a book of its proceedings, has been considered an important early step in the direction of an interracial cooperation movement.[105]

Lily's reputation as an expert on racial matters also garnered her an academic publication. *The Annals of the American Academy of Political and Social Science* published "The White Man's Debt to the Negro" in 1913. Directly critical of the South's educational funding, Hammond also reminded her readers than the South held no monopoly on racial prejudice. She urged whites in the North and South to cease thinking of the "task of Negro uplift" as a racial problem:

> Our Negro problem is . . . our fragment of the world-problem of the privileged and unprivileged, of the strong and the weak, dwelling side by side. It is human, and economic. We say, here in the South, that the mass of the Negroes are thriftless and unreliable; that their homes are a menace to the health of the community; and that they largely furnish us our supply of criminals and paupers. And most of us believe that all this is the natural result, not of the Negro's economic status, but of the Negro's being Negro. . . . But the mass of the Negroes are still in the economic morass; and we [whites] of the South do not yet realize that conditions such as it furnishes produce exactly the same result in men of all races, the world around.[106]

Now at the height of her reform career, Lily published in 1914 the fullest exploration of her racial views yet. *In Black and White*, her most important and probably most controversial work, showed the development of her ideas at their most eloquent. While others of her generation saw difference as disability, or difference as testament to inferiority, Hammond saw difference as a sign of sophistication. Evolutionary theory suggested that life forms grew ever more diverse over time, as more and more species diverged. The emergence of races of men, she contended, represented a higher stage of evolution. Much like our contemporary "celebration of diversity," Hammond believed that races were different and should be different, and that those differences were God's design for improving the world. Each race had its own contributions to make, even if God had not made those contributions known to us.

In Black and White began where Hammond's social awakening began: in the tenements. Her statement that poor blacks "live in the slums we have built for them" grew out of Hammond's earliest convictions about the economic origins of poverty, and she carefully teased out the role of economics in racism. She made clear her belief that poverty was the South's central problem. She linked poverty to crime, disease, juvenile delinquency, and a host of other social problems. Hammond's solutions included street improvements, housing regulations, public health programs, a regional prison commission, and other legislative initiatives. Her assessment of segregated railroad cars and the profits they generated was very sophisticated, leading her to call for publicly owned transportation.

In Black and White simultaneously indicted and challenged southern whites. Its author considered the book something like an assessment of fifty years of emancipation. But she asked not "how are blacks doing after fifty years of freedom," but rather "how far have whites allowed them to advance in fifty years of freedom?" In answer to her own question, Lily's demands—the end of lynching, respect for African American women, the end of Jim Crow streetcars, improvements in housing and public health—placed the burden of change squarely on the shoulders of the white South. Blacks had not created these problems, nor did they have the resources to solve them. "They live in the slums we built for them," she wrote.

Hammond's language can sometimes fall uncomfortably on twenty-first-century ears. She could, for example, depict poor blacks as "childish and undeveloped creatures" (124) and could blithely acknowledge "the lack of morals among the mass of the negroes" (125). But unlike most southern whites, she quickly noted the presence of "chaste negroes and honest ones" (125). Hammond also pointed out that the South had its share of ignorant whites who could be as easily manipulated by politicians as were blacks. She suggested that if the solution for this problem was disfranchisement, it should be applied to whites as well as blacks.

Hammond also argued that southern whites carried the lion's share of the burden of race relations. When her contemporaries spoke of that burden, they generally described it in paternalistic terms of "superior" and "inferior" races—the white man's burden. But Hammond's interpretation of the "burden" was grounded in a different political and economic worldview. She argued that whites controlled educational access, employment opportunities, and the legal system. They were responsible for lynching, racially discriminatory laws, and a culture that disrespected black women. The white burden, then, was to disassemble the structures of racial inequality that they had built. The language of "white burden" may sound paternalistic today, but Hammond's reasoning was anything but paternalistic.

Hammond's language on the Civil War and Reconstruction can also be unsettling to twenty-first-century readers. In most points, her interpretation of those events was pure "Dunning school." The "Dunning school" refers to the generation of scholars who provided an academic imprimatur for the Lost Cause movement. William Dunning, Claude Bowers, U. B. Phillips, and others crafted a powerful narrative of the superiority of southern civilization, the benevolence of southern slavery, the innate moral and intellectual inferiority of African Americans, and the heroism of all southern soldiers. In the viewpoint of Dunning school adherents, the war was not over slavery, but rather over states' rights. Although she did not defend the institution of slavery, Hammond did not believe that the war was necessary to end it. Like the majority of Americans in her generation, North and South, she saw Reconstruction as a dark and painful period of history, and while Hammond agreed with the major outlines of this historical narrative, she rejected its underlying racial components. She did not justify slavery on racial grounds; she did not believe in the innate inferiority of blacks; she did not agree with race-based disfranchisement or with legally imposed racial segregation. As for white supremacy, Hammond cleverly twisted the concept: she wrote that her fear for white supremacy was that whites would prove unworthy, because "supremacy is for service" (38).

Although not reviewed by most southern periodicals, *In Black and White* merited a positive assessment by the *Annals of the American Academy of Political and Social Science*. The reviewer (identified only as C.K.) called Hammond "a southern woman who has caught a clear vision of social responsibility" and stated that the book was "most indicative of a new spirit with reference to the duty of the whites to the blacks." Hammond was "courageous and optimistic" and wrote with "a delightful sense of humor." The *Annals* review suggested that *In Black and White* would "open the eyes of many at the North to the extent and depth of the interest of the South in social questions."[107] The book became an important text for those committed to interracial cooperation and was immediately made recommended reading for all staff of the YWCA.[108]

Shortly after the publication of *In Black and White*, simmering problems at

Paine began to boil over (although no evidence suggests that the book had anything to do with the crisis). Paine had suffered from chronic funding difficulties, and the institution had a hard time keeping faculty and staff. In 1907, the financial situation had worsened, as three conferences of the C.M.E. Church decided to discontinue their support of the white-dominated institution, and the MECS had difficulty finding funds to replace the loss.[109] Although many had been hopeful that the fortunes of Paine would be "greatly enhanced with the arrival of John and Lily Hardy Hammond,"[110] the challenges proved greater than John could handle.

John inherited numerous problems at the college. When the Hammonds arrived in 1911, Hammond found the account books were carrying a four-thousand-dollar debt, which he believed to be the fault of the matron of the girls' dormitory, Mrs. J. A. Walker. The wife of a presiding elder in the C.M.E. Church, Walker had considerable clout in the institution, and Hammond lost a great deal of moral capital when he fired her. Hammond also fired a science teacher for his "unfit moral character," after learning that the teacher "was attempting the ruin of two girl students." The teacher, a Mr. Waddell, also happened to be a C.M.E. minister with strong ties to the black members of the board of trustees.[111]

Other faculty caused John difficulty as well. He hired the daughter of a trustee, Elder H. L. Stallworth, as a teacher for the grade-school department. When he concluded that she "was not worth her salt," Hammond fired her, despite her father's power in the institution. Stallworth was infuriated. The father "claimed that as a trustee he had the right to the position for his daughter. He seemed to feel sincerely that I had cheated him out of his just rights," wrote John later.[112]

Although widely heralded as a successful interracial effort, Paine was nevertheless plagued by racial tensions, some of which Hammond handled poorly. African American supporters of Paine, mostly from the C.M.E. Church, had frequently expressed frustration with the white domination of the institution. (The withdrawal of financial support by several conferences in 1907, mentioned previously, was one such expression.) Many of them also believed that Paine should protect and reward its own. When there were openings on the staff, African American supporters believed that Paine graduates should be given preference over "outsiders."[113] John Hammond, however, refused to treat the Paine jobs as sinecures for the black trustees, which antagonized the institution's most important supporters.

By January 1915, the situation had reached a crisis level. Sue Walker—widow of the previous president of Paine, George Williams Walker—wrote Bishop Warren Candler that she believed it was time for Hammond to leave. (As the Methodist bishop, Candler had the power to hire and fire in his district.) "Many of the best friends of the school," she argued, were "bitterly opposed to Dr. Hammond for many reasons." Walker wrote that a change should take place as soon as possible, to save the institution.[114]

Assessing the role of Warren Candler in these events is difficult, given the absence of any smoking-gun documentation. Candler and Hammond had known each other for decades, through their official positions in the Southern Methodist church, but they represented two very distinct wings of the church—with Hammond grouped in the liberal/social gospel branch and Candler very firmly in the camp of traditional evangelicalism. In recent years, Candler had become more strident in his opposition to the trend of socializing churches, as well as in his disapproval of many other progressive movements. (A staunch prohibitionist, Candler nevertheless refused to cooperate with the WCTU, because the organization had gone on record in support of woman suffrage.) Candler opposed the unification of the northern and southern Methodist churches partly because it would mean union with a church more thoroughly committed to the social gospel.[115]

On the other hand, Candler had been a long-term supporter of Paine College. Among the original incorporators of the institution, Candler had served as a member of the board of trustees for thirty years, and had actively raised money for the college.[116] Candler had been president of the board at the time of John's appointment as president.[117] But now, with Hammond's troubles bubbling up there, Candler abruptly resigned from the board.[118] One might see this as an attempt to distance himself from Hammond (or from the Hammonds). Privately, Candler began working to find a new position for John, so that he could be removed from Paine. He wrote to a fellow bishop, who was looking for a minister for a church in Alabama: "Please let me suggest that you appoint Rev. Jno. D. Hammond, D.D., to that pastorate. He ought to come away from Paine College, where he has never been successful, and he would fill Union Springs charge finely. In the pastorate he was a success, and he has never been effective in the highest degree with any other work."[119] Although this plan never materialized, its implications were clear. A move to this small rural church would not only have represented a demotion, it would also have involved changing conferences. Candler was trying to rid himself of Hammond (or the Hammonds) altogether.

Within days of posting this letter, the trustees of Paine College met and demanded John Hammond's resignation. As Hammond told it, "The charges were that I was so disliked and suspected by the colored people of Augusta, regardless of classes or denominational lines, and by the C.M.E. church at large, that I would kill the school if I stayed here; that I was the financial ruin of the school; and that the entire faculty, white and black, demanded my resignation, which I naturally gave."[120]

Although the claim has been made that the Hammonds were forced to leave Paine College because of their progressive racial views, the evidence does not support that conclusion.[121] Indeed, one rumor that circulated in Augusta at the time seems in direct refutation of this theory. John heard the story circulating that the Hammonds left because "Mrs. Hammond had 'forced' my resignation because she wouldn't live at a Negro school!"[122] (John's punctuation serves as recognition of the absurdity of this particular charge, given Lily's racial views.) Although it was not the Hammonds' extreme racial views that ended John's presidency, race was nevertheless part of the problem. Paine suffered from more racial difficulties than it publicly acknowledged. Black members of the board were demanding more control over the institution's policies; black faculty had disagreements with white faculty over standards of discipline. And John, who seemed to disapprove of the trend toward black "domination" of the school, as opposed to the ideal of a truly biracial partnership, stumbled through this racial minefield from the moment he and Lily arrived.[123] Subsequent events further suggest that liberalism had less to do with the Hammonds' departure than did school finances. John was the first of several presidents who succumbed to the financial problems confronting Paine in this era. One after another left in the turmoil of a growing debt.[124]

Lily herself gave no direct testimony about how the events at Paine affected her thinking on race relations, but it does appear that her views hardened during this decade. Her optimism about the potential for the white South to make rapid advancement on racial justice faded some. Her optimism about the potential for goodwill to prevail without legislative support also dimmed. Possibly, too, her optimism about the central role of the church in race relations faded, as she increasingly turned to secular organizations such as the NAACP and the Commission on Interracial Cooperation (CIC). Whether these changes reflected the frustrations at Paine or were a product of her recognition that the South was not making great progress in the second decade of the twentieth century is unclear. Both may have contributed to her disappointment.

Lily did not, however, give up entirely on the white South or on Methodist women. She continued to believe that "racial adjustment, like many other moral issues, waits on the leadership of these women," and she continued to press and prod them on racial issues.[125] In 1916, for example, she brought a resolution condemning lynching to the annual meeting of the North Georgia Conference. "We protest against being compelled to rear our children in an atmosphere so fraught with danger . . . ," she wrote. She offered a second resolution at the same meeting, proposing that the Women's Missionary Society "stand unanimously for respect for womanhood, whether white or black; and that we pledge ourselves, as Christians and as patriots, to do all in our power to help Christian colored women protect the homes and children of their people." Although many in her audience may have been more timid than she, Hammond's speeches were persuasive, and both resolutions were adopted.[126]

The following year, Hammond published *Southern Women and Racial Adjustment*, a booklet sponsored by the Slater Fund that served as a summation of current women's activism and a challenge to do more. Her tone in this pamphlet was notably sharper than a decade before. Southern whites must first change their views about African Americans, she said pointedly, before any improvements could take place. "One great obstacle to better racial adjustment has been the retention by many of us of the viewpoint of a day that is past: our ideal of a good free Negro has been too much like the one that fitted a good slave."[127] Although she noted the importance of church groups in past activities, Lily believed that the greatest energy in racial improvement at the time was coming from organizations other than the churches. The "initial inspiration has come from the churches and church teaching, but it is working out, in the main, through organizations outside the church. . . . Its flowering is outside the church, as its fullest fruition will be. The church women have created outside of their churches a free, flexible organization to which nothing that concerns human life is alien, and where denominational and class lines do not exist."[128] Lily's own activism certainly followed this arc: she started with Methodist missions but eventually moved to participation in the Southern Sociological Congress, the NAACP, and other secular or ecumenical organizations.

After the Hammonds left Paine, Lily became more confrontational in her approach. At a race relations conference in the summer of 1917, for example, Lily demonstrated her absolute fearlessness in debate. Dr. Marion M. Hull, a physician from Atlanta, gave a paper titled "The Relation of Depression to Health."

Despite the speaker's professional standing, Lily launched an aggressive attack on his presentation:

> As I understand the reader of the paper, he said that fifty per cent of the criminals were defective. That does not say all. Don't you think that if a man is in a state of nervous of physical unbalance which may go one way or the other, that that throws a good deal of responsibility on society for his environment. Bishop Berkeley said years ago about the children of the East side, East end of London, "They are damned into the world, not born." That is what I say when I go into the colored people's quarters—"damned into the world, damned into the world," and we white folks damned them.
>
> Some of you know of the report of the English prison of which Sir Edward Bryce wrote. Three thousand prisoners traced back, their ancestors and environment, and the conclusion of that report was that Lombrosco's criminal type does not exist, and that there was not a single one of those three thousand who approached the normal who would not, so far as human judgment could determine, have been useful members of society had they had anything like a normal environment, a normal chance in childhood. [129]

In another example of her newly more confrontational style, Lily attacked southern whites' facile praise of their "mammies." The turn of the century had seen an outpouring of memoirs and stories by southern white writers featuring a "mammy" character. [130] By 1917, Lily had apparently had enough. In order to protect black women, she wrote, the white South must "bury the Old Black Mammy. She may still be loved and honored. Her being dead is no bar to affection; but it certainly should bar a daily association with her corpse which threatens the corruption of sentiment into sentimentality. . . . She deserves a funeral, bless her; and she certainly needs one—a competent, permanent funeral that will not have to be done over again every few days. Her removal will clear the atmosphere and enable us to see the old soul's granddaughters, to whom we must in justice pay something of the debt we so freely acknowledge to her." [131] By challenging the basis for the reverence for "Mammy," Hammond was in fact challenging an important ideological underpinning of contemporary southern racial mores. She was also directly rejecting earlier leadership tactics of Belle Bennett, who had helped raise money for the women's annex at Paine by sentimental appeals to whites' love of their old mammies. (Bennett was much respected and widely considered a moderate in racial matters. Lily's frontal assault on the mammy myth was undoubtedly unappreciated by Bennett's supporters.)

Perhaps more important than the evolution in Lily's writing in these years was the evolution in her activism. No longer holding positions of leadership in the Methodist women's missions movement, Hammond began working more closely with secular organizations devoted to the race question. Early in 1917, Hammond agreed to work as a "secret" agent for the NAACP's Anti-Lynching Committee. Her assignment was to travel the South, interviewing leaders of southern white opinion and persuading them to attend a conference on the lynching question. In February 1917, the committee reported to the NAACP board that Hammond's trip "had yielded unexpectedly favorable results." American entry into World War I, however, derailed plans for the conference.[132]

Indirectly, the war produced an increased commitment to interracial solutions to the South's problems. World War I provoked tremendous racial tensions, especially as African American soldiers returned home to a region fearful of what they might now demand. The war had offered blacks mobility, high wages, and new experiences. White fears and black expectations clashed, provoked a virtual race war of lynchings, violence, and rioting. Several groups studying race relations morphed together to become the Committee on After War Cooperation. By 1920, the group had evolved again, this time into the Commission on Interracial Cooperation.[133]

The CIC, headed by Will Alexander, kept a purposefully amorphous structure and a purposefully low profile.[134] It had no single goal or program of reform, but rather worked in a loose organizational structure guided by a general set of assumptions. First, reflecting its progressive roots, the CIC placed great faith in the power of education to solve the South's racial problems. It conducted public relations campaigns to awaken whites and change their attitudes toward blacks.[135] Second, the CIC firmly believed that local communities should be allowed to work on their own unique problems. The central office set no regional goals or policies, allowing each local committee to decide its own immediate needs. Third, the organization was committed to working in the quietest way possible, desiring no fanfare or publicity that might scare away more timid white supporters. In fact, local committees might operate in such a way that the majority of whites remained unaware of their existence.

In the assessment of two contemporary supporters, the CIC "exerted a wide influence on racial attitudes. The method of the work in the Commission has been very simple. It has tried to bring together white and colored people in each local community, to think cooperatively about their particular problems. In one community they might study health problems. In another they work at the school situation. In others they might face the practices which brought friction and aroused antagonism. No national program was evolved, the one alone of getting leaders of the two races together to face their problems."[136] Tapping into funds available from northern philanthropies such as the Rosenwald and Carnegie foundations, the CIC became the most important of the several interracial efforts of the 1920s.[137]

The initial membership of the CIC was all white and all male. After black members were admitted, the issue of adding white women seemed even more delicate, given the region's obsession with protecting white women from contact with black men. Will Alexander, however, was determined that the CIC should be open to women, whom he recognized as having the most experience in interracial cooperation in the region. He turned to Methodist women for allies, and Lily Hammond played a central role in the formation of the CIC's women's division. The Methodist women's missionary council had created a Commission on Racial Relationships to study problems and to suggest avenues for cooperation. Alexander invited the commission to send representatives to the next meeting of the executive committee of the CIC. Lily Hammond was one of the three women present at the June 1920 meeting, which planned the famous Memphis gathering that took place the following October.[138] The story of the Memphis meeting has been told by several scholars; only a brief summary is necessary here.

Sponsored by the CIC, the Memphis meeting was held in the local YMCA over the course of two days. One hundred carefully chosen black and white women, all experienced leaders in social activism, talked and listened about life behind the veil of Jim Crow. Margaret Murray Washington, Elizabeth Ross Haynes, Charlotte Hawkins Brown, and Jennie Dee Moton were among the speakers. White women in the audience reported how moved they were by the eloquence of the black speakers, and how the experience challenged many of their assumptions about black women. The assembled group, reassured about the possibilities for women's interracial activism, agreed to create a women's division of the CIC.[139] Carrie Parks Johnson, a longtime coworker with Hammond in the Methodist missions movement, became the first director of women's work. The women's division hoped to spread that experience of social awakening in other women, by sponsoring small local gatherings that would re-create their meeting in Memphis.

Despite Lily's lifetime of commitment to this cause, her role in the new movement was destined to be small. In 1919, ill health had forced John's retirement from the ministry, and the Hammonds had moved to Islip, New York, to live with their daughter, Katherine Roulstone.[140] From such a remove, the Hammonds would no longer be at the center of events. They participated in limited ways: for example, Lily and John both signed the NAACP's call for a national anti-lynching conference in New York in 1919 (as did their longtime colleague W. D. Weatherford).[141] But John's active reform career had come to an end, and Lily's was severely restricted.

Lily found several ways to continue her work from New York. She became executive secretary for the Southern Publicity Committee, part of the still-amorphous interracial cooperation movement, and funded by the Phelps-Stokes Fund. The Publicity Committee was tasked with "putting before the public, through the Southern press, the hopeful, constructive things that white people and black people are doing together, thereby doing much to offset the wide publicity that is often given to instances of friction between individuals of the two races . . ."[142] Such a function was well suited to Lily's situation—living in New York, with her husband in declining health, but with the ability to conduct business by mail.[143] It was also an approach with which she had tremendous experience, having spent much of her career trying to educate southern whites about the needs and accomplishments of African Americans.

John's retirement might have made it easier for both of them to speak their minds more forthrightly. Before his retirement, Lily had acted surreptitiously on behalf of the NAACP. But in 1919, with John's ministerial career at a close, both of them could publicly sign the call for an NAACP-sponsored meeting. Their marriage and careers had much in common with those of Franklin and Eleanor Roosevelt. Both women gained prominence and a platform partly because of their husbands' careers, but both women had reform credentials of their own, earned through their many years of work with voluntary associations and women's groups. Both women were more liberal than their husbands in their views on race, and probably felt themselves restrained by the impact that their activities might have on their husbands' careers. Certainly Eleanor Roosevelt became much more outspoken after Franklin's death; had Lily's career extended as long after John's death, her own outspokenness may very well have been unleashed.

John died suddenly on December 12, 1923, at the age of seventy-three, in the Islip home they shared with their daughter and son-in-law.[144] In one of the shockingly few tributes to his long career in service to the Methodist church, a dormitory was named for him at the Mississippi Industrial College in Holly Springs, sponsored by the Colored Methodist Episcopal Church.[145]

Lily continued to live with her daughter after John's death, and she continued to write. Still sharp and outspoken, Lily wrote a letter to the editor of the *New York Times* in July 1924:

> Since women are in politics, one thing destined to pass from national conventions is applause for such childish and unethical remarks as those reported as coming from the Louisiana delegation, to the effect that whatever the Ku Klux plank adopted, Louisiana will vote for it. . . . I am one of millions of women allied by tradition to one or the other of our great parties who will vote for principles and for men who stand for them, regardless of party affiliations. We cannot be stampeded by noise or cake-walking; our enthusiasms do not work that way; and we want no pussy-footing in the name of religion or anything else. . . . Women cannot be bound by party traditions; and they care nothing for the success of political machines. They wish to meet the moral issues of today, and the party which holds their allegiance must do likewise, and without evasion.[146]

Even in these last years of her life, Lily produced two more books and several articles.

Lily Hammond died January 24, 1925, of pneumonia, at the age of sixty-five.[147] Her passing went mostly unmarked by her former coworkers. The Women's Missionary Council, to which Lily had devoted so many years of work, published a half-page memorial in its annual report. It noted only that she was "former First Vice President, Woman's Board of Home Missions, Editor 'Our Homes,' Author."[148] The contrast with the volumes published in honor of her contemporaries Mary Helm and Belle Bennett could not be more stark.

Lily did not live to see many of the fruits of her labors ripen. In the years after her death, the interracial cooperation movement, given shape by the CIC, flowered. In the assessment of historian Jacquelyn Hall, the CIC "encouraged and coordinated the first stirrings of racial liberalism in the region." In particular, the role of church women in the organization "rendered interracial work respectable in the conservative South."[149] The CIC, to which Hammond had played midwife, itself gave birth a decade after her death to the Association of Southern Women for the Prevention of Lynching.

Similarly, the Southern Methodist women's organizations continued their social welfare and interracial work. Under the leadership of Bertha Newell, a

protégé of Lily Hammond and her successor as head of the Bureau of Social
Service, Methodist women worked in cooperation with a range of secular and
nondenominational organizations. Newell, who had once attended the University of Chicago and trained under Jane Addams, now pushed Methodist women
to work for improved conditions for industrial workers, for protections for
working women, and for improved race relations. During her tenure, Southern
Methodist women "became widely recognized as leaders in southern industrial
reform." In 1935, the Women's Missionary Council endorsed the National Recovery Act, primarily because of the protections it offered to working women.[150]

In the same way that recovering women's activism has led us to reevaluate
the relative strength of the social gospel movement in the South, so it should
give us reason to reconsider the periodization of that movement. Paul Harvey
has recently argued that the social gospel continued to hold the attention of
Southern Baptist women much later than generally understood. He places that
interest well into the 1930s and 1940s, and notes the continuing efforts of Southern Baptist women in the area of interracial cooperation. When we add activities such as Lucy Randolph Mason's work with the labor movement, Bertha
Newell's work in race relations, Jessie Daniel Ames's antilynching crusade, and
the continuing growth of the YWCA and similar groups, then the activist stage
of the social gospel appears much longer lived than just the 1920s.[151]

It is also possible that Lily would have disapproved of some of the develop-
ments in the years after her death. The insistence of Jessie Daniel Ames that
the antilynching movement should be white only and her refusal to cooperate with black women's antilynching efforts[152] would likely have invoked Lily's
wrath. Hammond would also probably have regretted the way the Association
of Southern Women for the Prevention of Lynching (ASWPL) usurped the spot-
light from the CIC and focused on lynching to the exclusion of other issues.
Lily had always seen the "Negro question" as a spectrum of issues, all of which
had to be confronted. But the antilynching campaign under Ames's direction
threatened to draw attention away from other pressing needs, such as education,
playgrounds, hospitals, jobs, and housing.

Lily's last writing had nothing to do with race; it was a far more personal moment. In a letter to her children that accompanied her will, Lily wrote, "Think of
me as alive; alive beyond your furthest thought, and near, and loving you, and
well at last, free as the winds of heaven, and learning more and more the things
I want to know, and growing more toward what God wants me to become. I
think maybe John will have our home ready when I come, and we will have a

real home at last." Her final instructions to them: "Bury my body as cheaply as you decently can and forget it; don't wear mourning."[153]

Why Lily Hammond faded into such historical obscurity still is not entirely clear to me. Historians have searched for the "silent South" for more than a generation now, without uncovering Hammond's very public activism. One part of the explanation may be the absence of any collection of family papers. Although a widely published author and an activist for three decades, neither she nor her equally dedicated husband left papers behind. There is simply not enough documentation to tell the story of her life as well as we have those of other (sometimes less prominent) southern women. Another part of the explanation may be timing and geography. John's retirement and their relocation to New York took Lily away from the center of interracial cooperation activities just as the seeds she had helped nurture were germinating. The rise of the interracial cooperation movement after 1920 represented a partial fulfillment of her vision, but she was not present to help steer it. Whether her absence helps explain the apparent drift and lethargy of that movement cannot be answered.[154]

Jessie Daniel Ames may also be a part of the explanation of Lily's historical invisibility. Her more "instrumentalist approach" in the ASWPL pushed the organization into the limelight. She wanted attention and publicity. Ames had a "desire for concrete results and a visible impact on public life."[155] She grabbed headlines, and the CIC did not.

The diminished stature of the interracial cooperation effort, compared to the more celebrated histories accorded to the NAACP, the Congress for Racial Equality (CORE), and the Student Non-violent Coordinating Committee (SNCC) may also have served to minimize Lily's place in the historiography of the larger civil rights movement. The more aggressive, confrontational style of the major civil rights organizations provided historians with a record of vigor and accomplishment. By contrast, the interracial cooperation movement, with its aversion to publicity and its emphasis on behind-the-scenes activism, seemed passive and uninspiring. The largely masculine leadership of the major civil rights organizations and their dramatic showdowns in courtrooms and streetcars stood in marked contrast to the CIC and the National Urban League, with their focus on women, children, and social welfare. Lily's historical reputation may have suffered along with the gendered historical fortunes of her movement.

Yet all this does not adequately explain why Lily's place in the annals of

Southern Methodist women's activism has also been obscured. Although she was the most prolific author of the group, entrusted with writing several of the organization's official publications in the second and third decades of the twentieth century, Lily nevertheless disappeared from their chronicles after her death in 1925. There was no hagiographic tribute to her, such as those given for Belle Bennett and Mary Helm. Mabel Howell's 1928 history of Southern Methodist women noted Hammond's role as editor of educational leaflets but left her out of the section on interracial work.[156] Mary Noreen Dunn's 1936 history of the home missions movement mentioned her only once, and even then only to quote her praising Belle Bennett.[157] The same author's 1960 history seemed determined to write Hammond out of the story, reducing her to a bit player in places where she had actually been a leader.[158]

This particular distortion of the historical record—rising almost to the level of betrayal—is the hardest to explain. Extant sources offer no clues, and speculation is risky. But Lily's early prominence among Southern Methodist women was based on her broad commitment and activism on behalf of the full measure of Methodist women's missions. Her later concentration on "the race question" to the near exclusion of other causes pulled her more into the orbit of other organizations—the NAACP, the CIC, the Southern Publicity Committee—outside of the evangelical fold. Although Hammond never broke with the women's missions movement, her attentions were clearly directed elsewhere, and more singularly devoted Methodist women may have perceived this as some kind of a rejection. Lily's advocacy of governmental solutions for many problems—state-funded day care, public baths, labor regulations—may have offended still others, who continued to push for private sector/religiously centered solutions. From Hammond's perspective, it appeared that the church's conservative leadership had pushed her to work outside the denominational structures, but those still within the fold may not have seen it this way.[159]

The true reason for Lily's historical obscurity may never be known, but I do hope that this volume will in some measure restore Lily Hammond to her rightful place in the history of race relations in the South.

Notes

1. Anne Firor Scott, *The Southern Lady: From Pedestal to Politics, 1830–1930* (Chicago: University of Chicago Press, 1970). Scott noted that Hammond "held a mirror to southern society which must have caused some soul-searching among such of her readers as did not throw the book away in disgust" (95). In the second edition of *The Southern Lady*, Scott wrote: "Beginning with the accidental

discovery of Lily H. Hammond's *In Black and White*, I was able to trace their [Methodist women's] developing concern for what would be labeled interracial work" (Charlottesville: University Press of Virginia, 1995), 256. (N.B. All subsequent references are to the 1970 edition of *The Southern Lady*.)

2. John Patrick McDowell, *The Social Gospel in the South: The Woman's Home Mission Movement in the Methodist Episcopal Church, South, 1886–1939* (Baton Rouge: Louisiana State University Press, 1982).

3. Henry Warner Bowden, ed., *Dictionary of American Religious Biography*, 2nd ed. (Westport, Conn.: Greenwood Press, 1993), 223–24. This brief sketch is one of the few sources of biographical information available for Lily Hammond.

4. Lily regularly acknowledged that her parents were former slaveholders, a fact confirmed by the 1850 census for Camden County, North Carolina. Henry Hardy owned ten slaves that year, ranging in age from one to sixty years. What happened to the Hardys' slaves is not clear. A search through Camden County court records did not uncover any record of manumissions. Perhaps the slaves were taken with the family in their move to New Jersey, and became free then. Since the 1870 census reported three African Americans, all born in North Carolina, living with the Hardy family in New York, it seems reasonable to conclude that at least some of the family's slaves moved north with them in 1859 and became free in the process.

5. Lily Hardy Hammond, "Our Duty to the Negro," *Our Homes* 9 (January 1900): 1.

6. Examples of southern white hostility to "outside agitators" are legion, including Robert Ingalls, *Urban Vigilantes in the New South: Tampa, 1882–1936* (Gainesville: University Press of Florida, 1993, 1988); and Seth Cagin and Philip Dray, *We Are Not Afraid: The Story of Goodman, Schwerner, and Chaney and the Civil Rights Campaign for Mississippi* (New York: Macmillan, 1988).

7. The 1870 census lists both her father and oldest brother as "brokers" and a second brother (Caldwell) as a "clerk." Caldwell and a younger brother, Horace, later became bankers in Norfolk, Virginia. Lily's obituary identified her father as a member of the New York Stock Exchange, although it gave no dates. ("Mrs. Lydia Hardy Hammond," *New York Times*, January 24, 1925, 13. [All *New York Times* citations come from the online Historical *New York Times*, and use the page numbers from that source.])

8. Even if she disliked the pet names, it seems that the family continued to call her Lydia. She was listed as "Lydia" in the 1870 and 1910 censuses. Her obituary in the *New York Times* identified her as Lydia as well.

9. Lily Hardy Hammond, *In the Garden of Delight* (New York: Thomas Y. Crowell Co., 1916), 10.

10. Lily Hardy Hammond, "A Southern View of the Negro," *Outlook* 73 (March 14, 1903): 619.

11. Marion Talbolt and Lois Kimball Mathews Rosenberry, *History of the American Association of University Women, 1881–1931* (Boston: Houghton Mifflin, 1931), 48.

12. Janette Thomas Greenwood, *Bittersweet Legacy: The Black and White "Better Classes" in Charlotte, 1850–1910* (Chapel Hill: University of North Carolina Press, 1994), 81. See also William A. Link, *The Paradox of Southern Progressivism, 1880–1930* (Chapel Hill: University of North Carolina Press, 1992), chap. 3.

13. John Hammond Moore, "The Negro and Prohibition in Atlanta, 1885–1887," *South Atlantic Quarterly* 69 (1970): 38, 42. Although Moore noted the interracial nature of the campaigns, he did not argue that women were central to this interracial effort.

14. *Atlanta Constitution*, November 27, 1887, quoted by Moore, "The Negro and Prohibition in Atlanta," 53.

15. Greenwood, *Bittersweet Legacy*, 88–89, 97–98, 103.

16. Ibid., 110–11; Glenda Elizabeth Gilmore, *Gender and Jim Crow: Women and the Politics of White Supremacy in North Carolina, 1896–1920* (Chapel Hill: University of North Carolina Press, 1996), 49–50.

17. Writing in 1978, Darlene Roth put it this way: "Their social encounters were substantively different, and their club life-styles were dissimilar. Moreover, white and black women, isolated from each other, were ignorant of each other in those very associational situations they held dear in their

own experiences; at all levels of club life, there were no points of contact the between the races" (*Matronage, Patterns in Women's Organizations, Atlanta, Georgia, 1890–1940* [Brooklyn: Carlson Publishing, 1994], 67. Although dated 1994, this is the publication of an unrevised dissertation from 1978). Mary E. Frederickson, "Each One Is Dependent on the Other: Southern Churchwomen, Racial Reform, and the Process of Transformation, 1880–1940," in *Visible Women: New Essays on American Activism*, ed. Nancy A. Hewitt and Suzanne Lebsock (Urbana: University of Illinois Press, 1993), 308.

18. *Year Book and Minutes of the Fifty-Eighth Session of the North Georgia Conference, M. E. Church, South. Wesley Memorial Church, Atlanta, Georgia, November 19–24, 1924*, ed. H. C. Emory, 87. Information on Dennis Hammond's occupation and slave ownership comes from the 1850 census for Heard County, Georgia.

19. Only a handful of other southerners had preceded Hammond at Drew (William Pearson Tolley, ed., *Alumni Record of Drew Theological Seminary* [Madison, N.J.: The Seminary, 1926], 84). Drew prided itself on its progressive record, such as being the first seminary in the country to establish a Chair of Christian Sociology (Ezra Squier Tipple, ed., *Drew Theological Seminary, 1867–1917* [New York: Methodist Book Concern, 1917], 168).

20. The marriage date comes from the *Year Book and Minutes of the Fifty-Eighth Session of the North Georgia Conference*, 88.

21. As an example of this automatic leadership, Lily was chosen in 1897 as the "fraternal" representative of the South Georgia Conference to the annual meeting of the North Georgia Conference of the Woman's Parsonage and Home Mission Society. This meeting would have been within a year of the Hammonds' arrival at Wesleyan College in Macon (*Seventh Annual Report of the Woman's Parsonage and Home Mission Society of the North Georgia Conference* [Atlanta: Foote & Davies Publishers, 1898], 11). For a discussion of the challenges of being the wife of an itinerant Methodist minister, albeit in a frontier setting, see Julie Roy Jeffrey, "Ministry through Marriage," in Hilah F. Thomas and Rosemary Skinner Keller, eds., *Women in New Worlds* (Nashville: Abingdon Press, 1981).

22. See biographical sketch of John Hammond in Harold Lawrence, ed., *Methodist Preachers in Georgia, 1783–1900* (Tignall, Ga.: Boyd Publishing, 1984), 224.

23. "The Rev. John D. Hammond," *New York Times*, December 12, 1923, 21; *Year Book and Minutes of the Fifty-Eighth Session of the North Georgia Conference*, 88.

24. According to the 1900 census, the third child, Frances, was born in Georgia in 1893, but the family continued to live in Missouri. Either the entry is an error, or Frances may have been born during a visit to John's family in Georgia. Lily published at least four essays while in Missouri. "The Parsonage and Home Mission Reading Course," *Our Homes* 3 (September 1894): 1–2; "Woman's Work for Women," *Our Homes* 4 (September 1895): 6–7; "New Light on Social Problems," *Methodist Review* 42 (January–February 1896): 376–83; and "Our Debt to the Colored Race," *Our Homes* 5 (September 1896): 8–9.

25. *Ninth Annual Report of the Woman's Parsonage and Home Mission Society of the Methodist Episcopal Church South* (Kansas City, Mo.: Tiernan Havens Printing, 1895), unpaginated prefatory matter.

26. Josiah Strong (1847–1916), *Our Country: Its Possible Future and Its Present Crisis* (New York: Baker & Taylor Co., for the American Home Missionary Society, 1885), was one of the best-selling of all social gospel texts. Washington Gladden (1836–1918), *Applied Christianity: Moral Aspects of Social Questions* (Boston: Houghton, Mifflin and Company, 1886), was nearly equal in popularity.

27. Rauschenbusch was a prolific writer; his most influential book was probably *Christianity and the Social Crisis* (New York: Macmillan, 1907). See Paul M. Minus, *Walter Rauschenbusch, American Reformer* (New York: Macmillan, 1988).

28. Cecil E. Greek, *The Religious Roots of American Sociology* (New York: Garland, 1992), 24.

29. John Lee Eighmy, "Religious Liberalism in the South during the Progressive Era," *Church History* 38 (September 1969): 367, 370. Paul Harvey notes several Baptist figures active in the social gospel (Harvey, *Redeeming the South: Religious Cultures and Racial Identities among Southern*

Baptists, 1865–1925 [Chapel Hill: University of North Carolina Press, 1997]). Edgar Gardner Murphy was a leading southern social reformer, social gospel advocate, and Episcopal priest (Hugh C. Bailey, *Edgar Gardner Murphy, Gentle Progressive* [Coral Gables: University of Miami Press, 1968]).

30. John Eighmy began his account, "Religious Liberalism," 362–63, with Murphy and McKelway. As an illustration of this point, Ralph Luker's *The Social Gospel in Black and White* (Chapel Hill: University of North Carolina Press, 1991), does not even mention Lily Hammond, although more than a dozen references to Methodist Bishop Atticus Haygood appear.

31. Wendy J. Deichman Edwards and Carolyn De Swarte Gifford, eds., *Gender and the Social Gospel* (Urbana and Chicago: University of Illinois Press, 2003), 4–5; Mary Agnes Dougherty, "The Social Gospel According to Phoebe," in Thomas and Keller, *Women in New Worlds*, 200–201.

32. See Ingrid Overacker, "True to Our God: African American Women as Christian Activists in Rochester, New York," in Edwards and Gifford, *Gender and the Social Gospel*; Clayborne Carson, "Martin Luther King, Jr., and the African-American Social Gospel," in *African-American Christianity: Essays in History*, ed. Paul E. Johnson (Berkeley: University of California Press, 1994); and Evelyn Brooks Higginbotham, *Righteous Discontent: The Women's Movement in the Black Baptist Church, 1880–1920* (Cambridge: Harvard University Press, 1993).

33. Higginbotham, *Righteous Discontent*, 174–75; Paul Harvey, *Freedom's Coming: Religious Culture and the Shaping of the South from the Civil War through the Civil Rights Era* (Chapel Hill: University of North Carolina Press, 2005), 72; Gary Scott Smith, *The Search for Social Salvation: Social Christianity and America, 1880–1925* (Lanham, Md.: Lexington Books, 2000), 41, 224–27; Jacqueline Anne Rouse, *Lugenia Burns Hope: Black Southern Reformer* (Athens: University of Georgia Press, 1989).

34. Greek, *Religious Roots of American Sociology*, calls Strong's *Our Country* "one of the most nativistic tracts ever written" (90). See esp. pp. 47–50. See also Stephen W. Angell and Anthony B. Pinn, eds., *Social Protest Thought in the African Methodist Episcopal Church, 1862–1939* (Knoxville: University of Tennessee Press, 2000), 310; Harvey, *Freedom's Coming*, 65–66.

35. Greek, *Religious Roots of American Sociology*, 58–59; Janet Forsythe Fishburn, *The Fatherhood of God and the Victorian Family: The Social Gospel in America* (Philadelphia: Fortress Press, 1981), 122–23.

36. See especially Fishburn, *Fatherhood of God*, 32; Greek, *Religious Roots of American Sociology*, 86–87.

37. Greek, *Religious Roots of American Sociology*, 76.

38. Harvey, *Freedom's Coming*, 73, 82.

39. Sarah B. Cooper, "The Kindergarten and Crime," *Our Homes* 10 (September 1901): 1; "The Immigrant," *Our Homes* 19 (August 1910): 2; "The Question of Child Labor," *Our Homes* 11 (December 1902): 11; Lily Hardy Hammond, "Some Southern Factory Problems," *Methodist Review* 51 (May–June 1902), 349–59.

40. "In a package of old notes made for talks and addresses given in Missouri fifteen or twenty years ago, the editor found the following scribbled in pencil on a torn bit of paper in a handwriting strongly suggestive of the jerking of a railway train. . . ." Lily Hardy Hammond, "Home and Foreign Missions," *Our Homes* 19 (November 1910): 2. I have been unable to locate any information about these activities.

41. *Year Book and Minutes of the Fifty-Eighth Session of the North Georgia Conference*, 88.

42. John's job required him to attend annual meetings of all the different Southern Methodist conferences. In 1901, for example, he reported attending nineteen of the annual conferences (*Seventh Annual Report of the Board of Education of the Methodist Episcopal Church, South* [Nashville: MECS, 1901], 10). Lily's various positions within the women's missions movement also required her to travel. The Hammonds therefore had many opportunities to network with local and regional leaders, to observe organizations and institutions across the region, and to make connections with the leaders of movements and organizations throughout the South. Their speeches and writings reflect the Hammonds' deep knowledge of conditions in the South, and Lily in particular

made a point of including information about specific reform activities in her writings whenever possible.

43. Lily served as editor of *Our Homes* for several months during the transition to its merger with the *Missionary Voice* (Hammond, *Memories of Mary Helm* [Nashville: Woman's Missionary Council, M.E. Church, South, 1923], 46).

44. E. Charles Chatfield, "The Southern Sociological Congress: Organization of Uplift," *Tennessee Historical Quarterly* 19 (1960): 332 n. 12.

45. Don H. Doyle, *New Men, New Cities, New South: Atlanta, Nashville, Charleston, and Mobile, 1860–1910* (Chapel Hill: University of North Carolina Press, 1990), 265.

46. Floris Barnett Cash, *African American Women and Social Action: The Clubwomen and Volunteerism from Jim Crow to the New Deal, 1896–1936* (Westport, Conn.: Greenwood Press, 2001), 16–20, 26.

47. Raymond R. Sommerville Jr., *An Ex-Colored Church: Social Activism in the CME Church, 1870–1970* (Macon, Ga.: Mercer University Press, 2004), 47–49. The CME later changed its name to the Christian Methodist Episcopal Church, keeping its acronym intact.

48. See biographical sketches in Jessie Carney Smith, ed., *Notable Black American Women* (Detroit: Gale Research, 1992–2003). The sketch for Crosthwaite listed her as a member of the "Southern Interracial League," which may be an imprecise reference to the Commission on Interracial Cooperation.

49. Carole Stanford Bucy, *Women Helping Women: The YWCA of Nashville, 1898–1998* (Nashville: The YWCA of Nashville and Middle Tennessee, 1998), 5; John A. Simpson, *Edith D. Pope and Her Nashville Friends* (Knoxville: University of Tennessee Press, 2003), 130; Mattie Duncan Beard, *The W.C.T.U. in the Volunteer State* (Kingsport, Tenn.: Kingsport Press, 1962), 7.

50. Lily Hardy Hammond, *Southern Women and Racial Adjustment* (Lynchburg, Va.: J. P. Bell Co., Printers, 1917), 6. Hammond's comment is much more modest than Belle Kearney's better-known assessment of the WCTU: "The Woman's Christian Temperance Union was the golden key that unlocked the prison doors of pent-up possibilities. It was the generous liberator, the joyous iconoclast, the discoverer, the developer of Southern women" (Kearney, *A Slaveholder's Daughter* [1900; repr. New York: Negro Universities Press, 1969], 118).

51. Beard, *W.C.T.U.*, 12; Louis M. Kyriakoudes, *The Social Origins of the Urban South : Race, Gender, and Migration in Nashville and Middle Tennessee, 1890–1930* (Chapel Hill: University of North Carolina Press, 2003), 141–42.

52. McDowell, *Social Gospel in the South*, 9.

53. Ibid., 15; John Olen Fish, "Southern Methodism in the Progressive Era: A Social History" (Ph.D. dissertation, University of Georgia, 1969), 82; Mary E. Frederickson, "Shaping a New Society," in Hilah F. Thomas and Rosemary Skinner Keller, eds., *Women in New Worlds* (Nashville: Abingdon Press, 1981), 353.

54. Mrs. R. W. MacDonell, *Belle Harris Bennett: Her Life Work* (1928; repr. New York: Garland Publishing, 1987), 85.

55. Sara Estelle Haskin, *Women and Missions in the Methodist Episcopal Church, South* (Nashville: M.E. Church, South, 1920), 32; Scott, *Southern Lady*, 195.

56. Frederickson, "Shaping a New Society," 357.

57. Quoted by Harvey, *Freedom's Coming*, 67.

58. McDowell's *Social Gospel in the South* gives detailed coverage to the debate over women's roles in the Methodist Church. See also Virginia Shadron, "The Laity Rights Movement," in Thomas and Keller, eds., *Women in New Worlds*.

59. Will Alexander may have been the first to make this observation. In 1921 he wrote, "I have felt for several years that [the Woman's Home Mission Society] was the most progressive and constructive religious group in the South." Quoted by Jacquelyn Dowd Hall, *Revolt against Chivalry: Jessie Daniel Ames and the Women's Campaign against Lynching* (New York: Columbia University Press, 1979), 73.

60. *Seventh Annual Report of the Woman's Parsonage and Home Mission Society of the North Georgia Conference* (Atlanta: Foote & Davies Publishing, 1898), 26.

61. Local settlement houses created most of these institutions. Richmond's school of social work was the work of the Nurses' Settlement. See Elna C. Green, *This Business of Relief: Confronting Poverty in a Southern City, 1740–1940* (Athens: University of Georgia Press, 2003). In New Orleans, a school of social work grew out of the Kingsley House social settlement, and eventually became associated with Tulane University. See Elna C. Green, "National Trends, Regional Differences, Local Circumstances: Social Welfare in New Orleans, 1870s-1920s," in *Before the New Deal: Social Welfare in the South, 1830–1930*, ed. Green (Athens: University of Georgia Press, 1999).

62. The literature on the professionalization of social work in the early twentieth century includes most recently: Elizabeth N. Agnew, *From Charity to Social Work: Mary E. Richmond and the Creation of an American Profession* (Urbana: University of Illinois Press, 2004), and Ruth Crocker, *Mrs. Russell Sage: Women's Activism and Philanthropy in Gilded Age and Progressive Era America* (Bloomington: Indiana University Press, 2006). Classic texts include Roy Lubove, *The Professional Altruist: The Emergence of Social Work as a Career, 1880–1930* (New York: Atheneum, 1969), and James Leiby, *A History of Social Welfare and Social Work in the United States* (New York: Columbia University Press, 1978).

63. In 1896, Hammond wrote "New Light on Social Problems," which discussed a new book by Benjamin Kidd, titled *Social Evolution.* In 1904, she published a review essay titled "Present-Day Philanthropy," *Methodist Quarterly Review* 53 (January 1904): 25–35. I have been unable to determine whether Lily accompanied her husband to the Methodist Conference held in London in 1901, but John's presence there suggests the couple had some very direct ties to the transatlantic movement of ideas ("The Methodist Conference," *New York Times*, September 6, 1901, 6). On the Atlantic world of progressivism, see Daniel T. Rogers, *Atlantic Crossings: Social Politics in a Progressive Age* (Cambridge: Belknap Press of Harvard University Press, 1998); James Kloppenberg, *Uncertain Victory: Social Democracy and Progressivism in European and American Thought, 1870–1920* (New York: Oxford University Press, 1986); and Deirdre M. Moloney, *American Catholic Lay Groups and Transatlantic Social Reform in the Progressive Era* (Chapel Hill: University of North Carolina Press, 2002).

64. For example, Lily had a correspondence with Madeline McDowell Breckinridge about black women and school suffrage (Sophonisba Preston Breckinridge, *Madeline McDowell Breckinridge: A Leader in the New South* [Chicago: University of Chicago Press, 1921], 217).

65. Frederickson, "Shaping a New Society," 355.

66. See McDowell, *Social Gospel in the South*, 126–43.

67. Wilma Dykeman and James Stokely, *Seeds of Southern Change* (Chicago: University of Chicago Press, 1962), 85.

68. Lily's views thus paralleled those of the Southern Sociological Congress, which emphasized the social awakening of whites. Julia Anne McDonough, "Men and Women of Good Will: A History of the Commission on Interracial Cooperation and the Southern Regional Council, 1919–1954" (Ph.D. dissertation, University of Virginia, 1993), 21–28.

69. *Thirteenth Annual Report of the Woman's Home Mission Society of the Methodist Episcopal Church South* (Nashville: MECS, 1899), 98. Hammond was not the only one of her generation to argue that southern whites deluded themselves about their understanding of African Americans. See also W. E. B. DuBois, ed., *The Negro Church* (1906; repr. Walnut Creek, Calif.: Altamira Press, 2003), 164; and Guy B. Johnson, "Recent Literature on the Negro," *Journal of Social Forces* 3 (January 1925): 315.

70. Haskin, *Women and Missions*, 194–95; *Fifteenth Annual Report of the Woman's Home Mission Society of the Methodist Episcopal Church South* (Nashville: MECS, 1901), 51–52. See also the following year's annual report, 76.

71. Quotes come from pp. 619 and 620.

72. Lily Hardy Hammond, "Some Aspects of Southern Education," *The World To-Day* 9 (August 1905): 832–36.

73. Lily Hardy Hammond, "The Growth of Democracy in the South," *Methodist Quarterly Review* 54 (January 1905): 33–35.

74. Quoted by Willis D. Weatherford and Charles S. Johnson, *Race Relations: Adjustments of Whites and Negroes in the United States* (Boston, New York, and other cities: D. C. Heath, 1934), 526–27.

75. Hall, *Revolt against Chivalry*, 313 n. 39.

76. Quoted by Frederickson, "Shaping a New Society," 352.

77. Albert E. Barnett, *Andrew Sledd: His Life and Work* (n.p., 1956), 4; Henry Y. Warnock, "Andrew Sledd, Southern Methodists, and the Negro," *Journal of Southern History* 31 (August 1965): 267. Although Sledd returned to a position at the Candler School of Theology twelve years later, he never again attempted to enter the public discussion of race relations (Warnock, 269).

78. When publishing Mary Taylor Blauvett's essay "The Race Problem, as Discussed by Negro Women," the journal felt compelled to note that "the writer of this paper has no negro blood. She is a graduate of Wellesley and has done two years of graduate work in Oxford, England" (*American Journal of Sociology* 6, no. 5 [March 1901]: 662). The next essay was Paul S. Reinsch, "The Negro Race and European Civilization" (*American Journal of Sociology* 11, no. 2 [September 1905]).

79. Bucy, *Women Helping Women*, 42–43.

80. Ibid., 44.

81. *Nineteenth Annual Report of the Woman's Home Society of the Methodist Episcopal Church South* (Nashville: MECS, 1905), 14.

82. *Twentieth Annual Report of the Woman's Home Society of the Methodist Episcopal Church South* (Nashville: MECS, 1906), 16. Hammond's letter was dated April 24, from Steuben Sanitarium.

83. *Twenty-First Annual Report of the Woman's Home Mission Society of the Methodist Episcopal Church South* (Nashville: MECS, 1907), 17–18. This letter was reprinted under the title "A Letter from Mrs. J. D. Hammond to the Woman's Board of Home Missions," *Our Homes* 16 (July 1907): 11.

84. *Twenty-First Annual Report of the Woman's Home Mission Society*, 17–18.

85. Sommerville, *An Ex-Colored Church*, 55; Henry Y. Warnock, "Moderate Racial Thought and Attitudes of Southern Baptists and Methodists, 1900–1921" (Ph.D. dissertation, Northwestern University, 1963), 24, 69.

86. Eighth Annual and Second Quadrennial Report of the Board of Education of the Methodist Episcopal Church, South (Nashville: MECS, 1902), 16.

87. Haskin, *Women and Missions*, 194–95; Warnock, "Moderate Racial Thought," 43.

88. For an example of generous northern support of a white industrial training institution, see Victoria-Maria MacDonald and Eleanor Lenington, "Southern Poor Whites and Higher Education: Martha Berry's Philanthropic Strategies in the Building of Berry College," in *Women and Philanthropy in Education*, ed. Andrea Walton (Bloomington: Indiana University Press, 2005). See also Eric Anderson and Alfred A. Moss, *Dangerous Donations: Northern Philanthropy and Southern Black Education, 1902–1930* (Columbia: University of Missouri Press, 1999).

89. Luker, *Social Gospel in Black and White*, 23.

90. Quoted by Fish, "Southern Methodism in the Progressive Era," 156.

91. Willard Range, *The Rise and Progress of Negro Colleges in Georgia, 1865–1949* (Athens: University of Georgia Press, 1951), 72. It does appear that female students at Paine were pushed more into industrial training than men. Since few women were there preparing for the ministry, the law, and the professions, its administrators perceived that they had less need for the traditional college curriculum of Greek, Latin, theology, etc. See Mrs. R.W. MacDonell, "Tuskegee Normal and Industrial School, and Paine College," *Our Homes* 11 (August 1902): 5.

92. Fish, "Southern Methodism in the Progressive Era," 157.

93. *Eleventh Annual Report of the Board of Education of the Methodist Episcopal Church South* (Nashville: MECS, 1905), 23.

94. James E. McCulloch, *Battling for Social Betterment: Southern Sociological Congress, Memphis, Tennessee, May 6–10, 1914* (Nashville: Southern Sociological Congress, 1914), 138–45. The Ham-

monds also endorsed industrial training for whites. See Lily Hardy Hammond, "Woman's Work for Woman," *Our Homes* 4 (September 1895): 6.

95. Hall, *Revolt Against Chivalry*, 72.

96. Ibid., 313, n. 39.

97. Gilmore, *Gender and Jim Crow*, 50.

98. *Second Annual Report of the Woman's Missionary Society of the North Georgia Conference* (Augusta: Phoenix Printing, 1912), unpaginated prefatory matter.

99. *Third Annual Report of the Woman's Missionary Society of the North Georgia Conference* (Augusta: Phoenix Printing, 1913), 6, 30.

100. Chatfield, "Southern Sociological Congress," 347.

101. Ronald C. White Jr., *Liberty and Justice for All: Racial Reform and the Social Gospel (1877–1925)* (New York: Harper & Row, 1990), 235.

102. Eighmy, "Religious Liberalism in the South, 367.

103. James E. McCulloch, *The Call of the New South; Addresses Delivered at the Southern Sociological Congress, Nashville, Tennessee, May 7 to 10, 1912* (Nashville: Southern Sociological Congress, 1912), 361; Chatfield, "Southern Sociological Congress," 336–37.

104. James E. McCulloch, *The Call of the New South; Addresses Delivered at the Southern Sociological Congress, Nashville, Tennessee, May 7 to 10, 1912* (Nashville: Southern Sociological Congress, 1912), 361; Chatfield, "Southern Sociological Congress," 336–37; McCulloch, *The South Mobilizing for Social Service: Addresses Delivered at the Southern Sociological Congress, Atlanta, Georgia, April 25–29, 1913* (Nashville: Southern Sociological Congress, 1913), 455.

105. Warnock, "Moderate Racial Thought," 74.

106. Lily Hardy Hammond, "The White Man's Debt to the Negro," *Annals of the American Academy of Political and Social Science* 49 (September 1913): 68, 69.

107. *Annals* (January 1916): 292–93. There were no reviews in the *South Atlantic Quarterly*, the *Virginia Magazine of History and Biography*, the *Sewanee Review*, or other such southern periodicals.

108. Nancy Marie Robertson, " 'Deeper Even Than Race'? White Women and the Politics of Christian Sisterhood in the Young Women's Christian Association, 1906–1946" (Ph.D. dissertation, New York University, 1997), 149.

109. Harold Lloyd Fair, "Southern Methodists on Education and Race, 1900–1920" (Ph.D. dissertation, Vanderbilt University, 1971), 366 n120.

110. White, *Liberty and Justice for All*, 220.

111. John Hammond to Rev. W. F. McMurry, June 21, 1915 (Warren Candler Papers [hereinafter, Candler Papers], box 30, folder 1, Special Collections, Woodruff Library, Emory University, Atlanta). Hammond sent copies of this letter to several prominent Methodists, including Bishop Candler.

112. Ibid.

113. Sue G. Walker to Bishop Candler, January 23, 1915. Candler Papers, box 28, folder 2.

114. Ibid. It should be noted that Walker was not an entirely neutral observer to these events. Since many of John Hammond's actions represented changes in policy from those of her husband, and indeed some of Hammond's actions appeared as direct refutations of president Walker's policies, his widow may very well have resented her husband's successor.

115. Fair, "Southern Methodists on Education and Race," 498–99.

116. Mark K. Bauman, *Warren Akin Candler: The Conservative as Idealist* (Metuchen, N.J.: Scarecrow Press, 1981), 42–44.

117. "Rev. J. D. Hammond Named President," *Augusta Chronicle*, July 7, 1911, 2.

118. John Hammond to Bishop Candler, April 17, 1915, Candler Papers, box 29, folder 5.

119. Warren Candler to Bishop J. C. Kilgo, June 1, 1915, Candler Papers, box 29, folder 9.

120. Hammond to McMurray, June 21, 1915, Candler Papers.

121. The first to make this argument seems to have been Charles Flint Kellogg, *NAACP: A History of the National Association for the Advancement of Colored People* (Baltimore: Johns Hopkins University Press, 1967), 216, but Kellogg offered no evidence to support the claim. Despite the ab-

sence of evidence, other scholars have repeated the assertion, treating it as fact. See Morton Sosna, *In Search of the Silent South: Southern Liberals and the Race Issue* (New York: Columbia University Press, 1977), 14, and Donald L. Grant, *The Way It Was in the South: The Black Experience in the South* (New York: Carol Publishing, 1993), 241. Grant also claims that John Hammond "did not support higher academic education for blacks because he did not believe them capable," a statement refuted by the historical record.

122. Hammond to McMurray, June 21, 1915, Candler papers.

123. John used the term "domination" in this context. He also reported the friction on the faculty over discipline, noting that he disagreed with both black and white faculty over the proper standards of discipline (ibid.).

124. Range, *Rise and Progress of Negro Colleges in Georgia*, 174.

125. Lily Hardy Hammond, *Southern Women and Racial Adjustment* (Lynchburg, Va.: V. P. Bell Co., 1917), 5.

126. *Sixth Annual Report of the Woman's Missionary Society of the North Georgia Conference* (Augusta: Phoenix Printing, 1916), 17, 62.

127. Hammond, *Southern Women and Racial Adjustment*, 5.

128. Ibid., 15.

129. Willis D. Weatherford, ed. *Lawlessness or Civilization, which? Report of Addresses and Discussions in the Law and Order Conference, held at Blue Ridge, North Carolina, August 4th, 5th, and 6th, nineteen hundred and seventeen* (Nashville: Williams Printing, 1917), 92.

130. See, for example, Isaac Erwin Avery, *Idle Comments* (Charlotte: Avery Publishing Company, 1905), 78–80. On "mammy" in southern white iconography, see M. M. Manring, *Slave in a Box: The Strange Career of Aunt Jemima* (Charlottesville: University Press of Virginia, 1998), and Cheryl Thurber, "The Development of the Mammy Image and Mythology," in Virginia Bernhard, et al., eds., *Southern Women: Histories and Identities* (Columbia: University of Missouri Press, 1992).

131. Hammond, *Southern Women and Racial Adjustment*, 31–32.

132. Kellogg, *NAACP*, 220–21.

133. Link, *Paradox of Southern Progressivism*, 248–51.

134. Will Alexander was personally responsible for this "un-institutionalized" format, having come to distrust large institutions (Dykeman and Stokely, *Seeds of Southern Change*, 80).

135. Link, *Paradox of Southern Progressivism*, 252.

136. Weatherford and Johnson, *Race Relations*, 512.

137. Hall, *Revolt against Chivalry*, 62.

138. White, *Liberty and Justice for All*, 243.

139. Hall, *Revolt against Chivalry*, 89–95; McDowell, *Social Gospel in the South*, 88–93. This meeting was a who's who of women's interracial activism, including Lugenia Burns Hope, Carrie Parks Johnson, and Sara Estelle Haskin.

140. *Year Book and Minutes of the Fifty-Eighth Session of the North Georgia Conference*, 88. John continued to preach at a small mission church on Long Island until his death in 1923.

141. White, *Liberty and Justice for All*, 182.

142. Robert Russa Moton, *Finding a Way Out: An Autobiography* (Garden City, N.Y.: Doubleday, Page & Co., 1921), 277–78.

143. The records are frustratingly vague on this, but the CIC apparently took over this press function sometime around 1922. Robert Eleazer, an experienced journalist, served as the educational director for twenty years.

144. "The Rev. John D. Hammond," *New York Times*, December 12, 1923, 21.

145. C. H. Phillips, *The History of the Colored Methodist Episcopal Church in America: Comprising its Organization, Subsequent Development and Present Status* (Jackson: C.M.E. Church, 1925), 590.

146. "Woman Voter Protests," *New York Times*, July 2, 1924, 18. This insistence on nonpartisanship puts Lily squarely in the mainstream of women's political culture in the 1920s. See Lorraine Gates Schuyler, *The Weight of Their Votes: Southern Women and Political Leverage in the 1920s* (Chapel Hill: University of North Carolina Press, 2006).

147. "Mrs. Lydia Hardy Hammond," *New York Times*, January 24, 1925, 13.

148. *Fifteen Annual Report of the Woman's Missionary Council of the Methodist Episcopal Church South, for 1924–25* (Nashville: MECS, 1925), 6.

149. Hall, *Revolt against Chivalry*, 104.

150. Frederickson, "Shaping a New Society," 358–59.

151. Harvey, *Freedom's Coming*, 74, 82–87.

152. Hall, *Revolt against Chivalry*, 166.

153. "In Letter With Will She Bars Mourning," *New York Times*, April 22, 1925, 3. All three of her children lived in New York. Frances Hammond (who apparently had not married) and Katherine Roulstone both lived in the city; Henry Dennis Hammond lived in Binghamton.

154. Even sympathetic contemporaries sometimes saw the CIC as having only "tentative plans and no force behind them" (Hall, *Revolt Against Chivalry*, 126).

155. Ibid., 106, 127.

156. Mabel Katharine Howell, *Women and the Kingdom: Fifty Years of Kingdom Building by the Women of the Methodist Episcopal Church South, 1878–1928* (Nashville: Cokesbury, 1928), 71, 233–36.

157. Mary Noreen Dunn, *Women and Home Missions* (Nashville: Cokesbury Press, 1936), 60.

158. Noreen Dunn Tatum, *A Crown of Service: A Story of Woman's Work in the Methodist Episcopal Church, South, from 1878 to 1940* (Nashville: Parthenon, 1960).

159. Hammond's colleague Mary Helm appeared to understand. She protested the efforts of the Methodist hierarchy to restrain their women's activism, believing that it would push the most talented Methodist women to seek avenues for service outside the church (Shadron, "The Laity Rights Movement," 265).

Lily Hardy Hammond's Publications

"As Children See Us," *Babyhood: A Monthly Magazine for Mothers* 5 (December 1888–November 1889): 372–73.

"The Parsonage and Home Mission Reading Course." *Our Homes* 3 (September 1894): 1–2.

"Woman's Work for Women." *Our Homes* 4 (September 1895): 6–7.

"New Light on Social Problems." *Methodist Review* 42 (January–February 1896): 376–83.

"Knights Errant" [poem]. *Century* 56 (August 1898): 583.

"Our Debt to the Colored Race." *Our Homes* 5 (September 1896): 8–9.

"Our Duty to the Negro." *Our Homes* 9 (January 1900): 1.

"Book Review." *Our Homes* 11 (February 1902): 3.

"A Successful Marriage." *Harper's* 105 (October 1902): 747–52.

"Some Southern Factory Problems." *Methodist Review* 51 (May–June 1902): 349–59.

"A Southern View of the Negro." *Outlook* 73 (March 14, 1903): 619–23.

"Women Novelists and Marriage." *Methodist Quarterly Review* 52 (April 1903): 319–23.

"Footstep of Fear." *Independent* 55 (August 27, 1903): 2031–34.

"November Evening" [poem]. *Outlook* 75 (November 14, 1903): 655.

"Present-Day Philanthropy." *Methodist Quarterly Review* 53 (January 1904): 25–35.

"The Growth of Democracy in the South." *Methodist Quarterly Review* 54
(January 1905): 28–38.

"Typewriter Family" [children's poem]. *St. Nicholas* 32 (March 1905): 417.

"Aspects of Southern Education." *World To-day* 9 (August 1905): 832–36.

"Conqueror" [poem]. *Harper's* 111 (October 1905): 667.

The Master-Word, a Story of the South To-day.
New York: Macmillan Company, 1905.

"A Letter from Mrs. J. D. Hammond to the Woman's Board of Home Missions."
Our Homes 16 (July 1907): 11.

"The Rights of the Laity." *Our Homes* 19 (July 1910): 7–8.

"The New Philanthropy." *Our Homes* 19 (November 1910): 1–2.

"Our Work for Negroes." *Missionary Voice* 2 (March 1912): 181–82.

"The White Man's Debt to the Negro." *Annals of the American Academy of
Political and Social Science* 49 (September 1913): 67–73.

"Negro Boys Make Good." *Survey* 32 (May 16, 1914): 603.

"Wasted Power." *Christian Advocate* 75 (August 7, 1914): 10–11.

"The Work of the General Education Board in the South."
South Atlantic Quarterly 14 (October 1914): 348–57.

"Light on Negro Delinquency." *Christian
Advocate* 75 (October 16, 1914): 26–27.

In Black and White: An Interpretation of Southern Life. New York: Revell, 1914.

"A Black-and-White Christmas." *Christian Advocate* 76
(January 15, 1915): 26–27.

"Schools and Students." *Christian Advocate* 76 (April 2, 1915): 10–11.

"The Building of Homes." *Methodist Quarterly Review* 64 (April 1915): 315–21.

"Some Paine College Graduates." *Christian Advocate* 76 (May 7, 1915): 26–28.

"The Work of the General Education Board in the South."
South Atlantic Quarterly 14 (October 1915): 348–57.

In the Garden of Delight. New York: Thomas Y. Crowell Co., 1916.

Southern Women and Racial Adjustment.
Lynchburg, Va.: J. P. Bell Co., Printers, 1917.

M. Katharine Bennett, Grace Scribner, John E. Calfee, A. J. McKelway,
L. H. Hammond, Miriam L. Woodberry, and Walter C. Rauschenbusch.
The Path of Labor: Christianity and the World's Workers.
New York: Council of Women for Home Missions (1918).

"The City Negro." *Missionary Voice* 9 (March 1919): 83–84.

"Negro Condemnation of Negro Criminals." *Nashville Christian Advocate* 80
(August 22, 1919): 1080.

"Ignorance and the Eleven Million." *Nation's Business* 8
(December 1920): 38–40.

"Sure Foundations." *Outlook* 130 (March 29, 1922): 511–13.

"Believer in Happiness." *Outlook* 130 (April 5, 1922): 548–51.

"A Lover of All Races." *Missionary Voice* 12 (October 1922): 304.

In the Vanguard of a Race. New York: Council of Women for Home Missions
and Missionary Education Movement of the United States and Canada, 1922.

Saving an Idea. New York: Published jointly by Council of Women for Home
Missions and Missionary Education Movement of the United States and
Canada, 1922. (This is a reprint of chap. 4 of *In the Vanguard of a Race,*
a biographical sketch of Nannie Burroughs and the National Training
School for Women and Girls in Washington D.C.)

Memories of Mary Helm.
Nashville: Woman's Missionary Council, M.E. Church, South, 1923.

"Bible Lesson for January—The Task Christ Sets Himself and Us."
Missionary Voice 13 (December 1923): 382.

"Human Race and the Race of Man." *Methodist Quarterly Review* 73
(October 1924): 623–33.

Missionary Heroes. Nashville: Cokesbury Press, 1925.

The Negro in the New Working World.
Nashville: Woman's Department, Board of Missions, M.E. Church, South, n.d.

IN BLACK AND WHITE

An Interpretation of the South

BY L. H. HAMMOND

Author of "The Master-Word"

With an Introduction by
James H. Dillard, M.A., LL.D.,
President of the Jeanes Foundation Board,
Director of the Slater Fund

Fleming H. Revell Company
New York [et al.], 1914

To my mother and my father,

both slave-owners in earlier life,

whose broad thinking and selfless living

first taught me the meaning of human brotherhood,

I dedicate this book,

with a gratitude deepened by time, and a love undiminished by death.

Introduction

The problem of the South to-day is how to find voices and hearings for her best thoughts and sentiments. Especially is this true in regard to the relationship between the races. Public sentiment rules. It rules the attitude of individuals. It makes and unmakes the laws. It enforces or neglects the laws that are made. Public sentiment is mainly dependent upon the thoughts and sentiments that find expression in the constant utterances of pulpit, press, and political campaigns. On this question of race relationship the pulpit in the South is remarkably silent. The point is not raised whether or not the province of the pulpit is to discuss public and social problems. The fact is that the pulpit in the South is remarkably silent on the race question, even on the side of religion and religious duties. With few exceptions the direct contributions of the Southern clergy in establishing public sentiment on this question have amounted to little, and may almost be left out of count. It is the editor and the politician who, more exclusively in the South than in any other part of the country, influence public sentiment on the race question as well as on other public questions. The men of letters, the educators, the educated business men, have not counted appreciably in moulding public sentiment. I said editors along with politicians, but it is not so much the editorial writers as it is the managers who direct what news shall appear, and regulate the tones and head-lines of what appears. It is these and the politicians who are most responsible for public sentiment. For reasons that run back to the awful mistakes and hardships and outrages of the reconstruction period, the men who deal professionally in politics and public questions, and these include the newspaper men, have taken and still continue to take, not all of them but a large majority, an attitude of hostility and repression towards the Negro race. It is natural that it should be so.

But is it not time for a better note? The Negro is here, and so far as human vision reaches, he is here to stay, and to stay mainly in the South. He is not only here, but he is improving wonderfully in education and in the acquisition of property. There are exceptions. There are in fact large masses of Negroes who are not improving in their conditions; but the figures of statistics are beyond contradicting the fact that the race as a whole is making forward strides away from gross illiteracy and dependent poverty. Shall the white people wish it to be so? It seems to me that they should wish it to be so. It seems to me that our material prosperity depends upon the spread of intelligence and thrift among all the people, even the humblest. It seems to me that our public health demands this, because filth and disease extend their evils high and low. And how dare we say that humanity and religion do not demand it? If humanity and religion mean anything, they mean good will to man and the application of the eternal principles of justice and righteousness now and always.

It does not follow that any amount of good will and desire for righteous dealing does away with the fact of race. The Frenchman is not a German, nor the Jew a Gentile, and the difference of the Negro and the white is most of all distinctly marked. The problem of their living and working side by side in the same region is a problem, which no amount of optimism can deny. The problem is a problem which calls for neither a blind and hopeless pessimism nor a weak and watery optimism. The call is for facing facts, and dealing with them in the light of wise statesmanship and the holy principles of religious faith. Some advanced spirits would ignore the universal fact of race, and in the highest sense they are right in the sight of law and religion; but in the practical living of our lives there is no reason to ignore racial any more than other natural distinctions and affinities. There is a segregation which is perfectly natural and inevitable, and will surely take care of itself. Negroes as naturally and inevitably flock together as do the whites, and in my opinion their leaders oppose any denial of such natural segregation, and frown on offensive efforts to ignore the fact. Many doubtless question the truth of this attitude of the Negroes, but my experience leads me to the conviction that, however much we may think to the contrary, it is essentially and almost universally true.

For the white people the main point is that, with all recognition of racial feelings, we are bound to acknowledge the common rights of humanity. We are bound to acknowledge that all men are human, and have human rights and claims to life, liberty, and the pursuit of happiness. Are we not, we whites of the South, also bound by peculiar claims both of nearness and necessity? The Negro served us as a slave; in the providence of God he is now by law among us as a man. For his good, for our own good, is it not well for us to be helping him on to useful manhood? Grant that in the mass he is low down, can any low class, black or white, lie in the ditch and all of us not suffer?

It is because Mrs. Hammond's book strikes the good note that it is to be greatly welcomed at this time. I believe that our press and public will welcome it as a sincere, earnest, and able effort to tell the difficult truth. All may not agree with all she says, but that is not so important as to recognize that her book is one of the utterances which are needed at this time, and that she is seeking to help us all, North and South, to think rightly on this problem.

JAMES H. DILLARD

I

In Terms of Humanity

There is nothing except love itself which so adds to the richness and charm of life as a sense of wide horizons. One breathes in freedom under a wide sky, catching the proper perspective for life, and setting large and small in their true relations. The burdens and hindrances which press so close in a narrow, personal atmosphere drop away, and dwindle to their true size in those far spaces which include all human life. We never understand them till we see them so, set against the background of a world-experience, translated into terms common to all mankind.

We were made to be world-dwellers; members of our own small circle and section of country, loving and loyal to them all, yet members too of the whole human brotherhood: of our own race intensely; yet just as vitally, and more broadly, of the great Race of Man.

The best that can be said of an isolated man, cut off from his wide human relations, is that he has a capacity for life. A human stomach, or liver, or heart, may be cut out of the body it belongs in, and yet be kept "alive." It serves no end of use or beauty, poor unrelated thing, and is practically dead in its cold, colourless abiding place. Yet it has a latent capacity for living, if only it be placed again in vital connection with a human organism, and receive life from a working connection with the whole.

So many of us lead cold-storage lives, and find them, naturally, dull enough. So many more are vitally connected with but a fragment of life—our family circle, our neighbourhood or section. It is as if a heart beat in a mutilated body, legless or armless, perhaps without sight, or deaf to the far, sweet voices which call to the freest and happiest things in life.

We are made far-sighted. Scientists tell us that our increasing need of glasses is due to the fine, near-at-hand work imposed by civilization on eyes planned by nature for far-sweeping vision, for the wide look which goes from verge to verge of the high-arching sky.

It is much that we have acquired near vision; we would be savages still without it. Close observation, thought of little things, the constructive spirit at work upon details—these, inch by inch, through the ages, have built the road over which the race has advanced. Long sacrifice has gone into them, untold patience and endurance, the endless drudgery out of which character emerges, like a winged thing from its cocoon.

But we need not lose the wide look, nor work at details knowing nothing of their relation to the big world-life of man. How could we understand them so, or understand ourselves? How should we bear our griefs, or meet our difficulties, or work in hope and with joy? Life is such a dull puzzle to near-sighted folk; and so many of those whose lives touch theirs are sealed books to them, uninteresting because unknown. And ignorance breeds prejudice as a dunghill breeds flies.

The commonest prejudice of all, perhaps, is the near-visioned belief in the superiority of the people of one's own small corner to all the rest of the world. This frank and childish egotism is the hall-mark of the separated life, whether lived by Anglo-Saxon or Patagonian, Chinaman or American. We are the people, and wisdom will die with us! That is the world-cry of unrelated man; and it arrogates a superiority which implies antagonistic criticism of all dwellers without the small charmed circle of the crier's understanding.

This unsympathetic criticism betrays itself as ignorance by the very fact of its existence; for sympathy cannot fail if only one understands deep enough. It is the surface view, always, which breeds antagonism. If one could understand to the uttermost one would inevitably love to the uttermost: one's compassions, like God's, would be new every morning. It is because it is ordinarily so apart, cut off from sympathy, that criticism is so often shorn of renovating force. Its only chance for constructive service lies in being passed through the alembic of a living sympathy, which alone can transmute the inorganic matter of criticism into food for assimilation and growth.

For love, and not intellect, is the vital force; and no man is shut out by lack of knowledge from the widest human life. Things dim and confusing to the mind are clearly apprehended by the heart. If I venture to offer this partial interpretation of the life of that corner of the world which is home to me, it is not because of a belief that peculiar powers of any kind have been given to me, entitling me to speak of my people, or to them. It is because I am so truly one of the mass, living a small life in a small place, walled in by circumstances, like my brothers. For any sharer of the common lot whose deepest desire is to walk in love towards all the world will find, with the years, a way opening into the very heart of life, and will come upon the reasons for many of the things which perplex us, for much of the wrong we bear and the wrong we inflict, much which hedges us in, much which makes our brothers of a wider circle misunderstand and misjudge us. What is said must be incomplete and partly incorrect. One life may mirror the race life; yet the waves of personality inevitably refract the reflected rays. It is offered only for what it is: an attempt to translate some fragments of Southern life into world-terms; to set our sectional problems in their wide human relations, and so to see them as they really are.

When one lives on a little hill, all closed in by mountains, one cannot possibly see "the lay of the land"; and most of us begin life in a place like that. Some of us climb later to a mountain top, and live there with wide views, and heads near the stars. But the valleys look deep and dark from up there, the hills seem small, and the mountains fill the world. It is beautiful and splendid, and true, too: but it is only the half of truth—that most dangerous of all lies—until the mountains, too, are set in their wide relations. When men make them wings like birds, and fly high enough, they see something bigger than the mountains, and that is the earth to which they all belong. One can love the mountains after that without any childish pride in them, or childish scorn of the valleys and hills.

It is so with the races of men, and with that great, underlying humanity which binds them all in one.

Long ago, when I was young, I knew so many things that aren't so. I could label all the deeds of men as fast as I heard about them; and what was far more amazing, I could label the men who did them. Labelling deeds is really not a very complicated process. Even a child, for instance, can distinguish lies of a fairly simple type. But to put the right label on the man behind the lie—that is a different and most difficult matter. He may be a man who would die for the truth, who daily sacrifices for it as he understands it. He may be all hedged in with inheritances from which he has no way of escape—an example of "invincible ignorance." He may be just at the beginning of things: so many of us tell lies because we are not out of the kindergarten yet, and life exists for us only in relation to our own exuberant personalities. And he may be—though it isn't likely—a deliberate lover of lies. To label his deed is easy; but how shall one label him?

Yet youth has a passion for labels. It is such a fascinating way of displaying one's knowledge to a supposedly admiring world. And the more recently acquired our knowledge is, the more superficial, the more, in our youth, it refreshes our souls to display it, and to criticize the little folk of the family, who are still in those depths of ignorance so recently occupied by ourselves; and to criticize the old folks, whose knowledge has so fruited into wisdom that we cannot trace its connection with our own brand-new buds at all.

Dispensing information concerning its own shortcomings to a world that lies in darkness is, in fact, one of the natural and unforgettable joys of adolescence. Nobody ought to begrudge it to anybody. It is part of the glamour of youth, and dear, at one stage of life, to every soul alive. As we grow older we should remember, and smile. Poor young things, they beat against the walls of their ignorance so soon!

But one's wisdom must be ripe and garnered for this understanding. It is not to be expected of the younger young folks, whom older adolescence is so very hard upon. Their knowledge has achieved little more than a pair of cotyledons as yet, perhaps, and wisdom waits on the years. But they will be as big as the biggest soon, and know as much, or more: the younger ones "sass back."

That is the way quarrels start in families, as all long-suffering parents know. And I think something very like that has happened between the North and the South—between the big brother and the little one. For races are men writ large, and men are but larger children.

Sometimes we see twins whose individual development indicates a difference of years between the two. One had measles, perhaps, or scarlet fever, "with ulterior consequences," as the doctors say, and it has set him back a long time. His digestion was impaired, and lack of nourishment has stunted his growth. The other boy is full fed and vigorous, glorying in his strength as every boy must, and claiming the earth as his birthright. He wants to be nice to his little brother, but the child can't live his big-boy life at all; and he's grouchy, too—always getting his feelings hurt. It isn't the big boy's fault he's no bigger; and he's pig-headed and mean, anyway: just see the way he picks on folks that are weaker than he is!

The war was our measles; and we have hardly recovered from the ulterior consequences yet. But our Northern twin kept right on growing. He came to adolescence first: and in the last twenty-five years or so he has reached that later period of youth when one begins to look soberly out upon an ever-widening world, and to see a man's work and man's responsibilities shaping themselves from dreams.

I am sure that when I was a girl of fifteen, and first began to explore the purlieus of some Northern tenements, hardly any of my well-to-do, educated, and entirely respectable and Christian acquaintances cared anything whatever about them. Our rector was a man of visions and dreams, and he stirred his people to open a mission in what was considered the worst section of the city. I was a member of its regular working force until my marriage, a few years later. But to nobody connected with that mission did it exist for any purpose whatever except to save the souls of the tenement-dwellers out of this world into another one, and, incidentally, to show personal kindness, as occasion offered, to individuals of the district. Nobody dissented from the doctrine that whatever was wrong in the general tenement-house environment was merely the outward and visible sign of the tenement-dwellers' inward and spiritual lack of grace: if all their souls could only be saved there would be nothing left wrong with the tenements. There was no sense of responsibility on landlords, on the health authorities, the employers of labour, or the public at large. There was, in every one I was thrown with, a vigorous personal conscience; strong personal sympathy for individuals, who were to be got out of the general tenement-house mess if possible; much personal sacrifice; and a deep sense of personal obligation to be individually kind, and to save all the souls that were savable. But that was all. There was no glimmering of community consciousness, of community conscience, or of community sin. The North was growing fast, but it was still a many-individualed North. It responded keenly, as growing children will, to those stimuli which penetrated the area of its awakened consciousness. It was eager, alert, questioning, learning, immeasurably more stimulating mentally than my own beloved South: but it had not yet reached that stage of growth where a social conscience is possible. In the presence of appalling social wrong there was no response to stimulus whatever.

For myself, I was in wild revolt: but the only way out then conceivable to me was for the poor all to get saved in a hurry, and die and go to heaven. God might have known what He was about when He made slum people: but His reasons passed my understanding.

Just then I came upon some English magazines containing Miss Hill's earlier articles on housing, and God was cleared of the charges I had brought against Him.[1] The evils in the tenements were man-made; and if enough people would do the loving thing they could be stopped. It was all personal still—work, responsibility, and righted wrong; but saving souls included the changing of physical conditions.

1. Octavia Hill was a nineteenth-century reformer in London, and author of *Homes of the London Poor* (London: Macmillan, 1875).

But good people were not interested. Those to whom I talked considered Miss Hill's ideas visionary. They did not believe it possible to redeem slums— only to redeem some slum-dwellers' souls. I labeled them all on the spot, and "stupid" was the nicest word in the list. The indictment grew longer and blacker as the years went on. I was back in the South now—the beautiful, Christian country, where there were no slums, nor child labourers, nor sweat-shops, nor white slaves. It never occurred to me that we were too young and small, industrially, to develop these things; or that, like the North, we had to travel through the country of indifference to the evils we did have before we could grow old enough to care.

When Stead wrote "If Christ Came to Chicago" it was the last straw: respect for the North was gone.[2] They had money up there; they claimed to be Christians; and they knew. Yet nothing was done. The imprecatory Psalms made excellent reading.

And then, out of that vast welter of indifference, the emergence of a social conscience in the North! There had been already, here and there, a point of light—a man or a woman flinging an isolated life against embattled social wrongs. But now began a gathering of little groups; here and yonder one heard a word caught up by other voices until it rose into a cry: and now the sound of marching feet, and thunder which begins to shake the world!

The North is a glorious big brother: and as the hatred of newly-realized old wrongs grows within him, as that which is highest in him is more and more committing him to the doctrine and life of brotherhood, it is part of the law of youth and growth that he should have scant patience with those who are indifferent to conditions which touch him to the quick. The one unforgivable thing to him is that a people should be lacking in social conscience; the one inexplicable audacity, that without it they should dare to call themselves Christians. Our brother of the North is deep in the labeling stage.

And we Southern folk? If the big brother's contempt has scorched and burnt us, have we had no contempt for those who are younger than we? We had no smaller child in the immediate family to outlaw with labels; but providence has not been altogether unkind. For there is the cook's black baby: and it is so long since we were babies ourselves we can't be expected to remember that stage of our growth. Anyway, there is the baby; and the labels show up on him beautifully.

2. W. T. Stead, *If Christ Came to Chicago! A Plea for the Union of All Who Love in the Service of All Who Suffer* (Chicago: Laird & Lee, 1894).

The North, of course, thinks it had a social conscience fifty years ago: but that was a social conscience about other people's sins—a delicate variety for early forcing merely, as I know by my own experience. I once had a deal more social conscience about Northern conditions than about those of our Southern Negroes,[3] though my personal conscience about the Negroes was in a flourishing state. Besides, we had a conscience about slavery ourselves—a true social conscience in the germ. One of our sorest sore points is our Northern brother's irritating inability to grasp this fact, which is [a] matter of common knowledge in the South. Thousands of slave-owners, like my own parents, thought slavery wrong, and confidently expected the time, not far distant, when the states would themselves abolish it. The South did not fight for slavery. We have seen the day, down here, when we would have enjoyed putting that fact into our Northern brother's head with a pile-driver: and it really does seem, sometimes, that no lesser agency will ever get it there.

What the South fought for was its constitutional right to get out of the Union when it no longer desired to stay in it. We still believe the point was open to debate, though we have long since ceased to regret that the "Noes" won it.

As for the Negroes, we were developing a social conscience about them, a healthier growth, perhaps, though a slower one, than the vicarious conscience of the North. And because of that conscience, as well as because of natural human kindliness, the relations between black and white were in the main kindly and understanding. I make no excuse for slavery, nor for the terrible things allowed by it; but those things were the exception and not the rule. The conduct of the Negroes during the war proves that. They are a patient, gentle folk; but they are far from being superhuman. If the main product of slave-relations had not been kindliness the Southern armies would have disbanded to protect Southern homes.

These kindly relations were not shaken by Negro freedom. Nobody held it against the Negroes that they were free. And in the white men's hearts kindness was reinforced by gratitude for the faithful care the Negroes had given to the women and children of the South. In the ruin of the old order, and the desperate poverty of the new, readjustment would have been slow and difficult. It would have been, doubtless, many years before the polls would have been open to any considerable number of Negroes. But there were matters more vital than

3. The word Negro is printed with a capital throughout this book in obedience to the rule that requires all race-names to begin with a capital letter: *e.g.*, Indian, Teuton, Zulu, Maori, Anglo-Saxon, Filipino, etc., etc. [original footnote]

votes; and the readjustment, if slow, would have progressed normally, in mutual kindliness and patience.

But the North, with its social conscience about home conditions yet in embryo, and its social conscience for other folks, like a clock without a pendulum, working overtime, was bent on growth by cataclysm. If it could only have taken a world-look for a minute it would have seen growth never comes that way; but being so very busy doing things, it had no time to look. The North was a child as yet, and lived in a world fashioned out of its own thoughts. A child can take blocks of wood and put them into a barn or a castle or a ship: it is as easy as making fiat money. But when the blocks are men the fiat process never works: they will not stay put.

That was our great disaster—ours, and the Negro's and the North's. Children ourselves, how should we know the big, strong, overbearing North was but a child too? And we had all a child's keen sense of injustice, and keen resentment of it. We thought the North understood as well as we did what it was doing; we even thought the Negro understood. Hate sprang full-armoured in a night. The North called it reconstruction: it was destruction of a very high order. And in all that ruin of our dearest possessions the most precious, the most necessary thing destroyed was the old-time friendship between white and black. It shrivelled in the fires of hate; and from the ashes rose suspicion and injustice, all wrong inflicted and sustained, to curse both races yet.

The shock of those anarchic days is deep in the South's nerves to this day. Much which the North calls by a harsher name is a resurgence of an almost physical hysteria.

When I was a child my nurse put me to bed, and was supposed to sit by me till I went to sleep, but she never did. She was a white woman, by the way, and quite well educated: the older children's black mammy had stayed [by them]. She had a sweetheart waiting in the kitchen; and as soon she tucked me in bed she put out the light, and left me with the assurance that a lion and a tiger were under my bed, both friends of hers; and if I ever dared to get up to call my mother, or told her I was left alone, they would claw me under the bed by my feet and eat me up.

That was fifty years ago. But to this day, as soon as the light goes out my well-trained nerves try to jump me into bed. When I am least thinking of it there descends that sudden sense of impending claws.

We are like that about Negro domination. We know it is a foolish fear; yet we are so ready to start at it, both as regards our political and our social life.

Governor Northen, of Georgia, spoke the truth when he declared that "Social equality is a delusion set up by the demagogue" for his own ends: but demagogue or nurse, children are easily frightened.[4] And the South really felt the claws once; and the memory is deep in every nerve.

Beyond this, we have never yet set the Negro in his world-relations, any more than the North has so set us. We have looked upon our "Negro problem" as a thing apart, our strange, peculiar burden, the like of which the world has never seen; and our dominating thought about it is that this excrescence on Southern life shall never again threaten the existence of our civilization.

That this should be the main aspect the problems of our poorer classes present to us we owe partly to our memory of claws; yet largely too to that irresponsible, but inevitable, selfishness of youth, a phenomenon of growth not to be averted or shortened, which sees all life from a purely personal standpoint. We are just beginning, as a people, to touch that period of later adolescence where one glimpses the fact that a standpoint purely personal cannot, in the nature of things, be either kind or just, or true to our own best selves.

But while we are learning to admit this, to ourselves and to others, there are some things our kinsmen of a wider circle should remember. They should not forget that the first effect of sorrow is always isolation. After sorrow is assimilated, become food for expanding life, one may emerge and take one's place again, with no trace of past struggle except in a deeper sympathy with humanity, and a broader understanding of it. But assimilation takes place in the wilderness; and life passes one by at a time like that, an unheeded, alien, far-off force.

For years we lived in that wilderness, with no thought nor care for the wide world-life climbing, expanding, outside. Two things we had beside our sorrow: a struggle for bare existence which absorbed the energy of every fibre; and the pride of a high-spirited people who had been humbled in the dust. Sorrow, poverty, and pride: can any other three things produce such perfect insulation as these?

How should we have a social conscience? No nation has ever developed community consciousness while its members were battling for daily bread. A class possessed of a little leisure must be developed before that can appear, and must bear and rear children educated to a somewhat wider outlook than their fathers' bitter struggle made possible. The South is barely at this initial stage.

We knew the world—the polite world—pretty well before we had the measles. We were a cultivated folk. But the world of those days knew no more about

4. William Jonathan Northen (1835–1913), governor of Georgia, 1890–94.

a social conscience than it knew about "movies," or automobiles: it hadn't gone that far in the book. Individuals, it is true, were spending their lives, here and there, in the preparation of a soil where later a social conscience might germinate; but they were thought of, so far as they were thought of at all, as individual saints or individual cranks. The housing movement had a few disciples, both in France and in England; but they were not in the public eye. And the voice of the socialist was heard in the land only to mark him as a fit subject for the madhouse. England, foremost of all nations, had entered, half unwittingly, upon her magnificent and long-to-be continued course of social legislation; and men like Kingsley and Maurice were calling passionately to that void where a social conscience was soon to be.[5] But these were but the local affairs of a foreign nation, as we and the rest of the world saw them. There was nothing in America to parallel the conditions which had called their protest forth; and to us, as to the great mass of the privileged everywhere, nearly all of human life was foreign.

It was during the years of our sojourn in the wilderness that the privileged of earth began to discover humanity as a brotherhood, and shot beyond us. But our time of separation is ending. We have learned and achieved much in these years. Our sympathies are broader, our minds more mature, our hearts nearer a full awakening. But we know very little as yet about this new old world to which we have returned. We haven't learned about slums, or a minimum wage, or mending criminals instead of manufacturing them, or the abolition of poverty, or the connection between under-nourishment and the poorhouse. Even our churches are still inclined, many of them, to look askance at social service as an adulteration of the "pure gospel," and to regard the saving of souls out of this world into another one as the full measure of Christian duty. Some of us think if anybody says social service and Negroes in the same breath he must mean "social equality," and reach for a gun at once.

But the time of isolation is past with us. We stand ready to take our place in the world, and the powers of youth and health stir within us. We are ready for life in the open, for world-connections and a world-view.

What will we do with the Negro, our peculiar and heavy burden, our puzzle, almost our despair?

If we will quit thinking about him as peculiar he will cease to be either a

5. Charles Kingsley (1819–1875) was an English reformer, minister, and prolific author. He published several books detailing the horrific living and working conditions of the poor in mid-century London. Frederick Denison Maurice (1805–1872) was also an English reformer, minister, and writer in the same period. Maurice is considered the spiritual leader of the mid-century Christian Socialist movement.

puzzle or a despair. Are we the only folk on earth responsible for a "submerged tenth"? Burdens are peculiar in details, fitted to the individual or the race; but in essence they are the same for all mankind, and call for the same courage, the same sympathy, the same patience and hope and strength. National trials and difficulties are like personal sorrows and hardships: when we regard them as peculiar to ourselves they overwhelm us. Who are we, to walk in an unblazed path, to solve a problem new in the experience of mankind, to bear what man has never borne before? Human nature turns coward at the mere thought of it, and excuses its failure with the plea that it cannot be expected to be stronger or wiser than all the world.

But if the burden is not peculiar? If it is our part of a world-wide task? If everywhere men living under such conditions as do the majority of our Negroes are reacted upon by their environment just as the Negroes are? If we have mistakenly counted our poverty line and our colour line as one? If in every nation long neglect of the poor and the ignorant had piled up just such a weight of weakness, unthrift, unreliability and crime for a clearer-visioned generation to transform? If men in all lands, the best and finest, are spending themselves to solve problems such as ours?

When we see our problem in that light—see it as it is, see it in its wide human relations—we will set ourselves to its solution. We never have been "quitters" in the South. If this be our part of a world-task we will achieve it.

And our part of a world-task we will find it, as soon as we compare our poorest with the poorest of other countries and of all races. Skins differ in colour, heads are shaped differently; one man's mind runs ahead of his sympathies, perhaps, and another man's mind may creep while his emotional nature runs rampant. But under all outward differences their fundamental humanity is as much the same as is the earth under the mountain and the hill. The same things poison the minds and bodies of white and of black alike; the same elements nourish both. Honesty, purity, love, self-reliance and self-respect—who dare claim a monopoly of these for themselves? They are human, not racial, and to be built up in all races by the same processes: else Christ were a dreamer whom it were madness to follow.

We need to take the long look, as well as the wide one. We say—a church paper in the South said it only a few weeks ago—that in a whole long fifty years of freedom the Negro has advanced so little that his condition "is not encouraging." If that be true it is a grave indictment of us white folks: for the Negro has these fifty years accepted the conditions we have furnished for him, and been subject to us in all things. He has lived beside us, done our work. If there were no encouraging signs after our management of him for fifty years, the difficulty might lie with the management.

As a matter of fact, the statement was made without a proper knowledge of facts. Facts show remarkable progress, and under difficult conditions. But what is fifty years in the development of a race?—or two hundred and fifty, when it starts from savagery?

If we could go back to the skin-and-club days of our own puissant ancestors we would probably find that they made less progress from savagery in two hundred and fifty years than the Negroes have done in that time. Of course they had less outside help: they had to evolve many of their own forces of advance. But for centuries no one seeing then could have dreamed of the world-service waiting in the ages ahead for those wild Britains, who lived like beasts in their lairs. If we could go back and spend a few months with our forefathers, two hundred and fifty years after Roman civilization first touched them, we would probably be glad enough to get back to our black folks again: they would never be quite so black any more.

The truth is, we know nothing about what Negroes were made for or what they are capable of, except on the broad general ground that every human race has human power of development in some direction.— When any one says a thing like that old memories stir instantly in some of us, and we suspect the argument of carrying the sting of social equality in its tail. If we just could rout that old bogey out of our imaginations, and turn our minds from claws! Nobody can force on anybody associations undesired. And whatever Negroes may become, they will certainly not be white folks. They will be just themselves; something that will balance the white race and the yellow and the red, and that will render a racial service all its own. The higher they rise the more Negro they will be, the more the tides of their own race life will fill and satisfy and lift them—along their own path. To doubt that they have, beyond our vision, some world-service yet to render, something enough worth while to justify their long suffering and our own, would be to rule God out of history, and to put the thinking mind "to permanent intellectual confusion."

I would not appear to overlook the existence of race consciousness and of race prejudice, nor to blink the fact that the latter gravely complicates our portion of the world-problems of the unprivileged. Yet race prejudice, though necessarily local in its manifestations, cannot be charged upon the South alone: it is as wide as humanity, and as old as time. It is not confined, in the South, to either race. A thing so widespread, so deeply human, so common to all races, should move no man to bitterness, but to patience. And we are not denied the hope that humanity will one day rise above it.

Race consciousness is another matter. In every highly-developed branch of the great human race-stocks there exists a desire for the integrity of that stock, an instinct against amalgamation with any very-distantly-related race. It is true that with the majority of any such people the instinct shows itself chiefly as race-antagonism and race-prejudice; yet it is shared by those who are free from these lower manifestations of it. Despite individual exceptions this law holds good, the world around; and its violation, in the marriage of individuals of widely-different race-stocks, involves disastrous penalties.

As instinct so wide-spread and so deep may be safely credited to some under-lying cause in full harmony with the great laws of human development. The instinct for racial integrity, with its corollary of a separate social life, will doubtless persist in a world from which race prejudice has vanished. If one believed in an Ultimate Race which would be a blend of all races—a belief frequently adopted when one first recognizes the real oneness of humanity—one would necessarily regard this desire for racial integrity as but another manifestation of race prejudice, doomed, as such, to pass. But the wider and deeper one's association with life the more clearly seen is the law of differentiation in all development. In the light of this law the ultimate physical oneness of human races becomes as chimerical as the ultimate oneness of all species of trees or the disappearance of the rich diversity of winged forms of life in favour of an Ultimate Bird.

Life does not develop towards uniformity, but towards richness of variety in a unity of beauty and service. Unless the Race of Man contradicts all known laws of life it will develop in the same way; and whether white, or yellow, or black, they who guard their own racial integrity, in a spirit of brotherhood free from all other-racial scorn, will most truly serve the Race to which all belong. What we white people need to lay aside is not our care for racial separateness, but our prejudice. The black race needs, in aspiring to the fullest possible development, to foster a fuller faith in its own blood, and in the world's need for some service which it, and it alone, can render in richest measure to the great Brotherhood of Man.

II
The Basis of Adjustment

In a newspaper of a Southern city I read recently a report of the court proceedings of the day before. The first case tried was that of a white man, some thirty years of age, who had violated the white slave law.[1] He had abducted a girl of sixteen from her home, and was using her for immoral gain. The judge, in sentencing him, had dwelt at length on the preciousness of that of which the child had been robbed; but added that he had decided to make the sentence a light one, because the law was new, and not very widely understood. He gave the man one year in prison.

The next case, according to the paper, was that of a Negro boy of twenty. He had stolen eleven dollars and forty-six cents. The evidence was convincing; but the judge said he would give him also a light sentence. His reason was not, as it might have been, that the law against the offense was new. It is just as new as the other one, having been formally promulgated at the same time, on a mountain in the Sinaitic peninsula. But the judge's reason for mercy, he said, was that the evidence clearly showed that the boy had never had any chance in life. His parents had both died in his infancy, and nobody else had wanted him. He had grown up, no one knew how, beaten from pillar to post, uncared for, untaught. So the judge decided on mercy, and gave him three years.

I do not at this time raise the question of the wisdom of time-sentences, in these or any cases; that will be taken up later. The point is that the value of a child's honour and a mother's happiness, when stolen by a mature white man, was assessed at one year in prison; and the value of eleven dollars and forty-six cents, when stolen by a young Negro waif, was assessed at three years in the same place. The judge is a man who has, I believe, a sincere desire correctly to

1. The White Slave Traffic Act of 1910, commonly called the Mann Act in recognition of its Congressional sponsor, outlawed the transportation of women across state lines for immoral purposes.

administer the law in his high office; and law and justice are to him synonymous words. He thinks in terms of law, not in terms of humanity.

Some months ago I was visiting friends when a son of the house, a university student, came in with a story of a morning spent in the city court. Some case was pending in which the students were interested, and a body of them had been in attendance all the morning. A number of cases concerning Negroes had been disposed of before theirs was called.

"I tell you," he said, summing the morning up, "a 'nigger' stands no show in our courts."

He was evidently shocked by the fact, and so was the family. They are people far above the average in intelligence, in loving-kindness, in culture, in self-sacrificing personal service to the individual poor, both white and black. But courts of law were without the pale of their personal responsibility: their personal conscience, quick and beautifully responsive in any individual matter, merely condemned this wrong and laid it aside. There was no sign of social consciousness; of any sense that if anybody stood no show in their courts it was a community sin, for which all members of the community were responsible, and which the community could change if it would. They did not see that they had any duty in arousing the community to consciousness of social wrong. If any individual one of the many Negroes known to them had been brought before the court that morning, they would have done just what I have done in days when I had no more social conscience about Negroes than they had: they would have seen him, or his family, beforehand and asked some good lawyer, a personal friend probably, to see that the Negro had justice. The lawyer, who would probably not be in the habit of taking such cases, would do so cheerfully and without remuneration, partly to oblige a lady, but largely too for the sake of protecting a Negro who had become individually known to him, and who therefore appealed to his personal conscience.

Cases of both kinds are common all over the South. A Negro who gets in jail will send for "his white folks" first thing, if he is fortunate enough to have any. And they come, man or woman as the case may be, practically without fail. And often, when they come, the Negro gets less than justice in the courts in the sense that he is let off with a reprimand or a small fine when the law would call for something more. But none of us are sorry for that, for our penal laws, like those of most of the rest of the world, are archaic survivals, and recognize no relation between cause and effect where crime is concerned.

But the very great majority of Negroes who come before the courts have no white folks to send to. Our criminals, like the criminals of every country, come chiefly from the economic class which lives on, or over, the poverty line—from our "submerged tenth." Nearly all those in this economic class in the South are Negroes—a fact which has resulted in our confusing the poverty line with the colour line, and charging Negroes racially with sins and tendencies which belong, the world over, to any race living in their economic condition. But it is just the Negroes who belong in this economic class, these Negroes who from our submerged tenth, and who furnish the most of our criminal supply, whom we white people do not know, and who consequently have no white folks to send to, to see that they are protected in the courts.—Oh, there is the Negro problem, and the solution of it! The poorest, the most ignorant, the ones least able to resist temptation, the folk unhelped, untaught, who are born in squalor, who live in ignorance and in want of all things necessary for useful, innocent, happy lives—they do not know us, nor we them! There is no human bond of fellowship between our full lives and their empty ones; no making of straight paths for those stumbling feet, no service of the outcast by those who are lords of all!

In that one sense the Negro problem is peculiar. Otherwise it is an integral part of the world-problem of strength and weakness dwelling side by side, with the great Law overhead laying upon them both the necessity of working out a state of civilization which shall embody the spirit of human brotherhood, and secure justice and opportunity for all. There is nothing peculiar in that. The call to this duty is world-wide: the obligation we share with all the privileged of earth. The peculiar thing is that we alone, of all the privileged of Christendom, have no wide-spread sense of obligation to achieve this task. We even, many of us, look on the handful who respond to this world-call by service to our neediest as people half disgraced, who dishonour their high heritage in going where Christ would go, and in doing His will with all He has left on earth to do it—human feet and hands and hearts. That is peculiar.

For we honour the privileged of other places who do this very thing. Any of us would have been proud to know Tolstoi, not just as a writer of books but as a great man willing to forego greatness, and to give his life to ignorance and squalor and want. We are proud of Miss Jane Addams, formerly of Chicago, Illinois, but now this long time of the United States of America, North and South. But a Jane Addams among the Negroes—the slum Negroes, folk of that very economic class for which she spends herself at Hull House—! There is no more to be said.

Ah, but there is! We are only at that border-line of adolescence where a social conscience may stir in the heart's soil, and begin to reach upward to the light. We will know our slum folk yet. And that knowledge will be part of the basis of the adjustment which is to come.

A recent incident told me by a friend, one of the chief actors in it, throws light on present Southern conditions at several points.

This friend lives alone with her servants on her old family plantation, a few miles from one of our greatest cities. Her cook's husband, a trifling Negro and a steady drinker, had hired himself to a near-by farmer for whom the whites of the neighbourhood had scant respect. The man kept a plantation store where his "hands" could obtain provisions and whiskey as advances on their wages, settling with their employer at the end of the week, or the year. Until poor folk learn coöperative buying, after the English and continental method, these master-owned stores are a necessity in the South, as they are elsewhere; and here, as in Western lumber camps or Eastern mines and mills, monopoly tempts some to extortion. In such cases the Negroes are never out of debt, from year to year, their own fondness for whiskey being often as potent a reason for that fact as the storekeeper's greed. The storekeeper usually furnishes the whiskey which keeps them such unremunerative labourers; but his profit on the whiskey makes up for that.

The farmer in question appears to have been an employer of this type; and the Negro, whose poor wages fully paid for the work he did, was soon deep in debt. He decided to hire out somewhere else, and his contract troubled him no whit. He told his second employer of his debt to the first; and the man, according to custom, agreed to stand for it to the creditor by withholding part of the Negro's wages while in his employ, and paying it on the debt. Ordinarily this would have released the Negro, as few people try to get work out of one, contract or no contract, who is unwilling to give it. But the first farmer needed his "hand," and had, apparently, not even a personal conscience, or a rudimentary respect for law. So he kidnapped the Negro on his way to his new employer, gave him a hard beating, and set him to work on his own farm, threatening him, the Negro said, with far worse if he left the place again before the year was out. He even kept him at night until my friend, finding where he was, sent the farmer orders to allow the man to come home every night as soon as his day's work was done.

She is a frail little body, but accustomed to being obeyed; and the farmer did as he was bid. The Negro, however, shirked his work, and once more roused his employer's ire. This time the farmer came to the cabin in my friend's yard one night after she had retired. He brought a rope with him, without expounding his reason therefor, and ordered the Negro to get up and come with him. My friend went out and delivered, as her ultimatum, a demand that the Negro be formally released from his contract on the spot. Her simple fearlessness forced the white man's consent; and she gave him, in return, her personal check for eighty dollars—the amount claimed on the Negro's indebtedness.

The story shows the lengths to which the Southern personal conscience will go in befriending even a trifling Negro; and the fact that everybody settled down in peace as soon as the white man let the black one alone throws light on the state of our social consciousness. It is true my friend said the white man was practically ostracized by his own race; but that fact was the aggregate result of the action of many individuals, rather than the action of a community with a sense of community responsibility to uphold law.

The story naturally brings up the question of peonage, which is a logical outcome of our attitude to the Negroes since the destructive days of "recon- struction."

Country Negroes of the better type, hard-working, honest and thrifty, are pretty sure, sooner or later, to own their own farms and be their own masters. Negro ownership of Southern farm lands increased one hundred and fifty per cent. between 1900 and 1910—clear proof that the race is advancing rapidly, no matter how much that is undesirable may remain for future elimination. Proof, also, that notwithstanding mob barbarities and much unjust discrimination, Southern whites are better neighbours for black folk than some of our Northern brothers fear.

By this steady promotion of the best Negro tenants and labourers into the class of landowners, those left available for labour on white farms tend con- stantly to a lower level of character and efficiency. It would be hard to exag- gerate the shiftlessness and unreliability of many of them. The farmer who has employed them by the year may find himself deserted at the most critical pe- riod, and his year's work little more than a disaster. It is for protection against this danger that a number of men have resorted to the expedient of keeping the labourers forever in their debt, and, by agreement with other farmers, prevent- ing their getting employment elsewhere until that impossible time when their debt shall have been cancelled.

It is a surface remedy, which penetrates the skin of the difficulty only to set up inflammation. The basis of adjustment here necessitates an entire readjustment of thought and action, on the part of the whites, to the country Negro and his needs.

The two great assets of any country are the land and the people; and the people necessarily include those engaged in the basal industry of agriculture. The land produces increasingly as the people who till it gain in health, in morals, in intelligence, in the freedom and joy of life. It grows barren as they are debased. No man, however intelligent himself, can make a free man's crop with peon labour. For many years the South squandered the fertility of her fields. We are learning of late years, slowly and painfully, to build up the impoverished soil, and restore it to its former richness. But we have overlooked the other half of the problem—the squandered fertility of labour. Until we build up the worker the material on which his work is spent will never yield its normal return. The houses of very many farm labourers are more than enough to sap their vitality, to destroy ambition and self-respect, and to foster immorality and disease.

Conditions like these filch from the community its capital of human productiveness.

Added to this is our habitual neglect of the farm-hand's recreational life— the danger-place of all people of all races and all ages whose inward resources are limited, and whose power of self-control is not highly developed.

Even a locomotive, a thing all steel and brass, has to have its period of cared-for rest—its recreational life—if it is to live out in usefulness the normal lifetime of such an engine: and no man, of any race, will or can do first-class work if he is regarded as a machine while at work, and as a nonentity when his work-hours end. Drunkenness and immorality are the only resources of many of our farm-hands when not at work in the field. Peonage is no cure for debasement like this.

The Negroes need to be built up, like the soil. In cities and factories we are finding that it pays, in dollars and cents, to care for "the [white] human end of the machine." It will pay in the country, too, and when the human end is black. Christ's law of brotherhood is universal in its working, or it is no law at all. A Negro of this class, given a decent house and let alone in it, would soon bring it to the level of his former habitation. But if with the house he were given a friend—who according to Emerson's fine definition is "one who makes us do what we can"; if he were helped to start a chicken-yard of his own on intelligent principles, or a garden-patch; if the educational methods so successful at some points in the rural South were universally applied, relating the children rationally and happily to the land; if the schoolhouses were secured as social centres for older Negroes, and the better classes of coloured people were encouraged to cooperate in the movement; if the white men of the neighbourhood, farmers, pastors, schoolteachers and doctors, met them there occasionally to lecture on matters of community interest, and also to give them some real outlook in life, some glimpse of the wide relations of their narrow toil; if the white people would look into their religious life a little and do what so many white people did before the war—superintend their Sunday-schools and teach their Bible classes; if these simple and entirely possible things were done, the labourer would be built up along with the soil, and peonage would be seen for what it is—the device of selfish ignorance for meeting a situation which is caused by our own neglect of our poor, and is to be controlled only by service in a spirit of brotherhood.

It would not be as easy to do as read about, of course. There would be discouragement and failures. There always are when a thing is really worth doing. And we must expect, moreover, to pay a heavy premium for our fifty years' neglect of this simple duty to our country poor. The Negroes do not love us as much as they did fifty years ago, nor trust us as they did. No Southern white can turn in sympathy to the service of the poorer Negroes without being often startled, and sometimes sharply hurt, by suspicions and mistrusts which peer at him from hidden places, and sometimes threaten to bar his way. But that is our heritage from our own past, and it only emphasizes the danger of further neglect. It may go against our pride to recognize the fact, but we white people, if we really win our way with the mass of the Negroes, and pay in honour our share of the world-debt of the strong to the weak, must live down much of the record of our last fifty years.

But the lower class of Negroes, whether in city or country, do not present the only, nor, I often think, the most serious aspect of our Negro problem, so called. We have many classes of whites in the South, the lowest of which are little, if any, above the lower Negroes in education or morality. This class is not a large one, but it is widely scattered; and it is the most unstable element in our civilization. It is the nitrogen of the South, ready at a touch to slip its peaceful combinations, and in the ensuing explosion to rend the social fabric in every direction. It is the storm-centre of our race-prejudices, and generates many a cyclone which cuts a broad swath through much that the South cherishes. I know of no solution for this white side of our "Negro problem" but the one to be applied to the black side also—the gradual upbuilding of character by training and personal service, and above all by the example of just living in every relation of life.

But control of a situation need not wait on the solution of its problems. The existence of this dangerous white class is no excuse for the deeds its members are permitted to do; it but constitutes our duty and our reproach. There are a hundred law-abiding Southerners—oh, far, far more!—to every one of these lawless firebrands; yet individualistic as we are, unorganized by a social consciousness, half a dozen of them can sway the weak, the excitable, the unformed among us, can fire the mob spirit, and lay the honour of thousands in the dust.

We have lately had, in one Southern state, an extreme instance of this kind. A peculiarly atrocious murder had been committed by five Negroes, two of whom were lynched, the remaining three being hung by process of law. Some lawless white men, evidently too poor themselves to need the Negro's labour, then undertook to drive all Negroes from the country. Notice was served on the white people, in city and country, that dire and summary punishment would be meted out to all whites employing Negroes in any capacity after a certain date. The Negroes were warned that working for white people meant death, and were ordered to leave the country at once. A friend of mine who lives in the country town, which numbers several thousand inhabitants, told me the Negroes were pitiful to see. They went out in droves, young and old, often in rickety little wagons piled high with household goods; went out, not knowing whither, and leaving gardens behind them, and often homes of their own.

And the white people—the law-abiding majority of the population? They were thoroughly indignant from a personal, but not from a community standpoint. They condemned the outrage publicly, as individuals; and as individuals they each protected those Negroes personally known to them. Men carried pistols to protect their Negro chauffeurs, none of whom were molested as soon as that fact became known. Servants came to the white people's premises to sleep, and brought their relatives with them. It was the Negroes who had no "white folks" who suffered. Finally the matter dropped out of the newspapers. A year later two of the Negroes ventured back to their homes, which were promptly dynamited, though fortunately without loss of life. The two houses, the papers stated, were owned by white men; and the governor offered five hundred dollars reward for the perpetrators of this latest crime. They have not, however, been apprehended.

The papers of the state, like the whites of the outraged community, were outspoken in condemnation of these barbarous proceedings; yet there was no community conscience to weld the law-abiding majority of town or state into one strong will, fired with a determination to stop a hideous injustice, or to give the weak the protection of law which was their due, instead of the haphazard personal safeguards afforded by the circumstance of acquaintance with some white person.

It is scarcely a step from deeds like this to the murder, by mob law, of human beings. To a thinking mind there is nothing so sinister in our Southern life as the swift debauching of many of our people through yielding to the mob spirit. Time was when a Negro was lynched for one crime only; and the fearful provocation is still adduced, at least as the reason, if not as the excuse, for this savagery among us. But this lawless element has long since fallen below the point where such offense is necessary to set them baying for some Negro's life like bloodhounds on a trail. The curse of their own sins is upon them, and they drop nearer the beast's level every year.

But we of the law-abiding majority cannot lay on their shoulders our part of a community sin. If they do the deed, we, who could prevent it, permit them. There are, however, signs of a wide awakening. The individual consciences of the South are yearly more deeply stirred by these outrages. The outspoken condemnation of a few men and newspapers, years ago, is the common attitude to-day. And more than that, far more, is the stirring, by more signs than one, of a true community conscience at this most vital point. A few weeks ago the citizens of a town just disgraced by mob violence met in public assembly, confessed openly their sense of community shame, and pledged themselves as a people to see that the law was upheld in their midst henceforth. When the real South, the law-abiding majority, catches the contagion of that social consciousness mobs will be heard of among us no more.

A law has been proposed by some Southern man, whose name I am unable to trace, which would go far towards checking mob violence. It would automatically remove from office any sheriff who failed to protect a prisoner in his charge, and would render him ineligible for reëlection; and it would make the county liable for damages to the family of the murdered man. It would, in the writer's opinion, be wise to add to these provisions a requirement that the county tax for education be largely increased for a term of years following such a crime.

It was with the deepest thankfulness that I sat in a body of Southern women, gathered in Birmingham last April, when resolutions against lynching were brought in and unanimously passed. The overwhelming majority of Southern women have always repudiated the need of mob-murder for their protection; but it marks a great advance towards social consciousness when an organization representing over two hundred thousand Southern white women delivers a public protest against it. The occasion was the annual meeting of the Woman's Missionary Council of the M. E. Church, South. The resolutions "deplore the demoralizing influence of mob violence upon communities, and especially upon the youth of both races, who are thereby incited to a contempt of law resulting in moral degeneracy and the overthrow of justice." They state "that, as women engaged in Christian social service for the full redemption of our social order, we do protest, in the name of outraged justice, against the savagery of lynching;" and "call upon lawmakers and enforcers of law, and upon all who value justice and righteousness, to recognize their duty to the law, and to the criminal classes. We appeal to them to arouse public opinion against mob violence, and to enforce the law against those who defy it." The resolutions end by pledging the women "to increasing prayer and effort in behalf of those classes, the very environment of whose lives breeds crime."

Here is one vigorous development of social conscience in the South as regards the Negro. The Sociological Congress showed others. It is as contagious, thank heaven, as tuberculosis itself, once the patient's condition is ripe for it; and when we break out with it as we presently shall, we shall have a notable case. We never have done things by halves.

But the evil effects of the past are still with us. It is true that the crime of lynching is decreasing among us. It is also true that the number of Negroes lynched in the years made darkest by this wickedness was almost negligible as compared with the total Negro population. Negligible, I mean, not from a human, but from an arithmetical standpoint; and somehow, by that curious mental process of self-exculpation common to all men in the presence of embarrassing or shameful facts, many of us who yet abhor mob violence have unconsciously sought refuge from the horror in the arithmetical point of view. "It is horrible," we say, "wicked, shameful, inhuman; but at least, thank heaven, the crime is infrequent: the millions of Negroes never in danger proves that. As a race they are safe, and they know it."

But they do not know it; nor would we in their place. We have failed to use our imagination at this point. Every one of our millions of black citizens knows that every time this fire of death has flamed up from those depths where savagery still lurks in human hearts it has burst forth in a fresh place, without warning, dealing individual death, and sometimes suffering for many not even accused of crime. Lynchings do not come in the same place twice: if they did they could be avoided. The volcano bursts forth from what has been, in the memory of man, but a peaceful hillside. It is true the eruption seldom takes place: the awful thing to the Negro is that it *may* take place at any time, anywhere, even upon trivial, or, conceivably, upon unconscious provocation. That is lynching from the Negroes' point of view, which would probably be our own in their place. The possibility of illegal violence, the fear of it, is an ever-present thing in their lives. It hangs, a thick fog of distrust, between their race and ours. Through it they grope, misunderstanding and misinterpreting many of our most inno-cent deeds and ways. Individual whites they trust; but I think a few of them really trust us as a people. They know that nearly all of us feel kindly to them; that very few of us would ever harm them: but they also realize, taught by frightful experience, that when the very small lawless white element rises against them they cannot certainly rely upon protection from the rest of us.

This sense of evil possibly impending, with the deep distrust engendered by it, colours all the Negro's relations with us. It makes him shifty, time-serving. All of personal good that he plans or desires too often appears to him to be subject to the one imperious necessity of getting along with white folks—not of deserving or obtaining the respect of the better classes among us, but of avoid-ing the anger of individuals of our smallest and most dangerous class. To live in an atmosphere like that without moral deterioration requires a strength of character rare in men of every race.

Nor does the administration of criminal law in our courts always tend to lessen this distrust of white people. At each session of the Southern Sociologi-cal Congress Southern men high in office among us—judges, professors in our great universities, Y.M.C.A. leaders, and others, have stated that, despite indi-vidual exceptions, the trend of our courts is to mete out heavier punishment to black offenders than to white. It is not, they say, that Negroes are illegally sentenced; but that, for similar offenses, the Negro gets one of the heavier sen-tences permissible under the law, the white man one of the lighter. More than one Southern governor has defended his wholesale use of the pardoning power on the express ground "that the proportion of convictions is greater, and the terms of sentence longer, for Negroes than for whites." One Southern judge, a speaker at the Sociological Congress in Nashville, after stating that the white man too often escapes where the Negro is punished for a like offense, added the warning "that if punishments of the law are not imposed upon all offenders alike it will breed distrust of administration." Yes: and distrust of the race behind the administration. It will, and does.

A Southern bishop told me recently that at a banquet where several promi-nent Southerners were present, this judge among them, some of the guests questioned the accuracy of his statement in regard to discrimination in the courts. "And he just turned on us," said the bishop, "and gave us chapter and verse. He told what he had himself seen, in different courts. And he convinced his audience; when he finished nobody had a word to say."

It is not only the Negro's well-being that is at stake in this matter: it is the civilization of the South. Through all the ages, the country which denies the poorest equal justice is the one foredoomed to fall. It is doubtless true that our Southern courts are no more unjust to the very poor than are the courts of many other sections of our country, especially in our great cities. The poor immigrant without a "next friend" is liable to fare as badly as the Negro without any "white folks"; but that does not lessen our danger, or our responsibility. It ought to draw North and South closer together in the bonds of a common patriotism and a common public duty. It is because our poor are made conspicuous, and advertised, as it were, by their difference in colour that we seem to all the world greater sinners at this point than themselves. But while I would offer this suggestion, that others outside may feel more human sympathy for us while yet condemning our human sin, I would not have us at all excuse ourselves on the score that our sin is common to mankind. A social conscience, like a personal one, regards the moral quality of one's own deeds, and not what one's neighbours do, or fail to do. If we fail to achieve justice for the poorest, our doom is written in the stars: and we are neither helped nor hindered by other people's shortcomings.

Last of all in this connection, yet in their practical prevention of good feeling between the races not least, are the annoyances, discomforts and hardships laid upon the better class of Negroes by our failure to see under their black skins a humanity as dear to justice and to God as our own. There are many points for illustration; but one will suffice here—the matter of "Jim Crow" cars.

We who believe that the races should be kept racially, and therefore socially, distinct cannot advocate their mingling in the enforced intimacy of Pullman cars. It is enough for us to put up with ourselves under such conditions—and sometimes almost too much. But that does not at all excuse the traveling conditions which are forced upon Negroes of education and refinement, (I use the word advisedly), throughout the South. They pay for a straight railroad ticket exactly what we pay, and we force them to habitually accept in return accommodations we would despise one of our own people for putting up with.—And we say the Negroes are dirty! Miraculously, some of them are not, notwithstanding all the provision we make for confirming them in that condition.

Last year a young Negro girl came to the school of which my husband is the president—a school, by the way, founded, maintained and officered by Southern whites; and after she had been there some time she confided to one of her white teachers the fact that when she came to the city she had ridden in "the white folks' car."

"Were you with the white people?" she was asked.

No, she was not. She had paid her full fare, as usual, and had taken her place in the "Jim Crow" car, filthy with tobacco juice and incrusted dirt, foul with smoke both new and old, and containing a number of Negro men of the baser sort—the kind of car, in short, in which Negro women and girls, and clean, educated, well-to-do Negro men are so frequently expected to travel. There were no women that day, and only those rough men; and they began to molest the girl almost at once. Shrinking back in her seat in terror, she felt a sudden hope as the white brakeman came through the car: but he passed through, as unheeding as though dogs were squabbling over a bone. She stood it a few minutes longer, and then dashed frantically into the next car, the white day coach, dropped into the last seat, and burst into tears. Thus the conductor found her. On hearing her story he told her to stay where she was; that if any of the white people in the car objected he would explain her presence, and they would be willing for her to stay. No one objected, however, and she rode to her destination in peace.

Not all conductors are so humane. And it is practically impossible, as may be seen at a glance, for one white man, often a mere boy, to keep order among a car-full of Negroes like that, roused to evil by the presence of a girl evidently above their own social class. A white-boy conductor would be risking his life in such a case; and even if he saved it, if he started any "race row" on a railroad train by defending one Negro from another he would lose his job. So most of them harden their hearts and turn their eyes the other way—a performance for which I, for one, am slow to blame them. We have no right, as a people, habitually to permit impossible situations, and then to throw the responsibility for them on one man's, or one boy's, shoulders.

Last Christmas a coloured kindergartner[2] employed by some Southern white women in settlement work among her own people, went home for the holidays. There are several day trains, but some important home happening made her presence there necessary the morning after her work closed at the settlement; so

2. In the Progressive era, kindergartens were an innovative and still private reform movement generally directed at the children of the poor and the working class. To be a kindergartner was to be a specialized social worker, usually with specific training.

she took the night train, a thing she had never done before. The young woman is a college graduate, refined in speech and manner, modest and sensible in her relations with people of both races, and a strong and wholesome force in the lives of the poorer Negroes among whom she works. She took the Jim Crow car, of course, expecting to sit up all night, but with no idea of the experiences before her. The car was full of half-drunken Negro men off to enjoy one of the very few pleasures open to Negroes in the South—a regular old Christmas spree. There were one or two other women in the car, and they huddled together and endured the night in frightened silence. The train man, passing through, took no notice of the insults, or oaths or vile talk.

When she told the white women who had employed her about it, ten days later, she trembled as she spoke.

"I had never seen Negroes like that in my life," she said. "I knew there were such men; but my mother had spent her life keeping me away from them— Why can't the white people see it?" she burst out passionately. "Will they think forever that we are all like that? Why can't they let us be decent when we want to be?"

While my husband was Secretary of Education of the Southern Methodist Church, part of his work was to lay the matter of Negro education on the conscience of his denomination. One of the teachers at our one school for Negroes was a coloured man of unusual gifts and character, an honour graduate of a Northern university, and a man high in the respect and friendship of Southern whites in many states. To bring "the Negro question" closer home to our people the Methodist Board of Education paid this man's salary and travelling expenses; and for four years the white man and the black one travelled the rounds of our annual conferences, presenting the cause of the Negro to our white preachers and laymen, and finding, as time went on, much prejudice giving way to sympathy.[3]

The conference meetings are nearly all crowded into three months, several being held each week. When a secretary attends them his days are given to the conferences, his nights to travel; and it is a time of physical strain, even with all the comforts of modern travel. My husband, strong as he is, came home tired out at the end of each annual round.

"How Gilbert stands it, physically or religiously, I cannot see," he said. "He

3. This story refers to John Wesley Gilbert, the first black faculty member at Paine College. Gilbert was the first student to enroll when Paine opened. He then studied at Brown University, and was an expert in Greek and classical literature. He was hired at Paine in 1888.

goes half the time without lying down to sleep. If I were not with him, to dash into some white restaurant and buy him a cup of coffee and something to eat, he would often go hungry. And I have never once heard him complain, or seen his Christian composure ruffled. He is doing us white people a great service, freeing us from some of our worst prejudices: and we require him to do it at this cost!"

I know a Negro woman, the wife of a doctor, whom white doctors of the city tell me they respect both as a man and as a physician. He has a large charity practice, but a large paying one also. He is a man of considerable means, and owns an automobile. His home is thoroughly comfortable; and his wife is as amply provided for as the wife of a white man in similar circumstances would be. She is a refined, sensible, good woman, whose influence among her own people is of the best.

She told me not long ago that she went on a visit which necessitated a day in the usual Jim Crow car. I had asked her about the matter or she would not have mentioned it. We do not suspect the reserves of pride in Negroes of this class; and I count it a chief proof that my life among them is not a failure that they will speak to me frankly, as to a friend.

There had been no insult or terror in her case; simply filth, tobacco juice and smoke, coarse talk among other Negroes, and blinding, choking dust. When she reached her destination, she said, no one could have told the colour or texture of her dress or hat.

Somehow the hat gripped my sympathies. Women do so cherish their hats! I am never happy myself until the porter brings me a bag, and my head-gear is safe beyond reach of dust, with a hat-pin thrust through the gathered opening of the bag into the back of the opposite seat, to keep its precious contents from being waggled about. I can wash my hair; but a soot-filled hat is irretrievable; it can never look impeccable again.

Why should this other woman, who loves cleanliness as much as I do, and who is quite as willing to pay for it, be forced to travel in that disgusting filth? I know if I were forced to do it my husband and my children and all my friends would feel outraged about it, and would never have any use for the people who made me do it. Why should these people feel differently? It is nearly always the smaller matters of life which make its bitterness or its sweetness for us white people. We can bear great things greatly, often; but our courage and kindness and sympathies fail before the annoyances of life. Shall we expect more of Negroes than of ourselves?

A Southern state, a few years ago, required the railroads to provide equal accommodations for whites and Negroes in that state. They replied by a threat to take off all Pullmans for white people, as they could only be operated at a loss for Negroes: and the matter was dropped.

But day-coach accommodations are rarely equal. Even where the cars were originally alike, the habitual neglect of those in use for Negroes soon reduces them to a condition revolting to people of cleanly habits. The fact that many Negroes are unclean in their habits is no excuse for the condition of the cars. When white people are unclean, as they often are, the railroad is not excused from keeping the cars in a fairly decent condition, at worst. They may have to spend a little more for soap and water; but they must take their chances on that when they sell tickets.

The Jim Crow cars come under no one general description. I have occasionally seen a car for Negroes as clean as day coach for whites. Similarly, I have known personally of Negroes riding through Southern states all day and all night in a Pullman section, their presence known to all the white passengers, none of whom voiced any objection to them. But neither occurrence is the rule.

Sometimes there is a clean day coach for Negroes, and also a separate place for Negro men to smoke—usually a cut-off end of the smoking-car for whites. This is the best accommodation on the best roads. Sometimes this half of a smoking car, with its single toilet, is the only part of the train open to Negroes at all. Sometimes there is no place for Negroes except in the car with white smokers, though this again is unusual. The average conditions, undoubtedly, are far below those provided for white passengers paying the same price: and the spirit manifested by this treatment of Negroes is one people of any race or any class have the right to resent.

If whole Pullman cars cannot be profitably provided, one end of a first class day coach could be fitted up as a Pullman, and put in charge of the men on the white people's Pullman; and the other part of the car could give the Negroes what they now so often lack—day-coach accommodations equal to those for whites.

I believe the railroad people themselves have little idea of the number of Negroes who could and would pay for first-class accommodations. We know little about the educated, prosperous members of the race. As fast as they enter this class they withdraw into a world of their own—a world which lies all about us white folks, yet of whose existence we are scarcely aware. It is largely the inefficients, the failures, or the immature and untrained who remain with us. As they rise out of this class they disappear from our view. There are more prosperous Negroes who would pay for Pullmans than we imagine.

But if the railroads claim that they really cannot provide decent day coaches and comfortable sleeping accommodations for Negroes, a commission should be appointed to look into the matter: and if their contention proved just, fares for everybody should be raised by law to a point which would allow the roads to maintain standards of comfort and decency for all their passengers. We cannot afford, as a people, to let the Negroes pay for our cheap fares: for that is just what it amounts to when the railroad takes the same amount of money from both of us, and gives us better accommodations than it can afford to give them. We are not paying for all we can get in our day coaches, evidently; and if the Negro isn't footing the bill for the deficit, who is? As for the Pullman company, if half the published tales of its dividends be true, it could furnish cars for Negroes and pay its employees a living wage, and yet be in no danger of bankruptcy. Public utilities should be subject to public control.

It should be pointed out that not one of the Negroes whose cases I have cited, nor any Negro I ever spoke to on the subject, had any desire to share cars with white people. They have their pride, too; and they are not going where they are not wanted. They want safety, cleanliness, and comfort, not white company; and they are willing and ready to pay for them.

There is another grave injustice, wholly different from any I have touched upon, which I believe has had a profound effect for evil upon a large class of Negroes; yet scarcely any one, white or black, thinks of it as injustice at all. We Southern white women are greater offenders in the matter than the men; and I myself must plead guilty to the common charge. Yet I scarcely see how a woman very far from strong could sometime do differently; and if one be excused on the score of illness, it looks ugly to call her neighbour lazy for the same offense.

We demand too little in the way of honest work of the Negroes in our employ. Shirking, untidy habits, petty, and often serious, pilferings—we wink at them, and continue to pay honest money for dishonest work. We do not like to discharge Negroes. It grates on our pride to be talked about by a "darkey": and talk about us they certainly will, frequently with scant respect for truth. And as to discharging them, where will we get a better one, we ask; they are all alike. And you can't possibly do the work yourself; yet if you make them mad they may keep you out of a cook for weeks. And besides, "darkies" are "darkies": white people always have put up with them, and always will.—So we mourn in secret over the departed flour, and sigh for the lard that used to be in the bucket, and tell Jane or Lucinda how nice her cake was last night, and give her the cold biscuit to take home to her grandmother, and a few cookies for the children. And when Eliza Ann brings in the wash with three of the best towels gone, and half the handkerchiefs, and tells us blandly that she know she done brung back ev'y las' thing she took out, 'cause she hung 'em on her own line an' dey ain't been nobody near 'em but her an' de chillun, we falter meekly that it doesn't matter, and that the tablecloths look nice; and we give her a pair of stockings with just one tiny hole in them, and the dress she has scorched in two in the back breadth to make over for little Susan; and we pay her the full week's wages.

In our hearts we feel that we are "quality," and so cannot afford to hold Negroes to a strict account. For fifty years we have trained those of them with whom we have come in contact to rate both our friendship and our gentility in exact proportion to what we put up with from them, and what we give them without expectation of return. They think none the less of Northern people who require a return for well-done work for money received; but Southerners are "our white folks," and such exactions from them arouse instant distrust in the average Negro's breast, the least of his suspicions being that his employer has no connection with the "quality."

A year or two ago I had a bright little coloured girl about sixteen years old as extra help while company was in the house. I never have locked things up. I would rather have a dishonest servant steal from me than hurt an honest one's feelings: so I take my chances. But things did so vanish out of the pantry! Cake and fruit just melted into air. The cook was as honest as I was; and my little housemaid was getting fat. Finally, when a basket of high-priced peaches lost two-thirds of its contents before appearing in the house at all, I knew, like Brer Rabbit, that something had to be done. I talked to the child seriously about honesty as an asset of character. She turned on me with round-eyed wonder, and with what I still believe to have been genuine scorn.

"Well, if ever I had white folks talk to me like that!" she exclaimed. "*Honest!* I been honest all my life! I ain't never worked anywhere since I was born"—she had been at it, by spells, ever since she was ten—"where white folks grudge me what I et before. Ef it belongs to my white folks hit belongs to me, an' I takes it. I ain't goin' to work for no other kind." And she put on her hat and went home: I was beneath her services.

I felt ashamed. I had put up with her pilferings a long time before I spoke; and I and others like me had been training her, and tens of thousands more, to shiftlessness and dishonesty ever since they were born. The wonder is not that so many of them are worthless, but that there are so many honest, painstaking, trustworthy ones among them. They have attained to honesty with little help from us.

I once praised a cook of mine for her exquisite cleanliness, and the economy with which she evolved the most delicious dishes. She really was a jewel of a cook. She laughed amusedly when I spoke.

"I worked up North twelve years, an' I learned things," she said. "If I was dirty, or wasted, I lost my place. And I'd have lost it in a minute if I'd taken things. Yankee women don't put up with nothin'; they fire you an' do the work themselves."

She turned on me suddenly.

"It's you white people's fault we coloured people are so triflin'!" she burst out. "You-all scold us, but you put up with us. We don't need to do any better, because we get along just as well as if we did honest work. You-all say, 'Oh, what can you expect of darkies?' But we can be honest, and up there they make us. I wasn't no manner of account till I went North. An' if the Yankees had some of these other servants 'round yere they'd learn 'em somethin'. We can do better— if we must!"

Now in all these matters, great and small, and in dozens more which may not here be touched upon, what basis for living does white example furnish? Outside of personal and often unreasoning kindness, where we are prone to take the attitude of feudal lords who give *largesse*, what is there in our treatment of the Negro to inspire him with respect for justice and the law? If we will lay aside our preconceived notions for a little, and go over all the complex web of racial relations in the South as they might appear to a gentleman from Mars, for instance, newly landed on the earth, what is there, outcome of the fifty years, commensurate with the obligation of a strong people to a weak one? What have we done to bind them to us? What to lift them up? What foundation have we as a people laid for dwelling with them in honour and mutual good will?

I do not mean to imply that no basis of justice exists: if it did not, our civilization would be falling of its own weight. It does exist between many individual lives, both white and black. But as a people for a people the foundation is yet to be sought: and other foundation than justice there is none.

There is no sense in mincing matters. We are no longer children. It is the first step that costs, always; but the first step is very plain. It is to put away childish things—unreasoning prejudice and unreasoning pride—and to look truth squarely in the face, as men and women who love it at all costs. There is no truth in a detached view of the Negro, or of any human being. Everybody on earth is human first and racial afterwards. We must see in the Negro first of all, deeper than all, higher than all, a man, made in the image of God as truly as we ourselves. If in the race that image be less developed than in our own, in some individuals of the race it is certainly more highly developed than in some individuals of ours. And whatever grows is growable.

The only basis of living between man and man, whether low or high, which is safe for either is justice. And where there is less than justice, the danger is ever greater for the oppressor that for the oppressed. If white civilization is to endure, in the South or anywhere else, it must strike deep roots into the soil of our common humanity, and reach down to that bed-rock of justice which makes the framework of the world.

And one thing more is needed. For justice is a hard, cold thing; stable and strong; yet must it be softened to nourish a people's growth, and pass through the alembic of life itself before it can mount to light and warmth, and flutter brave banners in the sunshine, for the joy and refreshment of mankind.

There are some elements of the inorganic world so diverse that they can never join hands for useful work except in the presence of another element which, in some way beyond our knowledge as yet, removes the unseen barriers, and allows the two to meet. We call it catalytic action, by way of labelling our ignorance; and that which allows the unrelated fragments to exert their latent power for common service is a catalyser.

We are not left without a catalyser in our diverse human life. In an atmosphere of sympathy, of human brotherhood, of care for all of whom Christ died, the races of men—all races—may come together, for service of that great Race which climbs upward to the light.

My only fear for white supremacy is that we should prove unworthy of it. If we fail there, we shall pass. Supremacy is for service. It is suicide to thrust other races back from the good which we hold in trust for humanity. For him who would be greatest the price is still that he shall be servant of all.

III
Houses and Homes

Long ago, when I was a child, a grown-up cousin took me driving one afternoon behind a pair of his thoroughbreds. As we swept over the long shell road through autumn sunshine, with the pine trees singing overhead and the wind whitening the waves in the harbour beyond, I came on one of those experiences known to us all, when something long familiar yet never noticed stands suddenly forth, challenging eye and soul in a manner never to be forgotten.

Beside the road was a one-roomed Negro cabin, built of logs and chinked with mud. Its one door swung wide, and showed the rotted floor within. At the side was an unglazed opening like an eyeless socket, through which I glimpsed a tumbled bed and a broken cook-stove. A woman stood by the door, a little child beside her. Their rags were thick with dirt. The child looked at us with the wonder and interest of life yet in his young eyes; but the woman's black face was expressionless, her murky eyes unquestioning, unexpectant. She saw us because we crossed her field of vision, just as an animal might see a passing bird.

The day was glorious, our swift flight intoxicating; the swaying pine called to the blood, and the sea sang of wonders yet to be; but the stolid woman and her eyeless home blotted everything else. I had looked at the like a thousand times; but somehow that day, in my riot of physical and mental exaltation, I had eyes to see; and the shock of it made me gasp.

"Why must they live like that?" I demanded. "Why do I have everything, and they nothing?"

My elderly cousin laughed a little, and then, realizing my excitement, spoke soberly.

"Don't take other people's troubles too seriously, my dear; try to understand how much being used to things means. If those darkies had to live in your house they'd never rest till they got it as dirty and broken up as what they're used to. Then they'd be comfortable. They like what they've got: they're made that way."

I considered this comfortable doctrine in silence. Then:

"Why didn't God make them another way—some clean way? It would have been just as easy."

"That's too deep water for a person of your inches," he replied. "You must take God and folks like you find them. But that little darkey has as much fun as you do—maybe more: don't worry your head over nonsense."

A year or two afterwards my father's business took us to a great city of the North; and I was soon hard at work, on Saturdays and Sundays, at a church mission in the tenement district. Not content with the class work at the chapel I visited my small pupils in their—no, not their homes; I could never call them that; their dens. There were long stairs slippery with dirt, where blows and curses from the foul, dark rooms assailed my ears; there were rooms with one tiny window, and rooms with no window at all; there were beds and tubs and stoves and sewing-machines and babies and rags and tin cans and children and dirt and noise in one horrible confusion.

My mother was dead, and I kept my expeditions to myself. But I turned back to what my cousin had said about the Negroes for comfort. Did these white people like the way they lived? Were they made that way too?

The more I saw of them the more dubious I became; but my sociological researches, becoming known to the family, were summarily put a stop to. So I dropped the biological method and took to books.

But through those early experiences I came unconsciously to regard slum-dwellers as of one class. There were people of many races in those tenements; but their differences sank out of sight before the common degradation of their lives. And always with the thought of these came the memory of that Negro woman and her not-yet stolid child. They were human too; and there was something in them deeper than being Negroes—something that was kin to these emigrants of the tenements, and to me, and to all the world. They were a part of human life, like the rest: their fundamental needs and their fundamental reactions to environment were the same in kind. Whatever differences existed, they were differences in degree.

It is this recognition of human oneness that opens the door of understanding into the Negro slums. One slum interprets another; each slum-dweller helps to explain all the rest, whatever their nationality, wherever their abode. We can see this when we get rid of the deadening influence of the old political economy, and recognize the Negro slum for what it, and all slums, are—the joint product of ignorance, greed, and the monstrous old doctrine of *laissez faire.*

The old political economy was a science of investigation, not one of construction, and still less one at all concerned with morality. It observed the methods of human business intercourse much as one might examine the ways of earthquakes, or any other natural phenomena, with a view to deducting therefrom certain fixed laws as inherent in the nature of things, and as unmoral, as the attraction of oxygen and hydrogen. Thus, for example, the old doctrine concerning wages—that the employer would inevitably drive the workman as close to the edge of starvation as he possibly could while still keeping him alive to work; and that the workman would resist as much as he dared with the fear of losing his job before his eyes—was accepted as a basal law of a world where, apparently, whatever was was right. In such a world, the law of gravitation was no firmer or more respectable a fixture than the law that the landlord should get the highest rent he could for the cheapest shelter the poor could be induced to accept.

The watchword of the old political economy was that business is business—a territory roped off from human considerations, and governed by laws of its own. When human beings got into this district they were subject to the law of the land, which gave a chance only to him who could snatch and hold it. Religion and philanthropy might stand without if they would, and more or less liberally anoint the wounds of those who were worsted in the struggle, but otherwise they had no concern in the fray.

This conception of human relations had governed the world for ages before Ricardo formulated his "iron law." Its mark is deep in our life and thought to-day; and nowhere is it plainer, the world around, than upon the houses of the poor. In all countries where there is enough of civilization for society to have become divided into groups, the poorer folk, often without a sense of wrong on their part or injustice on the landlords', have been huddled together in a manner to bring property-owners the largest returns, regardless of other consequences.

Those other consequences have none the less left their mark also deep in human life. They are the same everywhere, regardless of country or race.

Cleanliness of body and of habitation is a fundamental preparation for cleanliness of mind, and water and fresh air exist in abundance to furnish it; yet the houses of those who most need cleanliness, and to whom it is the most difficult by inclination and occupation, are largely cut off from these two necessities without which human life cannot be normal. A well-to-do child, with generations of bath-tubs, outdoor sports, and sunny rooms behind him, might retain through life moral and even physical health under the conditions of the world's slums; but his children would show signs of breaking; and their children would be as truly of the slum as their neighbours. Generations of gain could be lost in one man's lifetime. Yet of the mass of the Negroes, who live in the slums we have built for them, where water is hard to come by and adequate ventilation impossible, we say that they are dirty by nature, and that to provide better things would result only in a waste of money.

We know little, as yet, in this our dawn of social consciousness, of the slums of the rest of the world. Our slum-dwellers are to us a race apart, a separate fragment of life, unrelated, a law unto themselves. They make their slums, we think, as a spider spins his web, from within. We all know, of course, that very many Negroes are far above the slum-dwellers. There are few communities in the South, however small, without a few Negroes whom the whites respect and trust. But we regard them, not as the natural outcome of a more normal chance in life, but as exceptions to the law of Negro development, through some personally-inherent exceptional quality, probably an infusion of white blood.

We need a wide horizon for the understanding of our slum-dweller. When we set him in his world-relations we see that in all mankind slum conditions produce slum results. Waterless, ill-ventilated houses, crowded beyond the possibility of decency because of low wages and high rents, make impossible the physical basis that is necessary for even the poorest home. And with this kind of housing go other evils, all working together to produce in any people, the world around, these characteristics which we believe to be racial and Negro. In a population racially homogeneous, like that of Rome or of Pekin, or racially heterogeneous like that of Chicago or New York, or in a bi-racial population like our own, the results are the same. Bad housing conditions, insufficient or un-nourishing food, vicious surroundings, a childhood spent unprotected in the streets, produce, in Europe, Asia and America, ill-nourished bodies, un-balanced nerves, vacant and vicious minds, a craving for stimulants and all evil excitements, lack of energy, weakened wills, laziness, thriftlessness, unreliability in every relation of life.

As life rises, it differentiates. Anglo-Saxon and Chinaman develop along different lines; and the higher their development the less alike they are. Each brings his own race-contribution to the great Race of Man. But in those lowest depths, where men are thrust back towards the level of beasts, acquired characteristics are in abeyance, and the old brute longings dominate once more. Men are wonderfully alike on this level—as alike as are vegetable and animal on their lowest plane: and yellow or white or black, there is little for any to boast of. But when normal conditions of growth are furnished, men of each race will come true to type; and the higher they rise the greater their differences will be. Just what the highest type of Negro race will be nobody knows; for as a race they have not yet had normal conditions, nor time for full development. But whatever it may be, it will not be a white type, nor a red nor a yellow one; and it will be something needed for the perfect development of the Race of Man.

These things being so—and a wide world-look is convincing—the places where our poorest live, our weakest and most tempted folk, take on new aspects and suggest new implications. Our slums are not the product of a race unrelated and incapable of development; they are our part of a world-wide morass where life capable of higher things is sucked under and destroyed.

The old political economy took no account of such matters; it accepted as a universal law the policy of exploitation, of individualistic commercialism, of cut-throat competition. It saw, not human beings, but profit and loss.

The new political economy is shifting the thought and the business of the world towards a basis of human brotherhood. It puts human rights above profit and loss, and holds conservation a wiser policy than exploitation. As to the human morass, it would drain it. And all this not as a matter of charity, not because Christ said men are all brethren; but because we *are* all brethren, and so lose more than we gain; in the long run, if we run things on any other basis. That thing Christ said is true!

When one sees in the slum-dweller a brother, what is one to do? If he really is a brother it will pay to treat him like one. Laws—the real ones—never do contradict one another. No law of true prosperity can be infringed upon by obedience to the law of brotherhood, if brotherhood is a real fact. It will work with any other real law there is.

A woman saw that, fifty years ago, and set out to demonstrate it in this very matter of housing.

"The people's homes are bad," she wrote, "partly because they are badly built and arranged; they are tenfold worse because the tenants' habits and lives are what they are. Transplant them to-morrow to healthy and commodious homes, and they would pollute and destroy them. There needs, and will need for some time, a reformatory work which will demand that loving zeal of individuals which cannot be legislated for by parliament. The heart of the English nation will supply it. It may and should be organized; it cannot be created."

Might not that have been written of the very poor of New York or St. Louis,

instead of the very poor of London? Or of the very poor of Atlanta or Birmingham, who happen to be black?

In 1866, three years after Ruskin's three thousand pounds made the beginning of her work possible, Miss Hill wrote again:

"That the spiritual elevation of a large class depended to a considerable extent on sanitary reform was, I considered, proved. But I was equally certain that
sanitary improvement itself was dependent on educational work among grown-
up people. . . . It seems to me that a greater power is in the hands of landlords
and landladies than of school-teachers—power either of life or death, physical
and spiritual.

"The disciplining of our immense poor population must be effected by individual influence; and this power can change it from a mob of paupers and
semi-paupers into a body of self-dependent workers."

It can change it because it did, and does; and Mr. Ruskin, "who alone believed
the scheme would work," was repaid in good English money for his investment,
as were the many others whose renting properties she and her trained assistants
managed during the fifty years between her first experiment in 1863 and her
death in 1912.

After twenty years of work she wrote, in 1883:

"I have no hesitation in saying that if a site were handed over to me at the
[usual] price, I would engage to house upon it under thoroughly healthy conditions, at rents which they could pay, and which would yield a fair interest on
capital, a very large proportion of the very poor."

And what was Miss Hill's scheme? Just a combination of the law of brotherhood with a sound business policy in collecting rents. With Ruskin's money she
acquired three houses "in a dreadful state of dirt and neglect." This was remedied, and an ample water supply provided. She herself undertook to collect the
weekly rent. At first her tenants regarded her as a natural enemy. Sometimes,
when she went on Saturday nights for her rent, she found them lying on their
filthy floors, dead drunk. The rent would often be thrust out to her through a
crack in the door, held fast against her entrance. The stairs were "many inches
deep in dirt, so hardened that a shovel had to be used to get it off." The people
were the poorest renting class, just above vagrants; they lived on the edge of
crime, and all too frequently passed over the fatal line. "Truly," said Miss Hill,
"a wild, lawless, desolate little kingdom to rule over."

"On what principles was I to rule these people? On the same that I had already tried, and tried with success, in other places, and which I may sum up as

the two following: firstly, to demand a strict fulfillment of their duties to me—one of the chief of which would be the punctual payment of rent; and secondly, to endeavour to be so unfailingly just and patient, that they should learn to trust the rule that was over them.

"With regard to details, I would make a few improvements at once—such, for example, as the laying on of water and repairing of dust bins; but, for the most part, improvements should be made only by degrees, as the people became more capable of valuing and not abusing them. I would have the rooms distempered and thoroughly cleansed as they became vacant, and then they should be offered to the more cleanly of the tenants. I would save such repairs as were not immediately needed as a means of giving work to the men in times of distress. I would draft the occupants of the underground kitchens into the upstairs rooms, and would ultimately convert the kitchens into bath-rooms and wash-houses. I would have the landlady's portion of the house—*i.e.,* the stairs and passages—at once repaired and distempered; and they should be regularly scrubbed, and, as far as possible, made models of cleanliness; for I knew from former experience that the example of this would, in time, silently spread itself to the rooms themselves, and that payment for this work would give me some hold over the elder girls. I would collect savings personally, not trust to their being taken to distant banks or saving clubs. And, finally, I knew that I should learn to feel these people as my friends, and so should instinctively feel the same respect for their privacy and their independence, and should treat them with the same courtesy, that I should show towards any other personal friends. There would be no interference, no entering their rooms uninvited, no offer of money or the necessaries of life. But when occasion presented itself I should give them any help I could, such as I might offer without insult to other friends—sympathy in their distresses; advice, help, and counsel in their difficulties. . . .

"When we set about our repairs and alterations, there was much that was discouraging. The better class of people in the court were hopeless of any permanent improvement. When one of the tenants of the shops saw that we were sending workmen into the empty rooms, he said considerately, 'I'll tell you what it is, Miss, it'll cost you a lot o' money to repair them places, and it's no good. The women's 'eads be druv through the door panels again in no time, and the place is good enough for such cattle as them there.' But we were not to be deterred.

"On the other hand, we were not to be hurried in our action by threats. These were not wanting. For no sooner did the tenants see the workmen about than they seemed to think that if they clamoured enough, they would get their own rooms put to rights. Nothing had been done for years. Now, they thought, was their opportunity. More than one woman locked me in her room with her, the better to rave and storm. She would shake the rent in her pocket to tempt me with the sound of the money, and roar out 'that never a farthing of it would she pay till her grate was set,' or her floor was mended, as the case might be. Perfect silence would make her voice drop lower and lower, until at last she would stop, wondering that no violent answers were hurled back at her, and a pause would ensue. I felt that promises would be little believed in, and besides, I wished to feel free to do as much, and only as much, as seemed to me best; so that my plan was to trust to my deeds to speak for themselves, and inspire confidence as time went on.

"The importance of advancing slowly, and of gaining some hold over the people as a necessary accompaniment to any real improvement in their dwellings, was perpetually apparent. Their habits were so degraded that we had to work a change in these before they would make any proper use of the improved surroundings we were prepared to give them. We had locks torn off, windows broken, drains stopped, dust-bins misused in every manner; even pipes broken, and watertaps wrenched away. This was sometimes the result of carelessness, and a deeply-rooted habit of dirt and untidiness; sometimes the damage was willful. Our remedy was to watch the right moment for furnishing these appliances, to persevere in supplying them, and to get the people by degrees to work with us for their preservation. I have learned to know that people are ashamed to abuse a place they find cared for. They will add dirt to dirt till a place is pestilential, but the more they find done for it, the more they will respect it, till at last order and cleanliness prevail. It is this feeling of theirs, coupled with the fact that they do not like those whom they have learned to love, and whose standard is higher than their own, to see things which would grieve them, which has enabled us to accomplish nearly every reform of outward things that we have achieved; so that the surest way to have any place kept clean is to go through it often yourself. . . .

"I mentioned our custom of using some of the necessary, yet not immediately wanted repairs as a means of affording work to tenants in slack times. . . . When a tenant is out of work, instead of reducing his energy by any gifts of money, we simply, whenever the funds at our disposal allow it, employ him in restoring and purifying the houses. And what a difference five shillings' worth of work in a bad week will make to a family! The father, instead of idling listlessly at the corner of the street, sets busily and happily to work, prepares the whitewash, mends the plaster, distempers the room; the wife bethinks herself of having a turn-out of musty corners or drawers—untouched, maybe, for months—of cleaning her windows, perhaps even of putting up a clean blind; and thus a sense of decency, the hope of beginning afresh and doing better, comes like new life into the home.

"The same cheering and encouraging sort of influence, though in a less degree, is exercised by our plan of having a little band of scrubbers.

"We have each passage scrubbed twice a week by one of the elder girls. The sixpence thus earned is a stimulus, and they often take an extreme interest in the work itself. One little girl was so proud of her first cleaning that she stood two hours watching her passage lest the boys, whom she considered as the natural enemies of order and cleanliness, should spoil it before I came to see it. And one woman remarked to her neighbour how nice the stairs looked. 'They haven't been cleaned,' she added, 'since ever I came into this house.' She had been there six years! The effect of these clean passages frequently spreads to the rooms, as the dark line of demarcation between the cleaned passage and the still dirty room arouses the attention, and begins to trouble the minds of its inmates.

"Gradually, then, these various modes of dealing with our little realm began to tell. Gradually the people began to trust us; and gradually the houses were improved. The sense of quiet power and sympathy soon made itself felt, and less and less was there any sign of rudeness or violence towards ourselves. Even before the first winter was over many a one would hurry to light us up the stairs, and instead of my having the rentbook and money thrust to me through the half-open door, my reception would be, 'Oh, can't you come in, Miss, and sit down for a bit?' Little by little houses were renovated, the grates reset, the holes in the floors repaired, the cracking, dirty plaster replaced by a clean, smooth surface, the heaps of rubbish removed, and we progressed towards order.

"Amongst the many benefits which the possession of the houses enables us to confer on the people, perhaps one of the most important, is our power of saving them from neighbours who would render their lives miserable. It is a most merciful thing to protect the poor from the pain of living in the next room to drunken, disorderly people. 'I am dying,' said an old woman to me the other day: 'I wish you would put me where I can't hear S—— beating his wife. Her screams are awful. And B——, too, he do come in so drunk. Let me go over the way to No. 30.' Our success depends on duly arranging the inmates: not too many children in any one house, so as to overcrowd it; not too few, so as to overcrowd another; not two bad people side by side, or they drink together; not a terribly bad person beside a very respectable one. . . .

"On Saturday evenings, about eight o'clock, the tenants know that we are to be found in the club-room . . . and that they may come to us there if they like, either for business or a friendly chat.

"Picture a low, rather long room, one of my assistants and myself sitting in state, with pen and ink and bags for money at a deal table under a flaring gas-jet; the door, which leads straight into the court, standing wide open. A bright red blind, drawn down over the broad window, prevents the passers-by from gazing in there, but round the open door there are gathered a set of wild, dirty faces looking in upon us. Such a semicircle they make, as the strong gas-light falls upon them! They are mostly children with dishevelled hair, and ragged, uncared-for clothes; but above them, now and then, one sees the haggard face of a woman hurrying to make her Saturday evening purchases, or the vacant stare of some half-drunken man. The grown-up people who stop to look in are usually strangers, for those who know us generally come in to us. 'Well! they give it this time, anyhow,' one woman will exclaim, sitting down on a bench near us, so engrossed in the question of whether she obtains a parish allowance that she thinks 'they' can mean no one but the Board of Guardians, and 'it' nothing but the much-desired allowance. 'Yes, I thought I'd come in and tell you,' she will go on; 'I went up Tuesday—' And then will follow the whole story.

" 'Well, and how do you find yourself, Miss?' a big Irish labourer in a flannel jacket will say, entering afterwards; 'I just come in to say I shall be knocked off Monday; finished a job across the park: and if so be there's any little thing in whitewashing to do, why, I'll be glad to do it.'

" 'Presently,' we reply, nodding to a thin, slight woman at the door. She has not spoken, but we know the meaning of that beseeching look. She wants us to go up and get her husband's rent from him before he goes out to spend more of it in drink.

"The eager, watchful eyes of one of our little scrubbers next attract attention: there she stands, with her savings-card in her hand, waiting till we enter the sixpences she has earned from us during the week. 'How much have I got?' she says, eyeing the written sixpences with delight, 'because mother says, please, I'm to draw out next Saturday; she's going to buy me a pair of boots.'

" 'Take two shillings on the card and four shillings rent,' a proudly happy woman will say, as she lays down a piece of bright gold. A rare sight this in the court, but her husband has been in regular work for some little time.

" 'Please, Miss,' says another woman, 'will you see and do something for Jane? She's that masterful since her father died, I can't do nothing with her, and she'll do no good in this court. Do see and get her a place somewheres away.'

"A man will enter now: 'I'll leave you my rent to-night, Miss, instead o' Monday, please; it'll be safer with you than with me.'

"A pale woman comes next, in great sorrow. Her husband, she tells us, has been arrested without cause. We believe this to be true; the man has always paid his way honestly, worked industriously, and lived decently. So my assistant goes round to the police-station at once to bail him, while I remain to collect the savings. 'Did he seem grateful?' I say to her on her return. 'He took it very quietly,' is her answer; 'he seemed to feel it quite natural that we should help him.'

"Such are some of the scenes on our savings evenings; such some of the services we are called upon to render; such the kind of footing we are on with our tenants. An evening such as this assuredly shows that our footing has somewhat changed since those spent in this court during the first winter.

"My readers will not imagine that I mean to imply that there are not still depths of evil remaining in this court. It would be impossible for such a place as I described it as being originally to be raised in two years to a satisfactory condition. But what I do contend is, that we have worked some very real reforms, and seen some very real results. I feel that it is in a very great degree a question of time, and that, now that we have got hold of the hearts of the people, the court is sure to improve steadily. It will pay as good a percentage to its owners, and will benefit its tenants as much, as any of the other properties under my management have done. This court contains two out of eight properties on which the same plans have been tried, and all of them are increasingly prosperous. The first two were purchased by Mr. Ruskin.

"It appears to me then to be proved by practical experience that when we can induce the rich to undertake the duties of landlord in poor neighbourhoods, and ensure a sufficient amount of the wise, personal supervision of educated and sympathetic people acting as their representatives, we achieve results which are not attainable in any other way. . . . It is not so much a question of dealing with houses alone, as of dealing with houses in connection with their influence on the character and habits of the people who inhabit them. . . . The principle on which the whole work rests is that the inhabitants and their surroundings must be improved together. It has never yet failed to succeed.

"Finally, I would call upon those who may possess cottage property in large towns to consider the immense power they thus hold in their hands, and the large influence for good they may exercise by the wise use of that power. . . . And I would ask those who do not hold such property to consider whether they might not, by possessing themselves of some, confer lasting benefits on their poorer neighbours?

"In these pages I have dwelt mainly on the way our management affects the people, as I have given elsewhere my experience as to financial matters and details of practical management. But I may here urge one thing on those about to undertake to deal with such property—the extreme importance of enforcing the punctual payment of rents. This principle is a vital one. Firstly, because it strikes one blow at the credit system, that curse of the poor; secondly, because it prevents large losses from bad debts, and prevents the tenant from believing he will be suffered to remain, whatever his conduct may be, resting that belief on his knowledge of the large sum that would be lost were he turned out; and, thirdly, because the mere fact that the man is kept up to his duty is a help to him, and increases his self-respect and hope of doing better.

"I would also say to those who, in the carrying out of such an undertaking, are brought into immediate contact with the tenants, that its success will depend most of all on their giving sympathy to the tenants, and awakening confidence in them; but it will depend also in a great degree on their power of bestowing concentrated attention on small details. . . .

"It is the small things of the world that colour the lives of those around, and it is on persistent efforts to reform these that progress depends; and we may rest assured that they who see with greater eyes than ours have a due estimate of the service, and that if we did but perceive the mighty principles underlying these tiny things we should rather feel awed that we are entrusted with them at all, than scornful and impatient that they are no larger. What are we that we should ask for more than that God should let us work for Him among the tangible things which He created to be fair, and the human spirits which He redeemed to be pure?"

I have quoted at length from Miss Hill's little book, partly because her work is so little known in the South; partly because her own words make so clear the basis of human sympathy on which the success of all such work must depend. That sympathy is a world-principle, a world-need, and a world-power. If she proved with these people—as she did for fifty years—that business success is entirely compatible with a spirit of brotherhood; that housing reform and the reform of immorality and vice go hand in hand; that paupers and semi-paupers can be changed into a body of self-dependent workers; then surely there is hope for slum-dwellers elsewhere.

The Octavia Hill plan has been tried in a number of cities in England and Scotland; and in New York, Boston, and Philadelphia. The work has been to a remarkable degree both financially and humanly successful.

Mme. Montessori's work in Rome is among this same tenement class. Her Houses of Childhood are in re-made tenements, where good business and brotherhood go hand in hand. The children who have astonished the world are from this same class of paupers, semi-paupers and criminals. Until opportunity was offered these who have been denied it, who could have guessed the measure of their response?[1]

The Negroes of this same economic class need what their class needs the world around. They will respond in the same way. The colour of one's skin, or even the shape of one's head, cannot change the working of a principle. The trouble in lifting up this lowest class of Negroes is that we have not yet paid the price. Things worth doing always cost; and to do this thing among us will take, in somebody's heart, that same passion for justice and opportunity for the weak that it takes everywhere else.

But the doing of it need not wait until that passion rises in all hearts, else one might well despair. Prove that a thing pays—in money—and it goes. Men and women who cared little for humanity were glad to turn the management of their tenement property over to Miss Hill as soon as they found returns by her methods were better than by theirs. She was so overwhelmed with offers that she and her assistants had to refuse much of what the owners urged upon them. Many of the great manufacturers of this and other countries frankly admit that their reason for the extensive welfare work they carry on among their working people is purely a business one: they have found that it pays, in money, to care for "the human end of the machine."

That is the way the world moves. The people with love in their hearts, the seers, pay the price, open the new way, and prove it better than the old; then people walk in it, because it is proven good.

There is nothing to do with many of the shanties for Negroes, in city and

1. Maria Montessori's first book on her now-famous educational methods, *The Montessori Method: Scientific Pedagogy as Applied to Child Education in "the Children's Houses"* (Cambridge, Mass.: R. Bentley, 1912), did not appear in English until 1912, only two years before the publication of *In Black and White*. The project that Hammond describes here, with children from tenements in Rome, began in 1907.

country, but to condemn them by law and tear them down. As our social conscience becomes aroused this will inevitably be done. Many houses now in use
would do very well if given a water supply and some extra windows, provided
the rent-collecting were done, not by an indifferent or contemptuous real estate
agent, but on the Octavia Hill plan.

Negro women of force and character should be trained under white auspices
to do this work. Two or three owners of Negro renting property could together
employ such a rent collector for what the real estate agent would cost, or less.
Their property would improve as well as their tenants; and the frightful waste of
humanity that goes on in our slums, the drifting of wreckage into prisons and
poorhouses, would not only be checked, but these now broken creatures would
become a community asset, as every real worker is.

We need an experiment station in the housing of Negroes of this class. An
ordinary city block, two-thirds of it covered with decent little houses, could
carry the interest on the whole investment, though one-third be given over to a
playground, on a corner of which should stand a community house with rooms
for clubs and industrial classes, as well as a decent meeting place for young people in the evening. Such a plant would demonstrate that healthful housing of
the very poor could be made a paying investment; and the income from it, if
made available for such a purpose, would provide for the training, under the
best of white management, of the Negro social workers so sorely needed in the
homes of our poor.

Calls for such workers are already coming from white people in several
Southern states. The owner of a lumber camp in the Southwest, who has long
carried on welfare work among his white employees, has tried to get a Negro
woman to help his coloured employees; and similar efforts have been lately
made by several others. A Southern white woman wrote me recently of conditions in a camp of Negroes where electricity was being developed from water
power. The workmen had their families with them—fourteen hundred black
folk in all, herded like cattle there in God's clean mountains, and living as untaught, helpless people will. Drinking, vice, and immorality were rampant. The
women knew nothing of home-making, had homes been possible. The children
were born like flies, and grew or died in moral and physical filth. A breeding-
place for criminals! And the right kind of Negro woman, properly trained, and
backed by a corporation merely selfishly intelligent, could have brought outward order and decency, lifted the workers to a far higher efficiency, and created

many real homes there, each one a point of contagion for life and hope and health. It would pay in dollars and cents.

It is impossible to speak of housing for Negroes without a word about the better classes among them, and the fight these must make for decent homes.

The thrifty working people, who constitute a large and ever-growing class, make heroic sacrifices to own their own homes. This is easier to do in the country than in the city, and the home, when won, is far safer; for if one owns even a very few acres one need not fear the placing of a saloon next door, or a low dance-hall, or a vice resort for white people—evils which constantly threaten every Negro owner of a hard-won city home. Sanitary conditions, too, are under one's own control, and with intelligent parents it is possible for children to grow up in robust health, which they can scarcely do in those parts of our cities open to Negro homes. The country is the place for poor Negroes, not because they are Negroes, but because they are human, and of like needs with the rest of the world.

But before they will be permanently content in the country they must have what any race of people must have under like conditions: perfect security for life and property; and such education as will relate them to country life in an efficient, social and joyful way.

Neither of these things is beyond attainment. The trend towards better education in the Negro rural schools is noted elsewhere; and the effects of this movement will be powerfully reinforced by the decision of the United States Government to use its eight hundred Southern farm-demonstrators for work among both races. There is also a strong element in the Southern state universities which favours the inclusion of gatherings of Negro farmers in the agricultural extension work of their lecturers and demonstrators. When these things bear fruit, and when not merely a large part of the South, but absolutely all of it, is as safe for Negroes as for white people, the housing of the country Negro will be a problem practically solved.

The city dwellers are in a harder case. The poorest share the fate of slum-dwellers of all races. They live in those sections which are morally and physically the least desirable, and are neglected habitually by the city health authorities. Cleanliness and decency are alike beyond them. But in addition to these things, in far too many of our cities, both the respectable working man and the prosperous, educated Negro are forced to live in surroundings from which men of any other race, of their economic status, would be allowed to escape.

It is even worse that that. When by their own efforts a few Negroes secure a respectable neighbourhood, families of the better class building up a little community of their own, they are peculiarly liable to have saloons and houses of ill-fame thrust upon them by a low class of whites whom the upper classes do not restrain. The Negro owner of a city home, whatever his education or business success, whatever the sum invested in his property, cannot be sure, from month to month, of retaining for his family surroundings compatible with moral health and safety.

I know a Negro, an honour graduate of Brown University, a winner there of the fellowship in the American School at Athens, Greece.[2] He is a man of wide attainments, of blameless life, of modesty and good manners. He is in full sympathy with the best Southern thought concerning race relations; and his wide influence among his people is a thing for white Southerners to be thankful for. He has turned aside from money-getting all these years, to serve his people in return for a very simple living. By what effort one can imagine he bought a little home. It is far from his work, on the outskirts of the city, placed there in the hope that his children might grow up in safety. His home attracted other homes, until the neighbourhood became good enough for a white man's house of ill-fame, which he found was to be erected on the lot adjoining his own. He has three daughters, the oldest barely grown. He saved himself by buying the lot, at a cost of long saving and strain.

"But I am not safe any more," he said. "There are still vacant lots there; and I can't possibly buy them all."

If I were a Negro I should do just as Negroes do—resent with all my heart our stupid white assumption that when they attempt to buy property in our own desirable sections they are trying to force themselves upon us in impudence, and to assert their belief in and desire for "social equality."

What these Negroes of the better classes want is first of all a neighbourhood of assured moral decency in which to rear their children. Their passionate desire for character in their children we do not begin to understand. Next to that they want sanitary conditions, and avoidance of the lower classes of their own people, just as we do ourselves. To get these things some Negroes are willing to thrust themselves, if they can, among white people, and to endure their resentment and contempt.

"If you white people could only understand!" a Negro woman said to me not

---

2. This would again be John Wesley Gilbert, to whom Hammond referred in chap. 2.

long ago, her face fired with feeling. "We don't want our homes where we're not wanted. But we want to be decent too. And it's the same all over the country—anything will do for a 'nigger.' You think we're all alike, and you don't care what happens to us just so we're out of your sight. My husband and I were living in Denver; and we had money to pay for a comfortable house. But there wasn't a place to rent to Negroes that a self-respecting Negro would have. And how will my people ever learn to be decent if they must live in the white people's vice district?"

We have no right to treat people like that. In one large Southern city, with high taxes and a big revenue and an expensive health department, a white friend of mine counted one morning twelve dead cats and dogs, in various stages of decomposition, in one short Negro alley. It was not an uncommon sight, except that the corpses were rather numerous. The outhouses are vile beyond description, a menace not merely to the Negroes but to the entire community. Yet if a Negro tries to buy a home in a healthful part of town we think his one motive is to thrust himself upon us, socially, just as far as he dares.

The way out of a situation like that is so simple, so plain! What is needed to solve the problem is not a segregation law, to force those who would be clean back into the bog we ought to drain out of existence; it is just to put ourselves in the Negroes' place and do as we would have done by. If we white people could only have a Negro's consciousness for a day or two it would clear up so many things. As it is, we can at least use our imagination.

If the city's health laws were enforced where they are most needed, punishing those who break them if necessary, till they learned better; if streets could be set aside in a district capable of being made more attractive, and a fair share of city improvements put there; if the Negroes who built good homes there were protected as well-to-do white people are from the fear of saloons and other vice resorts; if it were all done not in contempt, but in a spirit of justice and human consideration, there would be no need for segregation laws. Negroes, like white people, like to live among their friends. The overwhelming majority of them believe, as we do, in the social separation of the races; and beyond that, they do not want their children to grow up among those who look down upon them.

I am told that a well-to-do Negro in Kansas City, understanding his people's feeling, bought a considerable tract of land there, some distance out, and improved it as white men do for white buyers. The lots were sold under restrictions which guaranteed the neighbourhood morally, and went, my informant said, "like hot cakes." The place is to-day the most desirable for Negro homeowners in Kansas City. The man who bought the land originally made a handsome profit. His example could be followed by real estate men, white or black, in any large Southern city with an assurance of success. It is really not bad business to do justice.

I have dwelt at length on this matter of Negro homes because it is fundamental to justice, and therefore to any lasting adjustment between the races. No people can rise higher than their homes. And we criticize unsparingly the Negro's weakness and faults, yet fasten upon him living conditions which, the world over and among all races, breed just those things for which we blame him most.

IV
An Ounce of Prevention

There is practical unanimity in the South regarding the low moral standards of the Negro race as a whole. We admit that there are exceptions to the rule; we always know a few personally. But the overwhelming consensus of opinion is that Negroes generally are dirty, untruthful, and immoral; and beyond and above and below everything else, they are by nature dishonest.

However exaggerated such statements may be as applied to the whole ten million Negroes in America, very many of whom are practically as unknown to us whites as though they lived in another country, they are dangerously true of a large part of that class with which we come most frequently in contact. But have we ever asked ourselves why? Have we gone into their homes to find what drives them? Do we know anything of the wants in their lives? Have we any idea of the tremendous forces of wreckage which gather in those great empty places where human need cries with none to answer?

If we would look a little into the lives of those who live below the poverty line in communities where there are no black people, we would find that there is a certain degree of pressure under which human character, in the mass, tends to break. The ideal of humanity is the man who will meet all tests, endure all pressure, surmount all difficulties, suffer all loss, and pass out at last still pure in heart, unspotted, undefiled. However we fail ourselves—nay, because we fail—we cling to this ideal as the standard by which men should be judged. Whatever soil of sin be on us, we know, in our inmost hearts, that men and women were meant to be like that. It is for this that we honour our heroes and martyrs, who, wherever they have come to birth, belong first of all to humanity, and not to any one race. It is not for what they bore that we love them most, nor for what they have achieved: they are to us revealers of our own possibilities. We see in them the heights to which we ourselves, and all humanity, were meant to rise.

But is a child's power of resistance to be tested like an adult's? We are learning that premature burdens will strain young muscle beyond the possibility of future vigour. We found out long ago that young colts and calves must be shielded from undue strain: we lost money unless they were.

Later, and more slowly, the world is waking to the money loss involved in straining children's muscles too soon. We find that a child's muscles are a national asset, or ought to be, as well as a colt's. But character is a more precious asset still. It is a driving-force scarcely to be measured in national life, a productive source of wealth, as well as of happiness, beyond any other one thing. It is of far slower growth than muscle, and strain is more fatal, care more vital to it. Even the highest races are still so undeveloped morally that in any heavy, widespread stress the cartilaginous honour of thousands will give under the pressure, until men hitherto counted blameless seem little better than beasts. Times of war disclose conditions like that, invariably; and times of wide-spread panic, or famine, or disaster of any kind. The San Francisco earthquake furnished a recent and spectacular example.

Now when these things are true of favoured folk, of those who have had something of a normal chance in life, we may be sure, even before we look to see, that those cut off from a normal chance will not, in the mass, develop much power of resistance to undue strain. They, of all men, have least to bear strain with. Their moral muscles, undernourished and over-strained from birth, are uncoordinated with one another, or with their wills. The will itself hangs loose and undeveloped, shaken by vagrant desires and passing storms of passion. These are the people, the world around, who strew the path of civilization with wreckage. Crime is but the extreme manifestation of conditions which create vast swamps of incapacity, shiftlessness and immorality, in which human character is engulfed as in a quicksand, and out of which crime emerges as the topmost blossom of its rank and fetid growth.

What are some of the main causes of this human ruin and waste? Not here in the South, but everywhere. We have no peculiar laws of life down here, any more than we have peculiar laws of physics. If an apple falls to the ground in England because of the attraction of gravitation, one will fall in Maine, or in Georgia, or in Kamchatka, for exactly the same reason. And if certain conditions in New York wreck physical and moral health in human beings, and result in all unhuman ruin, those same conditions will produce similar results, in any climate, upon any fragment of humanity exposed to them.

We are a pious people here in the South—perhaps, like our brethren elsewhere, more pious than we are Christlike. There are very many of us who, when the effect of conditions on character is asserted, begin at once to defend God's almightiness, and the power of grace to save to the uttermost. To some among us it seems a reflection on grace to suggest that men ever need anything else, or need grace itself anywhere but in their own lives. But they do need it elsewhere, nevertheless—in the hearts and lives of other people, and expressed in the conditions which surround them. One of the best women I know, one of unusual intelligence and education, said to me not long ago, in a hesitating, doubtful voice:

"And you heard her say, that doctor, just as I did, that when she examined the blood of those thirty fallen girls the average for the thirty was less than three million red blood-corpuscles where five million were normal; and that blood so impoverished lowered the vitality, starved the nerves, lessened their resistive power to temptation and impaired their wills, as well as their energy and ability to work. She said they were not fallen women: they were felled women—felled by social conditions to which we Christian women assented. —It did sound reasonable, I know, and dreadful. I felt like a criminal myself, almost. But doesn't it leave out God, and salvation? Where does sin come in when you look at society like that? And surely God is almighty; and His grace—" She looked at me, a puzzled frown between her eyes.

I do not doubt God's almightiness; nor do I pretend to understand why, being almighty, He has chosen to so limit His own power that His own will cannot possibly get done in this world until men are willing to do it. I do not doubt that He can do a great many things which I feel sure He never will. He never will, for instance, enable a man to make two hundred bushels of corn to the acre on land uncleared of weeds: and He will not return to any people, or any church, a harvest of "saved souls" in bodies whose living conditions defy all His laws of health and growth and decency, moral and physical. A few ears of corn may come to maturity, even among the weeds; and a man or woman here or there may rise to newness of life despite surroundings which deal death on every side: but the law holds good, all the same. It would be quite as effective, and fully as religious, so far as I can understand, to kneel beside the untouched weeds and pray for a bumper crop of corn as it is for us Christians to pray for the souls' salvation of the poor, and go comfortably home to dinner without one rudimentary intention of furnishing them surroundings in which love and righteousness can flourish. To look at community life like that does not, to my mind, do away with sin. It fixes it on us, the supposedly righteous, who know and do not, rather than on those who neither know nor do, and whom we fail to enlighten or protect.

I know the feeling is very strong in the South against any attempt at regeneration by man-made law instead of by spiritual processes; and I would not seem to fail in reverence to that best and greatest of all miracles, the redeeming life of God in the soul. I believe, in the brave words of Dr. Wines, spoken at the International Prison Congress after forty years of labour for prison reform, that "reformation is never accomplished until the heart has been reached and regenerated by the grace of Almighty God."[1] I also believe that our neglect of the living conditions of the poor has raised barriers between them and that grace which can no more be removed by prayer alone, or by faith not "made whole with deed," than weeds could be removed from a corn field by the same process. To destroy those barriers by arousing a community conscience, and recording its awakening in community action expressed in statutory law, is more religious by far than any amount of prayer for the salvation of the poor offered by folk who go home to idleness. We have thrown on the poor, and on God's grace, responsibility for the results of our own sins of neglect: and until the churches shoulder their share of responsibility for community conditions which defy the Bible law of human brotherhood here and now, I do not believe they will make any great headway, in the world outside their borders, in preaching the fatherhood of God or salvation for the world to come.

Where, then, should one apply the hoe in order to earn the right to pray unashamed for a harvest of salvation among the poor?

The matters of housing and sanitation have been already touched upon; inadequately, yet enough, I trust, to set wiser minds than my own to thinking, and stronger hands to work. Next to it, and closely connected with it, is the fundamental question of recreation.

The negations of life are the deadly things. Overt acts of wrong have inflicted untold miseries in every age; yet for blight upon humanity at large they cannot compare with the steady, persistent, accumulated results of perfectly respectable neglects. And the neglect of the human desire for recreation, age-long, worldwide, has been so often not merely respectable, but a virtue of the highest standing! We have talked much of the universal instinct for God, so evident even among savages; and we have based on it one of our strongest arguments for the existence of a God: to such universal need, we say, there must be somewhere

1. Enoch Cobb Wines (1806–1879) was a national leader in prison reform in the nineteenth century.

an answer; the existence of the need demands it. But in this universal play-instinct, common to all races and all time, we have found no proof of a need that demands an answer, no trace of a wise Creator's handiwork, nothing at all of design. For centuries it was merely an elfish trick of youth, to be as nearly suppressed as possible, being dangerously akin to the devil and all his works. And even now many affectionate and otherwise intelligent parents regard it as a part of their children's childhood and youth merely, to be lived through until that safe stage of maturity be reached where children become sober and sensible, and put away childish things. Many provide dolls and balls because they enjoy giving their children pleasure, but with little idea that the love of play is almost the greatest formative power in a child's life, and that by it he may be shaped to the highest ideals, the widest usefulness, or be degraded to the level of the beast.

It is not merely that a child coördinates his muscles and mind in play; he coördinates his entire being with the world about him in play that is wisely detected. He finds himself as a citizen of his world. In team-play, in the give and take of success and defeat, in fair play and respect for the rules of the game, he learns self-control, respect for the rights of others, the adjustment of his own personality to those about him, and a deep regard for law and justice.

All these things are fundamental to a law-abiding, honest life. In families of several children, where the mother is willing and able to share the play life of the children, they may learn these things at home, even in cramped quarters and under unfavourable conditions: but few poor children have mothers of leisure. There is no place for their play in the cluttered house, or in the diminutive yard some poor people are fortunate enough to own. In the cities the streets are the playgrounds of the poor. They are such for our poor, the Negroes. There is little play possible there, even in smaller cities, that fits their need. Besides, few of them know how to play, in city or country. The play-instinct has been perverted or suppressed so long that its natural outlet, with many of them, seems closed. They are not peculiar in this: they have simply suffered the deprivation of a deep human need, as children of the very poor have done elsewhere; and they react under the unnatural condition exactly as does all the rest of humanity in a similar situation.

There are certain laws of spiritual physics which are universal in their oper-ation, and which seem closely akin to the physics of matter. One can compress the air, guide it according to its own laws in prepared channels, and work with it miracles of usefulness. One can compress it with no outlet at all, and defy the law of its nature up to a certain point. After that, something goes to smash. Those are facts at the North Pole, and at the South Pole, and everywhere in between. Similarly, one can take this race-wide play-instinct, and guide it according to its own law of development to the building up of body and soul far above the danger-line of human ruin. Also, one can suppress it with impunity—for a certain length of time. But like the air, it has to go somewhere; and if it cannot go the safe way, it will take some other: the energy which creates it must be expressed. To this crude young need with no adequate outlet all sorts of illicit adventures proffer their irresistible lure—petty thefts, trials of brute strength, the aping of older folk in obscene talk and vicious deeds, "crap-playing" in the streets, the smoking of cigarettes, surreptitious drinking, the stealing of older people's "dope."

We understand here in the South, those of us who are somewhat interested in such matters, that these are proven facts concerning the gangs of young toughs in Northern slums. It is perfectly reasonable to quite a number of us that a baseball ground and a boys' club, or an organization of Boy Scouts, will transform a crowd of budding white criminals into decent young humans who delight to obey the law and to require their companions to do likewise: but it does not seem to occur to us, as yet, that this law of the gang is operative except where humanity has a white skin. So instead of buying playgrounds for our poor with our taxes, and furnishing trained directors of play for them, we take many times the sum needed for this simple provision for a normal need, and build great court-houses with it, filled with expensive machinery, human and other, of what we are pleased to call justice; and put up endless local jails, every one of which is guaranteed, by every law of spiritual dynamics, to poison the folk put into it, and to smother their impulses towards a better life. And then we sit down and commiserate ourselves for being burdened with a people so bent by nature towards crime.

In the summer of 1912, in a Southern city, afternoon playgrounds for Negro children were opened by the combined efforts of a few people of both races. Negro women of force and ability were engaged to supervise them, and the whole venture was under the direction of a Southern white woman, a graduate of her own state university and of Columbia. The children gathered in the playgrounds like flies. None of them knew how to play, but they were still plastic with childhood, and responded as childhood everywhere does from the North Pole to the South. But older children came too—gangs of adolescent boys whose only idea of "fun" was to torment folk weaker than themselves, and to smash up whatever afforded others pleasure. They were a whole battalion of thorns in the flesh all summer long. The white women concerned, having exhausted their own resources, appealed to the local Y.M.C.A., and to the pastors of several of the churches, for a white man who would take the gang in charge and organize its members as a constructive force in their community. But though the Y.M.C.A. director and the pastors tried diligently to find a man to undertake the task, nobody was forthcoming; and the group continues its boisterous career towards the chain-gang, where so many of us believe Negroes gravitate by their own nature rather than by our neglect.

But children are only the beginning of the story. The play instinct is not an evanescent appurtenance of childhood: it is deep down among the primal needs of life, as real and as persistent as the need for air or food. We educated white people are perfectly aware of our own need for recreation. We turn to the woods and the mountains, to golf and tennis, fishing and camping, whenever we can possibly afford it, and just as long as we live. In between whiles we go to the theatre and the "movies," to baseball and football games, to the parks, on motoring trips—any and everywhere that promises us a break in the monotony of life, a bit of relaxation, a little laughter. We begin to understand that the need of these things is bedded so deep in the nature of white people that wage earners are actually more profitable to their employers, in dollars and cents, if they get their bit of vacation in summer time. It has long been customary in the North, and grows yearly more common with us, to give clerks and salespeople two-weeks' playtime a year, with pay; to close department stores at noon on Saturdays in summer; and to let everybody off on holidays. We are learning to do it not simply because we want other people to enjoy themselves, but because our enlightened selfishness is becoming convinced that a workman who never plays can never do the most efficient work.

But it has not occurred to us that natural laws have no special editions for skins of different colours. There are, of course, as many kinds of pleasure as there are individual natures; and some of them require not only certain temperaments, but certain stages of intellectual advancement, for their enjoyment. No one would claim that a slum Negro could be interested for a moment in much that would give a cultivated white man the keenest pleasure. But a need common to all humanity has somewhere an answer suited to each man's stage of development; an answer clean, healthful, and life-giving: and they who withhold it do so to their own peril as well as to the injury of him who needs.

The poor of every nation need play more than any other class, and are more injured by the lack of it. What else drives New York's wage-earning girls, by

scores of thousands, to the low dance-halls of commercialized pleasure? They
would rather go to decent places, as is shown by the way they crowd the few
which are provided: but recreation they must have, or snap under the daily
strain of work. Young men flock to the same places, decent fellows to begin
with, often, pitifully eager to meet "some nice girl." But the associations are
too much for their unguarded youth. It is the exhilaration of the liquor they
drink which lures them, not its taste. They want that glorious sense of freedom
which is its first effect, that power to rise in a tumult of life and energy above
all that cramps them in their sordid daily lives. It is the excitement of gambling that draws them—the ecstasy of bated breath, of pulses that throb and
thrill. They never intend to wreck their lives; only to bring into their poor dull
colourlessness a little of sheen and glamour and fire. The lower they are in the
economic and the moral scale, in every city of every land, the bleaker and duller
their empty lives, the more fiercely this need drives them. A man with a few of
the comforts of life, a few inward resources—only a few—may walk without
pleasure, maimed indeed, but in a straight path, to the end. But he who has
nothing, within or without, neither resource nor help, what shall he do, with
only his blank, dead life of drudgery, and his fierce human need for a little joy?

It is so simple it breaks one's heart. Such utter wreckage, such ruin and waste
and degradation, such lapsing of men into beastliness—and all for lack of a
thing like this, a simply human answer to a vital human need!

Sometimes when I think about us—us Southern white folks—I don't know
whether to laugh or to cry. We are good people. I've associated with us all my
life, and I know that is true. Ideals stir us as nothing else does. If there is anything
Southern people will do it is to spend themselves for an idea—once they catch
it. We caught the temperance idea years ago—it is really the germ of our late-
developing social consciousness—and we have fought for it as no other section
of American has. Somehow, by the blessing of Providence, our preachers got
hold of it by its individually religious end, and many of them have not thought
of it as "social service" to this day. So they welcomed it to the fold of orthodoxy,
and went forth to fight for it with never a Christian to say them nay, or to suggest
that social service was no concern of a church dedicated to the preaching of "the
pure gospel." As for results, a look at the wet-and-dry map of the United States
in this present year of grace will show that the South is the cleanest part of the
map. We do things just that way.

But like other grown-ups, we are mightily like children. A child will clean
up his playthings in a whirl of enthusiasm over helping his mother; and when

she comes in, by invitation, to admire the results, she will find the rubbish not cleaned up, but tucked out of sight, and perhaps ruining some of her most cherished finery in its novel seclusion. Only the obvious middle of the room is in order. We have gone at the drink habit just that way.

The Negro's propensity for drink does trouble us. That is one thing about his condition we are aware of. We even feel the menace to the community which drunken Negroes furnish; and we deplore a development still so low, after all these years of civilization. Nothing, we say, will eradicate the Negro's love of liquor. (We do not specify what we have tried as an eradicator; but whatever it was, it hasn't worked.)

According to our lights, however, and in all sincerity, we have done our duty. We have passed local-option and prohibition laws. We have made a *fiat* sweep of the whole miserable liquor business, with a view, largely, to removing from the play-hours of our very poor, both white and black, one of their three great resources, which are, for both colours in this poorest class, gambling, immorality and drink. But what we have taken with one hand we have given with the other: not something clean to take the place of the unclean; but the same uncleanness with the added smirch of lawlessness. In all our cities men, nearly all of whom are white, are allowed to open "near-beer" saloons for the open selling of every known intoxicant, and to make a living from the degradation of our poor, both white and black, with the consent and protection of the authorities. When the poor, who are mostly black, go as the drink drives them, we dive into our pockets for more taxes to build larger court-houses and jails; and the women, whom the prisoners might have supported if they had had a better chance to stay sober, are left to choose between the streets for themselves, or work for themselves and the streets for their children. And so the manufacture of criminals, one of our most stupendous industries, and certainly our most expensive luxury, goes bravely on.

Prohibition is good as far as it goes, even though in our cities it does not go at all. But it will never, by itself, do very much more than just slick life up on the outside. It is a purely negative measure, a gigantic Thou shalt not. It has its place in positive life, as many other negations have: but a negation can never construct anything; its utmost is to clear the ground for construction. And if those who clear the ground construct nothing, somebody else will. Human life, being part of nature, tolerates no vacuum. Temperance measures, to be effective, must be constructive: they must offer something to take the place of what they have driven out. Until the human craving for relaxation, for exaltation of body and spirit, be cleanly met, it will spend itself on the unclean. And out of uncleanness will come waste and wreckage, for present and future generations.

What is there in the South that offers clean amusement, clean play, to Negroes young or old? In a recent investigation made by an International Y.M.C.A. Secretary, himself a Southern man, four cities were found having public parks for Negroes. Four public parks for Negroes in fifteen Southern states! Out of seventeen cities eight reported having picture shows for Negroes, and nine none. Of the picture shows reported half were "very low and degrading, with the vilest vaudeville attachment." In five cities there are theatres for Negroes— character not specified; and in several they are allowed in the peanut gallery of white theatres; but the investigator reports "the better class of Negroes say they will not go unless for some special attraction, as they are put with lowest class of whites." The report further declares that the "principal places of amusement for the male population [Negro] are the saloons, pool and billiard rooms." The saloon people are the quickest of all whites to recognize the Negro's humanity. They see that Negroes become slaves of drink exactly as white men do, and spend their last nickel for it in the same manner. In my own city the very large majority of cases in the recorder's court are Negroes, and nearly all their infractions of law are the results of drinking. The city is in a prohibition state. It contains eighty officially licensed near-beer saloons, and seventy-nine of them are run by white men. In practically every city of the South we white people set this object lesson regarding respect for law before the Negroes, and then deplore and despise the innate lawlessness of the black man's nature.

But if diversions other than drinking and lewdness are hard for adult Negroes to come by, what is done for the children? Louisville has two or three playgrounds for them, not very well equipped, but under the direction of the City Park Commissioner, as are the far ampler playgrounds for white children; and New Orleans has recently opened one with semi-official recognition. So far as I can learn these are the only cities in the South which have officially recognized this basal human need as common to white and black. A prominent church and club woman of Nashville gave a playground to Negro children in that city a few years ago; and whites and blacks together have now for two summers provided vacation playgrounds for Negro children in Augusta, Ga. That completes the list to date.

Laying aside all altruistic motives, turning our backs on Christ's doctrine of human brotherhood, and acting solely from the standpoint of enlightened self-ishness, it would pay the South, just in money, to put a three-acre playground next door to every schoolhouse for both whites and blacks, and to add to the teaching force a director of play for each county, under whose supervision the teachers of the various schools could in turn assume charge of the playground after school hours. Folk dances would take the place of games with the older children. We could call them folk games if some of our church people looked askance at the other word. If the universal enjoyment of movement in rhythmical time could be met in this clean and wholesome fashion it would do more to undermine "animal dancing" than any well-deserved philippic that could be hurled against it. The best way to get rid of an unclean thing is to put in its place a clean one which meets the need.

The schoolhouse should be the recreation centre for young and old. For years great corporations have been employing "social engineers" to work among the employees as a matter of sound business policy, to bring up the efficiency of the human end of the machine. A large part of the engineer's duty has lain in providing clean and interesting recreation for folk deadened by drudgery. Lately a city or two has taken the matter up and appointed a city Superintendent of Public Recreation, just as they have a Park Commissioner. There is no sentiment in such an act—no sentimentality, at least. Hard-headed business men have done it, and communities stand to it, and pay the necessary taxes to finance it, because it will pay in human character and happiness, and, in the long run, in dollars as well. So here and yonder, in the most unexpected places, it keeps cropping out in life that what we call Christian doctrines are not doctrines at all. They are laws of human life, and Christ's, not in the sense that He made them up, but in the sense that He understood them and put them into words. When we provide for the human needs of the weakest, we come not upon sacrifice, but on more abundant life for all. For we really are brethren, all of us, and the satisfied need of those who lack the strength and prosperity of all.

V

Human Wreckage

But what of the wreckage already achieved? What of that fragment of the world-wide ruin most in evidence to our consciousness—the criminals, young and old, of both races, who fill our Southern jails, and work in all possible publicity of disgrace, chained and striped, upon our streets?

For thousands of years the world has had two theories only about the relation of the state to crime. One is the theory of vengeance, originally the right of the individual, but as civilization progressed a right which became vested in the community. Among Christian nations Moses has set forth as the champion of this theory; and "an eye for an eye, a tooth for a tooth" is still widely quoted in justification of this outworn delusion, upon which the criminal law of the nations is founded.

It was doubtless a benevolent law in Moses' day which restricted vengeance, not to the limit of the avenger's power, but to that rough justice which measured the penalty by the offense. So far as we can decipher those old records, and those of far later generations, to inject into vengeance an idea of justice was not the least of the great lawgiver's achievements. Many, however, who quote Moses with gusto seem unacquainted with later Biblical literature, in which the exercise of vengeance is distinctly declared to be beyond the province of mankind.

Nevertheless, men cherish it to this day as a sacred and inalienable right. And lest vengeance unadorned should be insufficient, they have embroidered this first theory with the second—that punishments severe and ingenious beyond what vengeance might demand would act as deterrents to criminals *in posse*. On this altar of public benevolence the criminal *in esse* is still offered up, a useless and frightful sacrifice to the blindness and folly of men. It is true the law no longer condemns him to be broken on the wheel, nor burned with faggots of green wood, nor tortured in many of the thousand ways which make the prison history of the past such black reading.

But notwithstanding the rise and spread of a modern penology which is already profoundly influencing criminal procedure in many countries, the vast bulk of the world's criminals are still dealt with under a combination of these two theories. The criminal is punished because punishment is his desert and the state's right; and his degree of punishment must be severe enough to frighten anybody else from attempting a similar crime. That severity of sentence does not deter others from crime is proven by the criminal history of many centuries, and has long been openly acknowledged by authorities on crime in all countries. It is out of this self-confessed breakdown of the old system that the rise of a new one has become possible.

The foundation of the new system is, in the words of the eminent chairman of the English Prison Commission, "the accepted axiom of modern penology that a prisoner has reversionary rights in humanity." It regards a man convicted of crime not primarily as a criminal, but as an individual who, "by the application of influences or discipline, labour, education, moral and religious, backed up on discharge by a well-organized system of [oversight] is capable of reinstatement into civic life." It flatly denies the Italian theory of "a criminal type," pronouncing it a superstition, pure and simple. It offers abundant evidence that the criminal disposition is produced, largely in individuals physically or mentally weak, by social conditions which have forced their lives along lines of least resistance. It stands for the reformatory, for the indeterminate sentence, release on parole, the permanent separation of prisoners into groups according to type and criminal development, for education, moral, religious and industrial, for labour in outdoor life as far as practicable, for the abolition of prison stripes, and everything calculated to break down self-respect, and for life-detention of all who cannot be restored to society in safety to the community and to themselves.

Twenty-two nations were officially represented in the last International Prison Congress, which met in Washington City three years ago; three additional governments, Spain, the Transvaal, and Egypt, signified their desire to join; and negotiations were opened with the governments of China and Japan which indicate that at the next Congress representatives of those governments will take their place in the body as members, instead of taking part unofficially, as heretofore. The members of this Congress differed, as might be supposed, on many points: but they stood as a body for the principles of the new penology above stated. They also endorsed the principle that payment should be allowed the prisoner by the state for his work over and above the sum necessary for his own support; and that this remainder should be turned over to the prisoner's family if in need.

A point of deepest significance to Americans, North and South, was the unanimous conviction of all the delegates, home and foreign, that American local jails were the worst known to civilization. The United States government placed a special train at the disposal of the foreign delegates, and acted as their host during a tour of investigation which covered most of the country's great reformatories, adult and juvenile, and many local jails. It is said that Tombs, in New York City, reduced the foreigners to speechlessness. One of the most eminent said afterwards that the only thing to do with it was to tear it down; but the others found words incompatible with the minimum of politeness necessary in the presence of a host. The secretary of the Howard Association of London, when asked, did not hesitate to say that every jail he saw in America "ought to be wiped off the face of the earth," and that "nowhere in Europe do such conditions exist." The newly-elected president of the Congress, Sir Evelyn Ruggles-Brise, in extending an invitation for the next meeting to be held in England, begged the Americans "out of their humanity" to consider the case of "the thousands of petty offenders now passing through your city and county jails in such appalling numbers."

The reformatories of a few of the Northern states confessedly lead the world, and the principles of human restoration which they have demonstrated are spreading to the states of the West; but we of the South lag behind in every phase of reformatory and preventive work. The only point at which we are strictly up with the procession is in the matter of our local jails. They are like those of the rest of America, well adapted to the one specific end of manufacturing criminals out of that vast company of petty offenders not yet beyond the pale of citizenship.

I was talking with a friend not long ago about a certain local jail. A white woman who had once worked for her had been arrested on some charge, and had appealed to her for help. She had gone to the jail with a lawyer, a friend of hers, but had been refused permission to see the prisoner. The lawyer had been passed in at once, but the jailer stopped my friend.

"No ma'am," he declared with respectful positiveness; "you can't go in there. It ain't no place for a lady to be in, nor to see. It ain't fit."

"And he had a white woman in there!" exclaimed my friend; "a white woman, in a place unfit for a lady even to see! I told him if she could stand staying in it I could stand seeing it, but he wouldn't let me in."

I sympathized with her indignation: but was it any better for a black woman than for a white one? The white woman should have had a little better chance than the other to resist the moral contagion of the place, and should have been less of a menace to the community when she came out. But the Negroes, and many, too, of the whites, if they ever had a chance before the law grips them, lose it in the jail the law provides; lose it before they are even proven guilty of the crime with which they are charged. Men grown old in crime and debauchery are, in nearly all our jails, thrown with first offenders, often with mere boys. The accommodations provided for unconvicted American citizens violate the laws of decency and health in regard to the commonest physical needs. There is no privacy, no cleanliness. Everything in his surroundings combines to brand on the offender's consciousness the fact that he is no longer regarded as a being with human rights, reversionary or otherwise. His relation to life is purely that of the committer of a crime.

He may be just a boy, his offense a trifle; or, if more serious, the outcome, not of premeditated wickedness, but of a thwarted love of adventure, youth's natural flare of high spirits turned awry. In some of our cities such an offender would get what he needs—separate confinement beforehand, and an investigation, rather than a trial, before a specially constituted court. A real effort would be made to understand not what the boy did, but why he did it; and after being dealt with by the judge on that line chiefly, he would be turned over to a probation officer whose duty it would be to watch over him, and assist him to moral convalescence. The law should give the judge, as it does in Denver, certain powers to enforce, if necessary, parental coöperation in helping the boy, and in correcting wrong home conditions. With the right kind of judges and probation officers a vast deal of human wreckage is prevented by these courts.

But we have few of them in the South: and there is little of the kind of care needed given to young Negro delinquents. In what I am told is one of the best-managed juvenile courts of the South the probation officers for the Negro children are Negro women. That is an immense improvement on the old chain-gang way, of course; but adolescent boys, white or black, will not be very profoundly influenced by anything or anybody feminine. They need a man, and a wise one.

In only a few places, however, does the matter of probation come up. For the majority of our lawbreakers, young and old, one sure destination waits— the chain-gang, sometimes more euphemistically known as the convict camp. Here prisoners of all degrees of criminality are thrown promiscuously together, and clothed in stripes to advertise them to all beholders as outlaws from the human family. They wear individual chains in the daytime, which are fastened together at night. And they endure whatever of suffering, degradation, insult and injustice their individual keepers choose to bestow upon them.

A Southern Bishop, living in one of our largest cities, recently had a visit from a white man in a dirty, frowsy, unkempt suit, who announced himself as a convict discharged forty-eight hours before from the coal mines near by, which are worked by convict labour. Being questioned, he admitted that he had eaten but twice since his discharge. A Negro had given him some corn bread the first day, and a barkeeper on the next had given him a sandwich and a drink of whiskey. He refused the food and money the Bishop offered him. He had come, he said, to tell the story of what was done to the prisoners in those mines; he had promised the other convicts before he left that he would carry the story to some Christian, and see if he would take the matter up. If he took anything for himself, he said, it might cast suspicion on his tale.

He was a well-educated man. He said he had been an editor. A wrong had been done to a member of his family; in a blaze of anger he had shot and killed the offender; and he had been sentenced to three years at hard labour, which he had served.

The men were worked in gangs, under convict foremen, and each gang was assessed so many tons per day. If they mined more they were credited with the excess, to be paid for it when they left the camp. All credits, however, were given by the foremen, themselves convicts; and they could, and did, give the credits, not to those who earned them, but to those who shared with their overseers, or bribed them in other ways. The foremen carried horrible whips; and they used them constantly, unmercifully, without warning and without provocation. Men were beaten and kicked and injured until it was not at all an unknown thing, the convict said, for a man to put his left hand on the train rail and let the coal car run over it and crush it off. Then he had to be sent to some other camp, being useless for mining. It might be just as bad, of course; but there was always a chance. This convict had stuck it out. He had been told that he had no overtime pay coming to him. He had received the clothes he wore, taken from some newly-entered convict, instead of the new suit required by law, and had been turned out, penniless, to go back to the world in the newness of life, and conduct himself in such an irreproachable manner, after the lesson he had had, as not to get into a convict camp again.

The Bishop told his story quietly, as his habit is, while we sat gasping.

"What did you *do?*" we demanded.

"I made him take a little money, for one thing—as a loan. He wouldn't take much: but I followed him down the street and begged till he had to take a little. And I talked to some men who have influence. There is a public meeting called for the seventeenth. There will be men from all over the state, and I think the matter will be probed to the bottom. We may get our state laws reformed before we get through."

But one state is not enough. In my own state, which is not the one of the Bishop's convict, the leaders of the Men and Religion Movement in our capital city have published a list of the barbarities of our convict camps which sound like the Middle Ages. Twenty years ago, in the same state, an investigator appointed by the Governor reported exactly the same conditions. And these states are not behind some of the others. Four of our states, however—Kentucky, Missouri, Tennessee and Texas—are in the honour list of twenty-one states which have adopted the indeterminate sentence and the parole law; yet three of these retain the convict lease or convict labour system. In a few states the Governor had power to restore citizenship to a discharged convict. But in Texas, Kentucky and Tennessee no man convicted of crime remains an outlaw except by his own will. Citizenship is restored by law to every convicted criminal who, after due testing when released on parole, proves worthy of that trust. The last taint of his sin is cast behind him by the law, and he takes his place again, a man among men. "As far as the east is from the west—." Isn't that the normal way, the way that *works* because men are made to respond to it?

I was waiting at a railroad station not long ago when a frightened-looking Negro boy of about eighteen came by in the custody of three big policemen, who stood guard about him till the patrol wagon appeared and swallowed him up. After the crowd dispersed I learned from one of the policemen that the boy had been caught in the act of stealing a box of cigars. The policeman though he would get fifteen years for it; but seeing my horror, and wishing, evidently, to oblige a lady if possible, he reconsidered the matter and said maybe he would get off with ten years, seeing he was not really grown. I remembered the boy who was sentenced to three years for taking eleven dollars and forty-six cents: but that judge had especially pointed out that the sentence was unusually merciful. This boy's judge might well give him ten years of enforced criminal association for his theft: there was no telling.

I remembered another time, some years ago, when I was waiting for another train, at a junction in the mountains of a Southern state. The county sheriff was waiting also, with two white boys of seventeen or eighteen, moonshiners. The boys were chained together by their wrists and by their necks, with what looked like trace-chains. The sheriff had evidently imbibed their whiskey, probably for safe-keeping. He swaggered about, a coarse, not ill-tempered man, a pistol protruding from either pocket of his coat. He talked loudly, joking the boys about their capture and the becomingness of their present adornments. They tried hard to imitate his manner, and to wear an air of jaunty and amused indifference; but their eyes were frightened and ashamed.

Oh, the folly of it! The blind, stupid, brutal *uselessness* of it, the wicked waste of human lives and souls!

What had any of these boys, white or black, done, in their isolation, their ignorance, their stunted moral growth, unfriended, untaught—what had they done which gave society the right to seize their poor, starved lives and break and poison them in its foul prisons beyond hope of recovery for all time? Even if we had the right, what good does it do? The veriest madman out of Bedlam would hardly claim that our convict camps benefit the prisoners: but do they deter others from crime?

The census of the United States can answer that question: and the prison records of all civilized countries will join with the penologists of the world in confirming what the census says. Every year a vast number of arrests are made, and a less vast number of prisoners are discharged. *Less* vast. Each year our prison population receives an added permanent deposit from this great stream of human misery and ignorance and sin, as it washes through those black and awful places where men already injured are permanently deformed. Such measures have never lessened crime: they provoke it always, everywhere, since prisons were. The more cruelly or publicly a crime is punished the more surely it drives suggestion home to some ill-balanced nature, and rouses it to imitation. The punishment seems to add the last irresistible attraction to those on the border of criminality.

So far from stopping crime, our present system, with its public and private humiliations of the offender, propagates crime in both the criminal and the beholder. Whatever beats down a prisoner's remnants of self-respect is a blow not only at his manhood, but at the manhood of the state. Our prisons are great spawning-beds, where the crime of the community is gathered in that the crime of the state may pass over it and fructify it, sending out swarms of new evil influences to squirm and twist and spread in all the ooze and slime of the community, that our criminal supply may never fail.

We need more rational methods in our whole criminal procedure. When one has scarlet fever or diphtheria one is quarantined, not for a specified time, but until one can be safely restored to community life, as shown by one's personal condition. The criminal must also be treated as an individual. Something must be learned of his heredity, his environment, the causes which led to his crime. Only so may one attempt his restoration. To expect to attain it on any other basis than the one of sympathetic understanding is as unreasonable as to expect one course of treatment to cure every form of disease. Even the same disease requires different treatment for different cases; and to fix the term of a man's imprisonment by the crime he has committed is to ignore the dominating factor in the case—his personality. His personality, not his past offense, makes him a social menace. He should be imprisoned as long, and only as long, as his personality threatens danger to the community.

Dean Kirchwey, of the Faculty of Law of Columbia University, in a great address on "Ending the Reign of Terror" said:

"A demonstration of the fact, which we may well consider indubitable, that criminal conduct is usually, if not always, the result of conditions more or less beyond the control of the delinquent, cannot fail to shake the theory of moral responsibility upon which the vindictive idea of punishment is based, as well as to allay and in time overcome the feeling of resentment which such conduct now excites. And, on the other hand, a study of the psychology of the mob, and of the reaction of the existing penal system on the moral sense of the community will show how far it is safe to go in mitigating the rigours of the criminal law in a given jurisdiction . . . [until] such time as may be required to bring the community to a better appreciation of the nature of crime, and the conditions which determine it. . . .

"The doctrine that punishment is inflicted on the offender as a warning to others has come to be the orthodox view. . . . There is something touching in the unquestioning faith of the legal profession and of the man in the street in the efficacy of this vicarious suffering for crimes not yet committed. Yet it remains a matter of faith as yet unsupported by evidence. . . .

"The fact that a very large proportion—in some countries more than fifty per cent.—of criminals under confinement have previously undergone prison punishment seems to indicate that as a deterrent punishment by imprisonment leaves something to be desired. . . .

"The principle that punishment may . . . without reformatory influences be a means of moral amendment finds expression in many judicial utterances.

It is obviously a well-meant, but mistaken attempt to bring the sanctions of the moral law and of the ecclesiastical dispensation to the aid of the criminal law. . . . This imputes to the law a sanctity which the criminal would be the last to concede to it; and so quite apart from the vile and degrading conditions under which this work of grace was to be effected, it is not to be wondered at that we find no traces of its efficacy. . . .

"The principle of the reformation of criminals during imprisonment . . . does not assume that all criminals are capable of reformation, or even of improvement, nor that those who are can all be brought up to the level of good citizenship. It does assume, however, that most men and women, and all children, will respond to the steady pressure of a wholesome, uplifting environment . . . and it has already proven its faith by its works. . . . It must have cognizance of the life history of every individual committed to prison, with his heredity and environment. It studies him in prison—his needs, his capacities, his aspirations, his mental and moral equipment, his health, his reaction to . . . prison life. It follows him after his discharge. . . . It levies on all the sciences that deal with man—law, medicine, criminology, sociology. . . .

"The next few years will give us new data of great importance. . . . But there will be no facts for him who regards the criminal law as an instrument for venting wrath and hate on a fallen—and convicted—brother; none for him who would keep his fellow man in subjection to his iron law by terror; none for him who would work redemption through another's suffering. . . . The new moral atmosphere which has made every man his brother's keeper will be felt in the law courts as well as in the home and street. The new attitude of the state towards children of tender years will soon mark her attitude towards her erring children of a larger growth."

Those of us who can find comfort in a fact so painful may be assured that we of the South are not alone in the possession of a prison system outworn and barbarous. Nothing in our awful camps could be worse than what has been found, in most recent years, in the state prisons of several of the richest and most enlightened states of the North and West; and if they were all investigated the present black list would doubtless be longer than it is. But this fact concerns us only as it shows that our own conditions are part of a world-wide horror, which the best thought of the world has set itself to destroy. The reformation of our whole prison system is our part of a world-task.

We need a Southern Prison Commission, appointed by governors of the states, not to revise our prison system, but to study conditions, here and elsewhere, and to formulate a new system abreast of modern experience and founded on bed-rock truth and justice, instead of on the philosophy of the Middle Ages. The members of the Commission should be men of broad humanity and of strong common sense. Such men could, by the authority of their respective governors, make individual and unannounced visits, each to a number of prisons in his own state. Then they could examine the best the world can show them; the Denver juvenile court; the Colorado state farm, where "hardened" criminals are turned into men, without stripes, threats, chains or armed guards; the District of Columbia prison farm; the wonderful work for women at Bedford, N.Y., for men at Great Meadow, and for children at Industry, in the same state; the Kansas City municipal farm, a new idea in local government; the Massachusetts farms for vagrants and inebriates and many more.

This Commission would find at least three points in the South where Negro lawbreakers are being successfully trained towards good citizenship. In Virginia it is being done at the suggestion, and under the supervision, of a state officer, and with the backing of the legislature. In Georgia and Alabama it is being done by unknown and unlettered Negroes, whose loving hearts have led them into a wisdom not to be attained by any amount of unloving knowledge.

The State Superintendent of Charities and Correction in Virginia, a large-hearted, broad-minded man, fully abreast of the development of modern penology, has, in the last three years, taken from the Richmond penitentiary one hundred and fifty convicted Negro "criminals," all under fifteen years of age, and has placed them, under proper supervision, in good Negro homes, as members of the respective families. He tells me some hundred and forty-three of these boys are "making good." They are growing up into self-respecting and wealth-producing citizens, instead of becoming a recurring charge upon the state, which is the usual result of our ordinary methods of dealing with Negro first offenders.

At Ralph, Ala., is the Sam Daily reformatory, still called by his name, though Sam Daily himself has made his humble exit from life with no trumpets to proclaim him a hero, unless the angels sounded them on the other side. He was a full-blooded Negro, with no touch of efficiency as the gift of another race.

A white Alabamian, a city judge, moved with compassion for the young Negro delinquents brought before him, called for some good Negro of like compassion to give the boys a chance. Sam Daily responded, donating himself, his family, and one hundred and twenty-five acres of land to their use. First and last he took about three hundred boys from the Birmingham juvenile court, paid their way to the railroad station nearest his farm, fed them, clothed them, taught them industry, cleanliness and honour. I am told that ninety-five per cent. of his boys "make good."

The most curious thing about this enterprise is the fact that this poor Negro, who was never able to finish paying for his own farm, spent years of his life converting lawbreakers from a public liability to a public asset without receiving any public money to help bear the expenses of the process. Individual white men have helped him, and now help his widow, by making up deficits when they occur; but there is no regular public appropriation for this great and public service. The Southern Presbyterian Church, however, now pays regularly the salary of a trained Negro assistant at the reformatory. A white man, formerly a large slave-owner, who knows the reformatory well, writes me, in regard to its success with the boys, "I should call this forlorn effort to help the helpless a modern miracle." Only it isn't a miracle: it is natural law given a chance to work.

The third of these demonstrations of the response of Negro delinquents to good influences is made at the Paul Moss Orphanage at Augusta, Ga. Paul Moss is a Negro of rather limited education who gave up an excellent income as a skilled mechanic to devote his life to aiding Negro waifs and juvenile delinquents. He put all his savings into a small farm, where he has supported his charges with a little help from a few whites of the city and one or two Northern visitors. He is able to give the boys not much book education, but teaches them practical religion and a few trades. In the last six years he has sent out one hundred and sixty boys, half of whom were from the city juvenile court, the others being orphans and waifs in process of becoming delinquents. One hundred and fifty of these boys are "making good."

Each of these separate experiments shows that the response made by Negro delinquents to a helpful and sympathetic environment equals that made by the same class of other races—about ninety-five per cent. Would not our Southern Prison Commission consider this method of dealing with lawbreakers economically superior to the one now in general use? Even where we have reformatories for young Negroes under state or county supervision the inmates are treated as prisoners, dressed in some kind of distinctive branding uniform, kept under lock and key—and eventually landed, very many of them, in our prisons and convict camps. And we think that fact is explained by the Negro's criminal tendencies. The Commission, with all the evidence before it, might decide differently.

The Commission would look into the evils of convict labour as employed in many "model" prisons, so called, where men are driven beyond the limit of health under a contract system as vicious as our own, and turned out after years of alleged industrial training skilled only in some occupation employment in which is impossible outside of prison walls. They would go thoroughly into the question of the state's right, while attempting to restore a man to normal citizenship, to forbid his performance of the primal human duty to contribute to the support of his own family; and would examine the methods by which innocent women and children are beginning to be saved from this usual and unjust punishment.

They would learn what public services prisoners perform elsewhere, while being at the same time restored to manhood. We are too much in the habit of looking at the thing done, and ignoring the man who does it. Many of us feel, for instance, that in setting her convicts to work on the public roads—a most beneficent public service—one of our states has taken front rank in the treatment of her criminals. Yet that state clothes those men in stripes, as we all do, and works them in chains, on the public roads, under armed guards destitute of knowledge or fitness in the fine art of saving human wreckage.

In New Zealand in the last decade the convicts have planted 20,000,000 trees for the state, timbering waste lands, *and reclaiming the men.* But they do not wear stripes in New Zealand. The idea there is to deliver them from past degradation, not to sear it in for present and future injury. Denmark reforests her waste lands with men who, like the land, are in process of restoration. Prussia and Switzerland employ them to care for the great state forests: and they are employed in a number of our own Western states in various works of reclamation, though too often, with us, the uppermost idea is the reclamation, not of men, but of property.

All these things our Southern Prison Commission would consider; and far above the great and profitable work of reclaiming and enriching the wide waste lands of the South prison labour, they would set that greater and more profitable work of preventing the wide waste of human life, and reclaiming that already in process of ruin.

A prison system suited to human needs—the needs of prisoners, of their families, of the community at large—could be formulated, and presented to all our states, together with the information necessary, and with the weight of this South-wide Commission behind it. In principle, if not in all its details, it would be adopted in some states; and ultimately in all, as the experience of the foremost illuminated the wisdom of its provisions.

We need no revision of what we now have: we need a new penology, based on a conception of human life radically opposed to most that underlies our theory of punishment to-day.

We need to take up the call already being heard throughout the civilized world—a call for *trained* men and women to create the new profession of Healers-of-men-in-prison. We would not, even in our politics-fuddled cities put fifteenth century "leeches" (if we could get them) in charge of our public hospitals. Yet we count any ignorance competent to take unlimited control of sick souls and abnormal minds. In the recent Prison Congress America and Hungary joined hands to express the conviction of the penologists of the world that this professional training of prison officers—men already fitted by nature for such difficult and important work—was a vital need in the progress of humanity towards a sane and successful treatment of the world-problem of human wreckage.

VI
Service and Coöperation

If I were asked what the mass of the Negroes most need that we should give them, I think only one answer could be given which would go to the root of the whole matter. And that deepest need is not at all a Negro need, but a human one: we ourselves, as a people, share it profoundly.

They need ideals. The lives of so many of them seem just a chaos of wants, so that one stands at first dumb with bewilderment: so many fundamental needs, so much emptiness where there must be solid foundations if anything worth while is built up! But that which will open a way to fill all these empty spaces is a vision of something higher in their own souls; something higher, yet not too far or cold to kindle a spark of desire in their hearts, to quicken them, by vision and aspiration.

If we look back over the last fifty years we will see, perhaps, how little of this foremost essential of human advance we have furnished for them. Some things we have done, I know. We have paid millions for their education in the public schools: but have we cared how it was spent? The superintendent of education in one of our states, in a recent report, pronounces the Negro public schools of that commonwealth utterly inefficient.

He charges their wretched failure on the white county superintendents, many of whom, he says, never go near the Negro schools under them, nor concern themselves with the selection of fit teachers, nor with their improvement after they are selected. This story would fit more states than one. We could squander ten times the millions already spent in education like that without creating a single impulse towards better things: there is never any vivifying power in indifference.

Yet, our public schools for Negroes have done good—a world of it. Some of this must be credited to those among us who have honestly sought the Negro's good. The rest, I think, is due to the Negroes themselves, and to those once-so-hated "Yankees" who first made possible to Negro teachers a suitable preparation for their work.

Love is the world's lifting-force. It is like the light, which yearly lifts untold tons of cold, dead matter to the tree-tops in the beauty of green leaves. When we see leaves we know light has been at work: nothing else could lift matter up there so that leaves could be. And wherever we find a trace of spiritual quickening, a budding of dormant life, however scant, we know by the same token that Love has been at work: there is no other force which produces that effect. The uplift of the Negroes through the public schools, small as it is compared with what it might have been with the same expenditure of money, has chiefly come, not from our sometimes grudging provision, but from ideals kindled in some Negroes' souls by love and sacrifice other than our own.

The Northerners who came down here to teach the Negroes were ignorant of our past, of our conditions, of the underlying causes of our new antagonism to the Negroes—of all the circle of white life which looked to them so inexplicably cruel and wrong. They were only less ignorant about the Negroes, their traditions, their stage of race-growth, their true relation to Southern life. Few people had learned to be world-dwellers then; and these eager Northern folks, who saw a need and longed to meet it, translated neither white life nor black in world-terms. They made blunders, of course; and a good many Negroes acquired some knowledge at the expense of more wisdom. We have all seen white people do the same thing. And certainly the South never tried to help the situation. So far as explanation or assistance went we maintained a silence which was more than felt, while these from another world came and wrestled with our problems in all good faith, and according to their darkness and their light.

But with all the mistakes and friction, the energy wasted or turned to loss, these people brought one thing with them which is never wholly lost. It may be hindered, partly negatived, robbed of its full fruition by many things: but always love bears fruit. They brought with them that principle of life. They kindled a light in darkened hearts; they sent out thousands of Negroes fired with ideals of service to their race. And they have saved the situation, so far as it has been saved, for our Negro public schools.

We gave the Negroes ideals once. The North is dull of understanding at this point, as we are dull at others. It cannot take in the fact that slavery and ideals could exist contemporaneously. Yet once the North itself, and in the most strenuous days of its New England conscience, was unaware of any incompatibility between the two. It is the big brother again, forgetting his own so-recent ignorance, and ready with paste-pot and label for the younger child.

The existence of slavery we long accepted much as we did the weather—as a dispensation of providence which it were idle to inquire into. But we had a genuine affection for the Negroes, and out of it we met this need for ideals— an even deeper need than emancipation from physical slavery. Every Protestant denomination in the South had its white missionaries among the slaves, and all together they had nearly half a million slave members at the outbreak of the war. One church alone, the Southern Methodist, spent nearly two million dollars in missions to the Negroes prior to 1861, and had over three hundred white missionaries at work among them when the war broke out. The individual slave-owners, the very great majority of whom were Christian people, did even more. Men and women, they taught their slaves the Bible—not, as had been ignorantly suggested, to enforce the duties of meekness and obedience, but because the love of God in their own hearts necessitated their imparting it to those around them. My own mother was typical of her class, and no one who came in contact with her could have imagined that her service to the Negroes was caused by anything but the spirit which transfigured her whole life from day to day. Such women held regular Sunday-schools for their slaves, and often the white children of the household sat with the black ones to learn the Law which was over both of them alike. In times of rejoicing or of trouble the white people went to the Negro homes as friends; and in sickness they cared for them personally, often with their own hands.

Those among us who deny the Negro's capacity to respond to ideals should remember his faithfulness in time of war and temptation, and the beauty of character which even the most prejudiced of us admit belonged to "the old-time Negro." The admission, coupled, as it usually is, with sweeping charges against the character of the Negro of to-day, is the severest arraignment of Southern Christianity which can be brought against it. And we bring it ourselves, un-seeing.

But the truth has had its witnesses, all along. There were women all over the South who, like my mother, went serenely on in the path of love, even during reconstruction days, ministering to the sick and the poor about them, regard-less of the colour of their skins, and seeing only needs which love must meet. There were, in every state, men like Governor Colquitt, of Georgia, who as slave-owner, impoverished Confederate, and governor of his state, would tuck his

Bible under his arm any afternoon in the week, and go to some Negro cabin, where he would read and teach and pray, talking with the family as friend with friends, advising, comforting and inspiring them.

Nor did the next generation utterly fail. Through all the turmoil of reconstruction some passed the spirit of service to their children. An Alabama woman, for instance, who was widowed by the war, remained on her remote plantation, where she spent her life teaching the Negroes of the neighbourhood free of charge. Her daughters took up her work, and carry it on to this day. I know a brilliant Kentucky woman, daughter of a great slave-owner of that state who was at one time its governor, who has been a helper to Negro church workers, and to any Negro in need, her whole long, beautiful life. Another friend, a woman of wealth and influence, a leader among the women of the South today, taught a Bible class of Negroes for sixteen years, until her strength failed under her accumulating work for the unprivileged. Space fails for the instances known to even one person. One more must suffice.

Just after the war a South Carolinian, a graduate of Brown University and a devout Baptist, went to a Georgia city and gathered about him a little knot of Negro boys who wanted to become Baptist preachers. He taught them there for years, spending himself to give ideals to the ignorant and the poor, cut off from all other association. For the white people were bitter in those days, and despised him where they did not hate. It was one man's vision against a city's blindness—that world-old story of ignorance, and of light no darkness can quench. He is forgotten to-day by all but a few Negroes, one of whom, a fine, strong man who had felt his touch, told me his story. But the black boys to whom he gave ideals have gone out to give their people light. Their church is strong in Georgia, and these men lead it. One of them is its chief pastor in my own city; and so well has he responded to his teacher's efforts that the white people of the town are all his friends. When he was ill not long ago the daily paper reported his condition, and gave the names of several of the leading business men who went to his home to inquire how he did.

Yet few of the whites who speak of this Negro and of the others who were taught with him, as "the kind all Negroes ought to be" have any idea where the real springs of their lives were found. Some of us, turning away from the South's long tradition of service to the Negro race, knowing only the disjointed years of bitterness, feel only contempt, or at best a puzzled surprise, that any white Southerner should lower himself by stooping to help a Negro, or should persuade himself that they are worth the effort.

Yet we have never offered them ideals out of a living sympathy that they have not responded, for themselves and for their race. No one who knows the better class of Negroes can fail to be impressed with the spirit of sacrifice and service which is shared by nearly all of them. They follow that law of human life under which any race, in common stress of any kind, draws closer the band of brotherhood, and lives for the common good.

And oh, we white people are waking up! The thrill of the North's awaking, long ago begun, and not yet ended, is with me still; but these are my very own! Some of us have worked and waited so long. There have been years when the only warrant for hope was in the long look at the Race of Man, and the Love which leads it on. But that was warrant enough.—And now? Just a few of the signs—a few.

For long our churches have set a standard for us; and even though they themselves have not lived up to it, the pegs were down, and visible to the careful eye. In 1876 the Southern Presbyterians opened a theological school for Negroes at Tuscaloosa, Ala. For nineteen years the pastor of the white Presbyterian church of the town was also the head of this school, which has had only Southern whites as teachers from the beginning. The yearly income, provided by the denomination, had risen from four hundred dollars the first year to fifteen thousand twenty years later.[1] The theologues pay their board and tuition by working on the school farm under expert teaching. They go out to preach a gospel of love, morality, cleanliness, hard work, and modern methods of farming; also of friendliness to their white neighbours. I am told, by those who know the section about Tallapoosa, that race relations there are not of the problem kind. There has been response to ideals from both whites and blacks. The present head of the school is the son of a Mississippi slave-owner.

A few years after this school was started the Southern Methodists opened an institution in Augusta, Ga., for the training of Negro preachers, teachers, and other leaders for the race.[2] Its first president was a former slave-owner, who resigned the chair of English in a strong college to take the position at a most problematical salary. It cannot be denied that the school lived "at a poor dying rate" for several years: but the denomination was officially committed to it as a proper work for white Christians to undertake; Southern white college men and women have officered it from the first; and for eighteen years the church Board

1. The "income" is the annual appropriation from the church.
2. Hammond refers here to Paine College.

of Education has put its needs before the people, and, in coöperation with its president and faculty, has gradually won for it a better support.

These are, so far as I know, the only schools maintained exclusively by Southern whites for Negroes; but the Episcopal church has a number of schools for them in which Southern as well as Northern whites teach; and part of their support, which comes from their General Mission Board, is drawn from the Southern dioceses. The Southern Baptists, who have long made an annual appropriation for the education of Negroes at schools of other churches, are now preparing to open a theological seminary for them.

The first Southern settlement for Negroes is conducted by the son of an Alabama banker and former slaveholder. It is in Louisville, and is of late years jointly financed by the Northern and Southern Presbyterians. This settlement, I am told, is largely responsible for Louisville's Negro playgrounds and probation officers. This city also has a fine public library for Negroes,[3] with a Negro librarian and two assistants, all under the white librarian who is the head of the city system. A children's room is well patronized; and branches are maintained at some of the public schools. In a private letter the white head of the system declares the Negro library an untold blessing to the race. The use of a room in the building is allowed, free of charge, to clubs and other educational and recreational gatherings. The children, he writes, respond readily to guidance, and are eager for good books. The number of adult patrons grows steadily. The library, which is a beautiful building, was given by Mr. Carnegie, and cost $25,000.00. It is maintained by the city of Louisville. Libraries for Negroes have also been given by Mr. Carnegie to New Orleans, to Nashville, and to Meridian, Miss., the city authorities guaranteeing ample support.

I can learn of but two other Negro public libraries in the South. One, at Galveston, is the gift of a citizen of that place, whose will made provision for a library for each race. The librarian said that the children were being helped by it to a large extent. The response among adults was less marked. The other public library for Negroes is at Jacksonville, Fla.; and my last report from it, some time ago, stated that it was not as efficient as it should be, because only a room in a corner of the building for whites was available, so that it was impossible to make efforts to extend the work; but their present capacity was taxed.

Here is a scarcely-touched opportunity to create ideals for a race. These

---

3. Since this was written a second branch public library for Negroes has been opened in Louisville. [original footnote]

Carnegie libraries are among the wisest investments in the South. But some of us, like the children in the market-place, are hard to please. If the Negroes care nothing for books we say they are stupid and vicious-minded: if one proposes antidoting this dangerous condition with the best literature, sympathetically applied, we cry out against the Negro's uppishness, and want him taught to work.

He ought to be taught to work, no doubt. The great majority of Negroes, like the majority of every race, must always work with their hands. There is a deal more of what is called drudgery to be done in the world than of everything else put together; and most of us have our share of it to perform. But no one to whom work is drudgery has ever been rightly taught to work. I believe this lack of proper training is at the bottom of nine-tenths—or maybe eleventh-tenths—of all the laziness and shiftlessness of the poor which does not come from sub-normal physical conditions. Drudgery is not work: it is a mental attitude towards work which comes from ignorance or from physical weakness. The narrower the round of a man's life, or a woman's, the more they need outlook and horizon. The world over, the world's poor have been set to do the hardest work in a perfectly detached, unrelated way, without reasons, without background, without a trace of world-connections; and they usually find it a very boring job, and shirk it when they can, naturally.

We are learning rapidly to broaden the white worker's horizon through the industrial training given in our public and normal schools, and in our agricultural colleges; and in some of our cities part of this training is given to Negroes, some of it of a high order. In Richmond County, Georgia, this industrial work has been extended by the county itself, with no outside aid, to the Negro country schools. We have there a superintendent who looks closely after the schools of both races; and the county superintendent of industrial training gives as efficient oversight and help to the Negro schools, city and country, as to the white. I speak of this county because, living in it, I happen to know about it. That many others do as well I do not doubt.

But the great impulse towards rational training, towards an education which really educates, in the Negro country schools has come from the Jeanes Fund, given by a Northern woman, and administered by a Southern man, the grandson of a great slaveholder, a scholar and educator of distinction.[4] I know of no

---

4. The Jeanes Fund was established by Anna T. Jeanes of Philadelphia, with a $1 million endowment, to support black education in the South.

other one force in Negro life more beneficent than this. It is demonstrating in every one of our states the kind of work needed in their rural schools, and its quickening influence grows with the years. Virginia, first of all the South, appointed a superintendent of Negro rural public schools, a Phi Beta Kappa College graduate and a man for the South to be proud of. Kentucky, Georgia, North Carolina and Alabama have followed the example; and the other states are bound to do likewise or to see themselves out-distanced in the production of wealth in the not-far-distant future. For it is human nature to love work when ideals are put into it, when it has a background and a horizon.

The Y.M.C.A. is doing, through Southern secretaries, a work which can hardly be estimated. Six thousand students have been enrolled in Y.M.C.A. study classes in Southern colleges to study the Negro and the white man's duty to him. Already various forms of settlement and Sunday-school work have grown out of this study. In fifteen years these young men will be the leaders of the South; and even now the attitude of our colleges and universities, faculties and students, is an appreciable factor in the changing public sentiment.

The Y.M.C.A. has also a large coloured organization. Forty-one associations with over sixty thousand members are enrolled. Here again is a great opportunity to help create ideals for a race. In our cities there is no better way to fight intemperance and many other forms of vice among the Negroes, than to provide them with a good Y.M.C.A. building, and to help them get it fully on its feet.

The women of the Southern Methodist church are the only ones in the South as yet carrying on organized work for Negroes. For over twenty-five years they have been the South's women-pioneers along social service lines, first to whites and now to blacks. They opened the first settlement in the South, employed the first visiting nurse, opened the first free clinic, and introduced free kindergartens and industrial training at many points where they were previously unknown.

Twelve years ago they built two industrial cottages for girls at the church's school for Negroes in Augusta, and have since provided for the industrial training there, besides erecting recently a $25,000.00 dormitory. This sum was raised from several sources. Half of it was given by Southern white women, some of them giving as much as a thousand dollars each; five thousand was given by the General Education Board; and the rest was raised by a Negro man from the white Southern Methodist conferences.

In addition to this, these women will shortly open a farm school for Negro boys in Mississippi, five hundred acres of land having been recently given them by a Southern white man for this purpose.

In 1911 they appointed an Alabama woman, a college graduate, as secretary for Negro work. Her headquarters were located in Augusta, where she has opened the white South's second settlement for Negroes, the one in Louisville being the first.[5]

The Augusta vacation playgrounds, secured by the coöperation of people of both races, are an outcome of this work, which, inadequately housed and provided for as it is, is full of promise and interest. The children, nearly all from the poorest class, are as responsive as—well, as children, the world around: their development, in their various clubs and classes, is as striking as in any children of like class anywhere. The kindergartner is a coloured woman, a graduate of one of the best of the schools established by Northern missionaries after the war, and a power for good among her people.

But however institutions may be built up or multiplied, the South-wide need is a South-wide turning of the hearts of the strong to help the weak both by personal service and by coöperation with capable Negro leaders. To this need a number of Southern agencies at last begin to address themselves.

The will of the late Miss Caroline Phelps Stokes, a well-known Northern philanthropist, provided for the endowment of fellowships in the state universities of Virginia and Georgia "to enable Southern youth of broad sympathies to make a scientific study of the Negro, and of his adjustment to American civilization." These fellowships were accepted in the spirit of their founder, and in the belief that "any national program looking to the adjustment of relations must be based on a far wider knowledge of actual conditions than we now have." The university of Georgia has just published the results of the investigations made by its first Fellow under this foundation. He is the son of a member of the university faculty, and has spent a year in a close and sympathetic study of the Negroes of Athens, the university town, and of their relations with the whites. His report makes clear the community menace of conditions allowed in the Negro quarters, and calls for the coöperation of the educated whites in upbuilding the homes, churches and schools of the Negroes. Reports like these, coming

5. Mary DeBardeleben was the young woman who offered herself as a Methodist missionary to blacks.

from a great and beloved university, are sure to leaven the thought of an entire state. Miss Stokes's gift, like that of Miss Jeanes, proves the wisdom of Northern philanthropists who choose Southerners in sympathy with Negro betterment to administer their gifts. Such gifts, so given, draw together the North and the South, as well as the two races in the South.[6]

At the recent annual meeting of the Women's Missionary Council of the Southern Methodist Church the committee on Social Service brought in the following report, which was unanimously adopted:

"It shall be a duty of the Department of Social Service to promote the study of conditions and needs among the Negroes, locally, throughout the South; also to arouse the women of our auxiliaries to a sense of their personal duty as Christian Southerners to meet the needs and ameliorate the conditions of those of this backward race who are in our midst by personal service and sympathy. We recommend the giving of this sympathy and service in any or all of the following ways:

"(1) By learning the needs of Negro Sunday-schools, teaching their Bible classes, training their teachers in modern Sunday-school methods, helping to grade their schools, and offering such other assistance as may be needed.

"(2) By assisting Negro women in forming and directing missionary societies in their churches, giving them information and other help, especially in regard to home mission work among the poorer classes of their own race.

"(3) By looking into the needs of Negro public schools, requiring of the public authorities that their premises be kept sanitary, helping to secure coloured teachers of a high grade, and favouring the introduction of industrial training.

"(4) By looking after the recreation, or lack of it, of Negro children and young people; by endeavouring to interest the Christian women of all denominations in securing for them opportunities for clean play in playgrounds supervised by good Negro women or men; and by securing coöperation with Negro Young Men's and Young Women's Associations where these exist.

"(5) By securing from boards of education permission to use Negro schoolhouses as community centres, organizing and assisting the better class of Negroes in each community to take charge of these community centres and supervise them for the pleasure and instruction of their own race. By interesting white people in the movement, securing white physicians and others to talk

6. The Phelps Stokes Fund, still in existence today, was established in 1911. The mission is now broadened, to include education and interracial understanding around the world.

on personal and community hygiene, care of children, temperance, and other matters.

"(6) By visiting the local jails, by ascertaining the measure of justice accorded Negroes in the local courts, and by creating a sentiment for justice to youthful criminals whom wise treatment may reform.

"(7) By studying Negro housing conditions and their bearing on sickness, inefficiency, and crime; by bringing these conditions to the attention of the public; by insisting that the local authorities enforce in the Negro district the sanitary regulations of the community; by securing for Negroes a water supply sufficient for health and decency; by helping the Negroes of the better class to organize among their people civic clubs where the young may be trained in community cleanliness and righteousness.

"(8) By creating in the local white community higher ideals in regard to the relation between the two races; by standing for full and equal justice in all departments of life; by endeavouring to secure for the backward race not only the full measure of development of which they are capable, but the unmolested possession and enjoyment of all legitimate rewards of honest work; by standing, in short, for the full application to the Negroes and to ourselves of the Mosaic law of justice: 'Thou shalt love thy neighbour as thyself.' "

There are four thousand auxiliaries in this organization; and even though the work be taken up slowly, it will spread. The authorities at Paine College are urging upon the church the establishment of a training school for Negro missionaries and social workers who may be employed by the whites as well as by coloured churches in all these forms of coöperative effort. The need is so great we can but trust it will be met.

The secretary for the Home Department of the General Board of Missions of this church is working along similar lines. At his instance the Alabama conference has appointed a committee of ministers, laymen and women, to look into the condition of the Negroes within the bounds of the conference at all these points. A consistent plan of conference-wide help and coöperation is expected to result; and such committees will be asked for in the other conferences until all have taken the matter up.

The deepest significance of all these movements in the various churches lies in the fact that they all look towards coöperation between the better classes of both races for the uplift of the Negro poor. It is impossible to serve the best interests of either race without this personal communication between the two. Where we have had a disposition to help the Negroes the attitude of the whites, both North and South, has been too often suggestive of that of the rich burgher in the play of Rip Van Winkle—"Give him a cold potato, and let him go." We have but given where he and we need that we should share.

There are notable individual exceptions, but many of even the well-educated Negroes are yet unequal to the task of achieving unaided the spiritual emancipation of their people. These need the forming and inspiring touch of educated whites.

In some of our Northern cities more or less money has been contributed for the uplift of the local Negro population through Y.M.C.A. work or otherwise; but often, when the money is given, the Negroes are left quite to their own devices in trying to serve their people; and the result is rarely all that it might be under a system of sympathetic coöperation between both races.

A Northern Y.M.C.A. worker, in speaking of this fact not long ago, said that the Negroes of the North did not desire coöperation, and frequently resented it when offered.

I think some Negroes in the South feel the same way, and are quick to repudiate the suggestion that the Negroes are not entirely competent to take full charge of Negro education and Negro uplift in general. They want white people to furnish the money, and leave them to direct the work.

That some Negroes are entirely equal to such a task cannot be truthfully denied. The logical deduction from this fact is that the race has capabilities of development far beyond the position some of us would permanently assign it. But it is idle to make claims which are not borne out by facts. The finest and strongest Negroes, I believe without a single exception, have come to their high development largely through contact with broad-minded, large-hearted white men and women. For years to come few of them are destined to reach that plane by any other process. I think on this point the real leaders in the South, white and black, are agreed.

There should be some white teachers in every state school for the higher education of Negroes; but so far Alabama is the only state recognizing, in even a single institution, this statesmanlike and Christian principle. In Mississippi, however, whites have charge of the summer school for Negro teachers; and in my home county of Richmond, in Georgia, the county superintendent supervises in person the yearly institute for Negro teachers, lecturing before them from time to time. This is probably not unusual.

The need for such service is threefold. As the more highly developed race we owe this help to the other race; and unpaid spiritual debts issue, sooner or later, in spiritual bankruptcy. We must render such service for the sake of our own spiritual integrity. The Negroes need to receive all we can give them, that their own power to give, to their race and to the nation, may be enlarged. And beyond these needs is the fundamental necessity for both races to learn, however distinct they must remain racially, to work together in mutual respect, coöperating for the good of their common country, and for the kingdom of God on earth.

The exceptional Negro should be given the most responsible work as a teacher and leader of his people which his ability deserves. But the race would be superhuman if in fifty years of freedom it had become capable of taking its future entirely into its own hands. Some Negroes do not recognize this fact, and are quick to resent white assistance as white interference; and especially to distrust any measure or method which emphasizes the need for discipline of mind or spirit. Surely we are responsible here. Our long indifference weighs heavily against us; and our assistance, where offered, is too often tinctured—or impregnated—with condescension. If Christ had come to us that way I think we would be savages still. However fine it may look on the outside, there is no lifting force in any condescending deed. When we set about in our task in that entire simplicity and self-unconsciousness which are a necessary part of the spirit of Christian service, we will be oftener surprised by the depth of the response evoked than by a disposition to reject our help. Money alone, though we poured it into institutions for the Negroes like water, cannot settle our debt. The world around, the debt of the privileged involves their personality.

One of the straws which show our new consciousness of this fact blew across my path not long ago as I was returning from a trip to the North. In a travellers' chat with another passenger the subject of women's club-work came up; and my companion, knowing nothing of my own interests, told me of her recent experience as president of the federated clubs of her home town, a thriving city in North Carolina. The club-women had decided on a Clean-up Day, when it occurred to her that in order to make it a real cleaning day the city should be cleaned, and not merely that fraction of it which least needed cleansing. So she proposed to the club-women that for the health of their own households, as well as for other obvious reasons, they should invite the leaders of all the Negro women's societies to a conference, get them interested in the movement, and have a Clean-up Day which would leave the city clean. They expected perhaps a dozen Negro women, and seventy came. The mayor of the city and the president of the Board of Health addressed the gathering, and then the women talked, white and black.

"And you'd have been as astonished as we were if you'd heard those Negroes," she declared. "Some of them knew as much about parliamentary proceedings as we did; and they were so sensible, they talked so well, they were so glad to do all they could!—And I tell you," she added with a little laugh, "when it came to cleaning up, we had to hustle to keep up with them.—We don't expect much sickness in town this summer: the place—the whole place—is clean."

And Negroes do not respond to ideals? Let those who give them a chance—a growing group among us—testify.

The North Carolina club is not alone. On the Women's Club page of the *Atlanta Constitution* I read recently, in a single issue, accounts of three Georgia clubs which are cooperating with the Negroes of their respective cities to keep their towns clean and healthful.

The annual meetings of the Virginia State Board of Charities and Correction are open to both races. The Negroes report there their work among their own people; and the attitude of the Board is one of solicitude and helpfulness towards all dependents and delinquents in the commonwealth, rather than towards those of one race.

It is a Virginia town, too, which is demonstrating the wisdom of another form of coöperation; a form so simple, so needed, so obviously Christian, that one feels it should only be known to be adopted. I learned of it from a chance acquaintance whose relatives live in the town. The Protestant ministers of the town, both white and black, are members of the Ministers' Alliance. They meet once a month, as brothers of Him who came to serve all races and all classes of men, to pray and talk and plan for the spiritual uplift of the whole community. If Christ came again in the flesh, surely nowhere could He feel more at home than in a meeting-place like that.

It is puzzling that the local churches, of all denominations, all over the South, should fail as they do in leadership in this matter. Every large denomination has officially gone on record, in its highest legislative body, as recognizing the common brotherhood of the races, the common duty of the strong race to serve the weak one. No voice has been publicly lifted, in any denomination, to controvert this doctrine. White ministers have, undoubtedly, the kindliest feelings to Negroes. None of them, I think, would hesitate to accept gladly any invitation to speak or preach to a black audience. In my own denomination, when one speaks to a conference body of ministers about our duty to Negroes there is, of recent years, a deep, and often moving, response; and the presiding bishop never fails to press the duty home. And we are not double-faced, nor cowards. But I doubt if, in any state, a dozen ministers could be found, in all denominations put together, who make a practice of preaching, even once in two or three years, about race relations, or our duty to our black poor, or the connection between the Negro quarters of our cities and the interests of the kingdom of God. Yet these things enter into the warp and woof of daily life in the South, and help and hinder the growth in Christian character of every member of every church.

It is true the leaders of the South's best thought and action regarding the Negroes are church-members, grown up under Southern preachers; and in at least three great denominations the head of the work for Negroes is a minister, officially backed by his church. Yet the pulpits of the South rarely speak of those problems which press upon us all, and for which there is no solution outside the teachings of Christ. In this as in other things, the country over, the churches have yielded their crown of leadership to members who must do much of their work along lines largely ignored by the rank and file of the ministry.

Yet there are exceptions, each one a shining example of the leadership possible to our pulpits. Not long ago, after an outburst of race antagonism which was being chronicled and condemned in all the papers, I asked a Negro from a neighbouring state if such feeling existed in his section.

"No, ma'am, it don't," he answered emphatically; "not for a long time."

"Then it used to exist?"

"Oh, yes'm. We ain't had a thing but trouble till these last few years."

"What stopped it?"

"A white preacher stopped it. He thought some of the things done weren't right; and he got all the white preachers in town to agree to preach about Christ's way of treating coloured folks, all on the same day. They all did it again a month later, and once or twice more that year. And so long as he stayed there they all preached about it together that way, a time or two each year; and there ain't any trouble since. I heard tell two or three white folks got mad about it; but the preachers stuck it out. And now all the white folks treat us right, and we all are behaving better, and everybody is prospering a heap better than they used to."

Instances like this will multiply as our social conscience quickens. A fresh, clean wind stirs over the South before which old mists of prejudice are lifting. Insufficient and halting as the work of the churches has been, it has yet testified to the Christian doctrine of brotherhood. That all the churches must at some points, perhaps at many, be readjusted to conditions few who love them will deny: but in England, and in America, North and South, it is the churches which have created that social conscience which some deem all-sufficient without the churches, and at which the churches themselves sometimes look askance, as at a rival which would usurp their dominion. The Southern Sociological Congress is the first South-wide expression of this nascent conscience; and no one who attended the Congress meetings, in Nashville or in Atlanta, could fail to be impressed with the religious spirit in which men of many faiths had met to consider their common duties to the unprivileged of the South.

Out of the first meeting of the section on Race Relations came the appointment of a Southern University Commission on the Negro, with a representative from nearly every Southern state university. This commission met for organization in December, 1912. It reported to the Atlanta Congress a broad outline of investigation to be undertaken in regard to conditions—religious, educational, hygienic, economic and civic; the duty of whites in improving these conditions; and the ideal of race-relations towards which the South should work. No one who has heard these men speak, as several have already done in public, can doubt that large hearts and clear brains are at work upon the whole subject in a spirit of justice and service.

This is not the place to discuss the Congress at large; but it furnished many evidences of a social conscience at last astir on all community interests. The sectional meetings on Race Relations were a dream come true—a dream of a new South, with the old spirit of sympathy once more in the heart of the strong, and hands of human brotherhood held out to the weaker race. The privileged South has at last opened its doors of counsel and invited the unprivileged to enter in and talk over, men with men, the needs and duties which confront them both in making the land a home of justice and opportunity for all.

But that was not the whole story. With Southern white and Southern black speaking from the same platform, and seeing in so many things eye to eye at last, were men of that other class so long misunderstood and misjudged among us— the men of the North who came long ago to meet a great human need among those whom we, for the dark time being, had closed our hearts against. North and South and black and white met there, and pledged their common service to a common humanity, a common country, and a common God.

We stood, for those brief days, on one of those mountain tops from which the end is seen, near and beautiful and real. Afterwards, one turns to the rugged path again, and faces the long, long road. But the end is still real and beautiful, and as certain as Love itself. And as for nearness, shall one measure the life of the Race of Man by one's own narrow years; or the world-wide victory that awaits by one's tiny measure of personal failure or success? Though we ourselves pass not over, yet shall our brothers possess the land, and dwell there.

Sometimes a biologist, studying tissues under the microscope, will stain some cells and not others, that he may the better unravel some of life's obscure interactions.

I think God has done that in the South, dyeing our weak ones black, that it may be clear to the most careless what the weak have to suffer from the selfishness of the strong. Once we begin to see, it ought to be easier for us than for others to learn community righteousness, because the effects of evil are made so plain among us. And those who look on from afar should, rather than criticize us, watch more closely their own community life, where the strong may wrong the weak in less spectacular fashion.

It may be long before it is all stopped. The evil is great everywhere; and we of the South have been slow to start our part of the fight against it. But we have started now, at last—not as individuals only, as heretofore; but as a constantly-growing group of Southern folk who feel the common obligation of those who have to serve those who have not.

And having taken these first steps in recognition of our share of a world-task the main peculiarity of our Southern situation has vanished. For we have joined hands, we too, at last, with the privileged of earth elsewhere, to set free those without privilege; to serve our neighbour, not according to the colour of his skin, but according to his need.

VII
Those Who Come After Us

Being parents is the deepest thing in life. It runs away back of humanity, out into the wild, free places, where the bird broods high in air, and the weed pours all its being into its seed, and dies. It is doubtless this blood-kinship stirring in us what we yearn for the woods, and the mountains, and the sea; some inarticulate inner consciousness knows all these as homes of life, our common heritage, our common trust. With all the weight of suffering of those to whom the highest honours of that trust have been committed, and who have, as yet, failed to be worthy of them, we turn back to these haunts of simpler and more loyal forms of life for rest, and for strength and courage for the long road our feet have yet to go.

Parenthood is a thing to bind all life in one. It is not merely that nothing human is foreign to us afterwards: no life that grows by sacrifice is alien; and that is all the life there is.

It seems the miracle of the ages that we, on the summit of life, we humans, should have made this thing unclean: that the power to pass on the torch of life, to call out of nothingness those who shall shape the future of the race—that this, of all things, should be the force to make men beasts again, and to build for multitudes of the women of all races an age-long hell on earth.

At least one good should come of it: it should bind the women of the world in one. Being a woman goes deeper than being of this race or that, or of this or that social station. Red, yellow, or black, or white, we carry the world's sins on our shoulders, its degradation and anguish in our hearts. It all falls on the women, the lust, the degradation, the suffering. And what is a keener agony, a more intolerable shame, it falls on the women's daughters, whom they won in the valley of death. Have we not reason to stand together, we women of the world? A Chinese girl hawked publicly by her owner on the streets of Shanghai, an Indian maid betrayed in the forest, girls of our own race by scores of thousands,

Negro girls whom men of no race reverence—where is the difference? They are women, women all; and women bore them: women should stand together for the womanhood of the world.

It burns like fire when first we grasp that truth. It is inevitable, in the beginning, when the knowledge of broken lives first flares in our faces, and we reach hands of fellowship to draw some poor outcast back into the circle of human sympathy again, that women's standing together should mean to us their standing against the men. We are quick to hate, when we are young; and men are an easy mark. Nothing excuses them to us, nothing palliates. An honoured father, a brother whom we trust, a husband well-beloved—these are the accidents of the sex; creatures in whom, by some great miracle, a touch of their mothers' souls has turned dross to gold: but for men—. The sharpest trial of faith is no mental question to a woman; it comes straight from the heart of life, terrible and fierce: Would a good God make women as women are made, and shut them up in the same world with men?

And then, into such a woman's life, is sent a little son. He shall defy the law of his sex; he shall be pure, though all men else follow the common path.

She lives her son's life, and so she wins the freedom of his world. It takes imagination, and patience, and sympathy, and time. But when he begins to run with other boys she has his confidence; and so she learns, as we all must, by love, and not by hate.

What chance have they, these little boys, any more than the girls whose lives they poison? Before they know the meaning of words or acts their lives are poisoned, too. We care for everything about them, bodies and minds, except this highest thing, which we call unclean, and hide. It is not a question of a child's being taught or not taught; he learns, as surely as he lives and breathes. It is a question of how he shall be taught: in truth and cleanness, or in lies and filth. And because this power is the highest intrusted to us, because its perversion causes more misery and degradation than everything else put together, the right training of children in matters of sex is a basal necessity for the world's progress in righteousness. Shall we dare to remain prudes when we see what silence costs our children, sons and daughters both? Love takes no account of such childish shrinking, however much love may feel it: love serves the beloved unashamed, and at any cost. And love can find a way.

The future of both races in the South is more deeply concerned in this than in any other one thing. For to the pure all achievement is possible; and for the impure rottenness and decay are certain. There is no reason whatever for believing that any one country or section sins above the rest in this matter. Where two races of different colours dwell side by side, one strong, one weak, the evidences of sin are yet to be hidden: yet the sin exists no less, though less visibly, where strong and weak are of one skin. But there is no section of any country which is not implicated in the authorized statement of physicians of world-repute that seventy per cent. of the men of Christendom are, or have been, sufferers from vice-diseases. The meaning of such a statement staggers the mind: the stunted bodies and souls of children, women's long-drawn-out torments, the maiming of mind and flesh, the perverts, the paupers, the insane! Shall we be ashamed to remove burdens like these from those who shall follow us? Shall we shrink from sending the children of the South out unhandicapped, strong of body and pure in mind, to build the homes of the future; homes where white folk dwell, where black folk dwell, each secure from wrong and from fear?

For it can be so. There is a new day breaking. Old evils, hoary with the centuries until we have accepted them as inseparable from life itself, are being challenged, defied. The German Government believes the purity of young men not impossible of attainment. It orders the instruction in sex hygiene of every college student in the land. At a recent annual meeting of the American Medical Association one of their leading speakers, in a formal address, called on the churches of America to aid the doctors in their fight against the social evil by the teaching of sex hygiene. The doctors stood long, many of them, for the necessity of "wild oats." As an association they have now endorsed the movement for social purity as a necessity for personal and social health. That great, conservative organization, the Church of England, has undertaken a year's-long campaign against the social evil, with the avowed intention of uprooting it from English life.[1]

Time was when we thought yellow fever was providential. A providence which made yellow fever an integral part of the scheme of things would be benevolent indeed beside a providence which made this loathsome cancer a necessity of human life. We had yellow fever because we had not learned to destroy the breeding-places of the pests which carry it. We have the social evil for exactly the same reason.

---

1. The 1910s saw a great national discussion on the "social evil," or prostitution and venereal disease. States and cities across the country established commissions to study the problem. Contemporary literature included Katherine Houghton Hepburn, *Woman Suffrage and the Social Evil* (New York: National Woman Suffrage Publishing Co, 1914); Albert W. Elliott, *The Cause of the Social Evil and the Remedy* (Atlanta: Webb & Vary Printers, 1914); and Joseph H. Greer, *The Social Evil: Its Cause, Effect, and Cure* (Chicago: the author, 1913).

Its breeding-places are in the unclean thoughts of children and young people who were made to think cleanly. There is nothing more wonderful, more sacrificially pure, than the great law of life by which life comes from life, and like from like, strong life from pure, and weak from foul, which runs through all the organisms of earth. When a child begins to question he needs—and—she—not lies, but the clean truth. If the mother does not answer somebody else will; and then the poison will be at work.

A child can be taught *unconsciously* to reverence the life-giving power which he holds in trust. When the stress of temptation comes, swift and sharp, he may find himself prepared. He need not battle in the dark, ignorant of himself, of the meaning of life, of its dangers and rewards. A girl can be protected in all purity, that in time of danger she may so remain. Our parents did not know: but for an intelligent parent to send children out to-day defenseless against the contagions of school life is a neglect the child may find it impossible to forgive.

There is a little book by Ellen Torrelle, published by Heath, called "Plant and Animal Children, and How They Grow." One need not be botanist or biologist to make its stories clear to children's minds; and a child who understands its facts is unconsciously fortified against uncleanness. There is no room for impurity concerning the origin of life, not because it has been inveighed against, but because its possible place has been filled with thoughts beautiful and pure. Another book, which all adults and every adolescent boy should read, is Lavinia Dock's "Hygiene and Morality," published by the Putnams. In addition to these, and for many purposes, parents would do well to read Stanley Hall's "Youth," published by Appleton. There are many other books, large and small, a list of which may be had from the National Vigilance Committee, in New York.[2]

The time is not far distant when the teaching of such books as Miss Torrelle's will be obligatory in the earlier grades of the public schools; and when that is secured for those who shall come after us, the poor man's home, North, South and West, will be safer—yes, and the homes of the privileged too. For this hideous infection can never be confined, while it exists at all, to one economic class, or to this or that locality. It breeds misery and degradation for the community, just so far as it breeds at all.

But education is not the only measure; nor need we wait for a new generation

2. Ellen Torelle, *Plant and Animal Children: How They Grow* (Boston & New York: D. C. Heath, 1912); Lavinia Dock, *Hygiene and Morality: A Manual for Nurses and Others, Giving an Outline of the Medical, Social, and Legal Aspects of the Venereal Diseases* (New York: Putnam's Sons, 1910); G. Stanley Hall, *Youth: Its Education, Regimen, and Hygiene* (New York: Appleton, 1907).

to grow up to introduce wide-spread reform. Health laws should compel all physicians, as they already do those of a few states in other sections, to report not only cases of the lesser contagions, such as scarlet fever, diphtheria, and the like; but also the far more dangerous contagions of the vice-diseases. With this law goes a second, requiring a physician's certificate to the applicant's freedom from contagious disease before a marriage license can be issued. These laws are being widely advocated by physicians of the highest standing, by social workers everywhere, and by many health officers, parents, educators and ministers.

Another law urgently needed in many states, and no section more than in our own, is one raising the age of consent to at least eighteen years. In some of our Southern states it is ten years. The mere statement of such a fact would come as a shock to any but the more nascent social conscience. What of morality can we hope to evolve in the classes most in need of morality, white and black, when the defenseless childhood of the poor is held so cheap, *by law*?

But beyond all this, what can the privileged mothers do for those unprivileged, the strong to help the weak? For women should stand together, for the manhood and the womanhood of the world. Mothers cannot, if they would, break the tie which binds them to both sexes, to the whole human race.

Privilege exists for one end only—that it may become the common servitor of all. We pray such curious prayers sometimes, in the pulpit and out of it— prayers which automatically prevent their own fulfillment. We are so anxious for "especial" care and good, for "peculiar" blessings, for things which would mark us as a folk apart, or a family, or even an individual, sheltered from ordinary trials, lifted above the multitude who hunger, separated from the common lot, favoured of heaven beyond other folk!

A god who would answer prayers like those it should be beneath one's self-respect to pray to. If he be not equally the God of all flesh, he is no god for any flesh to petition. For there is a deep sense in which God Himself must be thought of in terms of humanity, so that no one who seeks fullness of life, which is fullness of love, may dare ask any protection, any mercy, any good for any aspect of our many-sided life, the giving of which would imply anything whatever "especial" in the sense that it is not open, to the limit of his need, to the least of all flesh who may ask for it.

But more than that. When we get this background of prayer in our minds, this true perspective of our own needs in relation to those of the rest of the world, we see the basis of justice on which the fulfilling of those needs must

rest. It is for lack of justice in our petitions that we have so largely been, in all
the ages,

"Bafflers of our own prayers, from youth to life's last scenes."[3]

Mothers should understand, because love costs them more, and so they
should be wiser in its ways. There can be no safe basis for prayer for one's child
except this basis of justice. If we desire protection for our daughters, or purity
for our sons, strong bodies for them and trained minds, a place for happy play,
freedom and joy in work, a life made rich by love and service, it is strange that
we should dare to ask these things of a just God except as we pledge our full
strength to effort to secure like good for all the children, the world around, to
whom it is denied.

What things that we desire for our children do Negro children lack? I do not
mean the luxuries, nor even many of the comforts of life: but those basal necessities to any clean, efficient, hopeful life, however humble and poor: abundant
water and fresh air, with a knowledge of their uses; houses where homes are
possible; sanitary surroundings; school training which really trains; a chance
for clean play; mothers who can approximate a mother's duties; religious instruction related to daily life. Without these things, what kind of people are
they foredoomed to be? And whose is the responsibility?

But more than that. Women make the standards for every community in our
land. North, South and West, community morals and ideals are exactly what,
consciously or unconsciously, the consciences of the privileged women of that
community permit. If the morality of the daughters of the very poor is to be
safeguarded anywhere, it must be done by the privileged women primarily. And
our very poor are black.

We need, in the first place, to see the women of our poor as women first, and
black afterwards. We need a new respect for them in our own minds, as children
of the one Father, even as we. We need more faith in the possibilities of the
poorest life which is born with a capacity, however limited, for divine things. We
need to use our imaginations, to put ourselves in the Negro woman's place. We
will find the exercise as broadening to our own lives as it will be beneficial to the
Negro's. We need to think of Negro womanhood as sacred, as the womanhood
of all the world must be. Thinking so, we will begin to honour its possibilities,

3. From Matthew Arnold's poem "Empedocles on Etna," pubished in 1852.

and try to bring them out. And if we hold up that standard, our men will come to it; they cannot help themselves. It is women who rule the world—or who can rule it, always, if only they will stand together. It is not merely that we have the men when they are babies. Beyond that tremendous fact men are dependent on women as women are not upon men. When women fix the terms on which men may secure their companionship and their love men must meet the conditions: they have no escape. Only, women must stand together, for womanhood, and for the race.

Let us plan for the future of the South we love under a wide sky. Let us plan, not for our children merely, nor for our race, else can the plans never bear full fruit. All that we want for our own let us plan for the children of the South, rich and poor, high and low, black and white: strong bodies, clean minds, hands skilled to labour, hearts just and kind and wise. Children do not grow like that of themselves, any more than roses grow double in the swamps: it is the children's power to respond to cultivation which lays upon us the duty of giving it.

I knew a family once where there were several normal children, and one little child, the youngest, whom epilepsy had reduced almost to idiocy. He was most repulsive to me when I first saw him, before I understood. He seemed that awful thing which some imagine they see in the world's undeveloped races—something in human shape without human capacity.

But his parents loved him so much! Their tenderness never failed for him, their care never abated. They loved the other children dearly, too; but this child needed them so much: they loved him according to his need.

Think of them for a moment—the hordes of the unprivileged of every race; those cut off from joy; the folk whose years are filled only with a great emptiness, with immeasurable ignorance and want; the mass of men and women, really, the vast majority of the human race. And God so loves the world—just so: according to the need.

VIII
The Great Adventure

I cannot close this little book without a word concerning those whose childhood is behind them, and who are soon to take their places in that great array of toilers whose hands are moulding the world's life in the present. Life looms before them as the Great Adventure, wherein difficulties and trials may await them, but which, in some unknown, far-off place, shall issue in achievement; in something which shall win them a place and honour which their own effort has secured for them, well-deserved.

We older people, the mass of us of least, look on as the raw recruits pass out, and smile, some of us kindly, some pityingly, some with bitterness, seeing their young enthusiasms, the high resolves and hopes which drive them, the gleam of the half-formed ideals which lure them on. Life will grip these over-confident children, we think, and trim them all to one sober pattern by the time they reach middle age. They will learn fast enough to accept its drudgery and to bow to its yoke. In the valley of old age they will stand much as their fathers stood, moulded by life, not moulding it, their laughter done; strong perhaps, but strong chiefly to accept and to bear the inevitable.

Is that the normal end of youth, the natural outcome of the Great Adventure; or are we so ill-adjusted to our environment that the abnormal is the usual and the normal the uncommon outcome of the quest?

Surely power is never intended for futility, and only ignorance can unmoved see it turned to waste. Yet if we measure in terms of human energy the advance of any one generation, and compare it with the force originally applied to secure advance, with that fund of energy, of hope and joy which we sum up as youth, the waste of power is staggering. It is only the smallest fraction of it which has been utilized: the rest has been absorbed by frictions which have largely wrecked the generators themselves. The energy of youth has gone to the destruction of all that makes youth young and wonderful. The one-time possessors of it stand broken, exhausted, numbed, in the valley of the Shadow; and the world they intended to lift has turned by a hair's breadth, and no more.

Yet some find youth but a gateway into a life which knows no age. Their bodies grow older, but only to reveal to the puzzled looker-on how very little years are concerned with either age or youth. Down to the very last their hearts are young, their fine enthusiasms unspent, their sympathies quick and keen, their joy unbroken, their hope a light no shadow can quench. Out of a long life filled, as we may know, chiefly with drudgeries and trials like our own, they come with young, eager eyes, out of which still looks the spirit of high adventure. Their message to youth is one of courage and hope:

> "Grow old along with me!
> The best is yet to be,
> The last of life, for which the first was made."

Surely that is the normal attitude of age, the natural outcome of youth and endeavour and hope. Wherever we see it, even the dullest of us, it appeals to some deep thing in us which, despite all our pessimism, justifies it, even against our will. It is so beautiful we know it must be true: all age was meant to be like that.

But how shall youth attain it? What subtle force has turned one life into this flashing diamond, and left another only dull, black coal, though they both are alike compact of a common humanity, and share its common lot? How shall we gear the spirit of youth, how band the individual to life in such manner that he may serve it without being broken by it; that he may drive on towards the fulfillment of his dreams, nor lose his hope, nor despair of the far achievement, but keep even in age

> "The rapture of the forward view,"[1]

and the spirit of immortal joy? If life be the Great Adventure how may one achieve it greatly, and know one's self a victor, even in the midnight of defeat?

One must live the normal human life to secure all that. We cannot expect human issues from a life lived on the animal's plane. An animal which is only an animal may come to the best of itself in isolation, an unrelated unit of its race. A young colt, or pig, or calf, left on an island where no other animal life existed, but provided with food and shelter the primal animal needs, would be

---

1. J. Harry Miller, *The Rapture of the Forward View*, 1905.

as perfect an animal as one reared in association with droves of its own kind. But a creature which is an animal and something more never comes to the best of itself when only those needs are met which may be satisfied in isolation. There are several authentic records of wolf-raised human young, and they have all reverted to animal type. Kipling's Mowgli, fascinating as he is, is inspired by his creator's own imagination; a real Mowgli could never have taken his place among human beings again, even on the edge of the jungle. Real wolf-children are like the Wild Man of Auvergne, whom a wise-hearted scientist laboured with so patiently over a hundred years ago. Cut off from human association the human in us atrophies beyond recall. For the primal law of human life is that to be truly human it must be shared with its kind.

When we get down to principles of life we are prone, unconsciously, to fall into Biblical phraseology; the roots of principles seem to run in that direction. It is literally true that no man liveth or dieth to himself: humanity is made that way. Whatever lives and dies some other way is not human, but animal. We live, we draw on the sources of life, we nourish and strengthen it, in exact measure as we share it with the race.

This is the secret of our wasted joy, our lost enthusiasms, our broken hopes: we have failed of the normal human life, the life of race-association, the life of brotherhood. The drop of water has lost itself and perished in the desert of individual desire, instead of finding itself in the stream of community life which trickles down through ever-widening associations to the great ocean of the Life of Man. In a most vital sense, the normal man, full-grown, has nothing to do with sections or boundaries, except as they help him to understand those of his brothers whom they dwarf and bind. For himself, he is a citizen of the world; and nothing in human life is foreign to him, past, present, or to come. The sense of race-life in himself, one atom of the mass, of the race-life whose laws govern atom and mass alike, opens all life to him, steadies his courage, heals his wounds, renews his youth, and feeds the flame of hope.

One's individual joy may be clouded so easily, and so soon; it is such a small, weak thing, taken by itself. It is part of the law of life that it should not be so; for he who would be man and not animal must be welded into one with his fellows; and love itself is not enough, without pain.

Suffering is so inexplicable, at first; it sets one apart while life sweeps by. But one has to be set apart to get the perspective of life, to see small and great in their true proportions, to learn the unshakable things, and to get one's own small personality properly related to them. At first, with all of us, it is the old

cry: Was ever sorrow like unto my sorrow, or difficulty like to mine?—That is
the cry of ignorance, of weakness, of selfishness, of egotism and provincialism,
the world around. It has come up in all ages, and will go up for ages yet to come.

But if one turns from one's atom-sorrow for a moment to take the race-wide,
age-long look, one sees that always, everywhere, such sorrows have been. They
are part of the race-lot. And everywhere there are, and have been, men and
women who have borne them bravely, and lived and died without bitterness
or complaint. Their lives are part of the race inheritance; their courage lifts us
up. What man has done we can do; they fought their battles not for themselves
alone. The strength of the race flows into us: we too can greatly bear; we too
can wear the badge of courage to hearten those who stumble by the way. If the
race must advance through suffering we will walk that path. We would not be
exempt, cut off. Shall we alone, of all the multitudes, bear no scars?

Personal success means something different after that. The Adventure itself is
different; greater, and more worth while. The quest one would achieve is fullness
of life; the path to it matters not so much. And fullness of life is never personal,
but human. One has cast in one's lot with the race; and in doing that, whatever
struggles are yet to come, the visible can no longer master the unseen. One is
delivered from that poverty of soul.

The greatest danger of education is that it may be twisted, just like ignorance,
to the service of intellectual arrogance, and so may breed spiritual decay. We all
need world-association; but especially those need it who are unusually gifted,
that they may escape the catastrophe of an emasculating egotism. The man who
is the mental superior of all his associates can neutralize that dangerous misfor-
tune only by finding his equals and his superiors wherever, in the race-life, they
have blossomed to the light. He must break the shackles of time and place to
commune with the mind of the race; and through that communion must learn
the humility inevitable to him who measures himself by universal, rather than
by provincial standards. Thus disciplined, he may add his atom of force to the
race-impetus towards righteousness without pride and without shame.

In such an association the race gains infinitesimally: the individual gains the
emancipation of his individuality, and walks henceforth at liberty and with joy.
The sting is gone from the thwarting narrowness of life; for the small task, set
in its large relation, is at once worth while. He is lifted enough above pettiness,
his own and that of others, to know it for what it is, and to be safe from the
hurt of it. Personal defeat, too, loses its bitterness. However his individual life
goes down in ruins, the great powers of truth and brotherhood to which he has

committed himself remain; that for which he struggled will triumph yet. His life, defeated though it be, is part of the victory of the race.

One's sense of joy is widened. Indeed, it has to be, or one could not endure the sharing of the sorrows of mankind. But the race is achieving, always. Each day sees something done which stirs the blood in the long

"World-war of dying flesh against the life."[2]

Each day somewhere the curtains of the dark are lifted and new knowledge gives new light. Each day men and women of all races, plain, simple folk like ourselves, are meeting difficulties with high hearts, unknown heroes in unguessed fights. And we are a part of all of it; we all work to one end.

Seen from the narrow window of a detached personal experience, life is confusing, baffling, coming no-whence, going no-whither, bound blind to the wheel of chance, and broken as it turns. It is the race-look which reveals the truth. The confusions are temporary, local, born of continued readjustments to higher levels. Whatever its weakness or its ignorance, life tends up. Men die, and races pass; but Man rises. One is no longer afraid of changes, though to the atom's unrelated consciousness the very foundations seem threatened. There is a Power that guides: and in the end, that which was planned from the beginning shall be.

So it is that the consciousness of race-life forms the rich background of our own small existence, giving depth and colour to our thin personalities, enriching and beautifying the poorest life which may be set against it. It saves us, too, in those times which come to all of us, when a sense of the futility of life descends upon us like a great black frost, shrivelling effort which had promised fruitage, and numbing the sources of energy and hope. It is then that we warm our hearts at the hearthstone of humanity, folded deep in the consciousness of a life which bears our tiny being on its breast, and which moves unerringly, if slowly, through seed-time and harvest, summer and winter, to one sure, high, far-off goal.

But the race-life is not only shelter and solace in days of suffering or defeat: it is also our inspiration and joy.

To him who walks in love among his neighbours in the little happenings of every day, and out into love's wider paths of community service, there comes, sooner or later, a day when every cloud is withdrawn; when he sees back to the

2. From Alfred Tennyson, "Merlin and Vivien," 1879.

low beginnings of life, and on, to its far fulfillment. He sees humanity in its first home, there in the mud and slime of things, pushing feebly forward here and there, driven by sharp necessity, inch by inch, dyeing the path with its own blood, yet slowly accumulating, out of its own sufferings, forces which purify and lift it. It begins to live not by bread alone: each least advance is purchased for it by some sacrificial life. From every rank of the vast savage mass the Givers come, offering up man's life, for the Life of Man. Seer and sage and warrior, king and peasant, master and slave, mothers whom no man may number, they pour out life like water, and thereby fructify the barren souls of the multitude, and create ideals for the race.

What else should life be for? What trace is left of all the beast-lives lived solitary in the mass, smothered in egotism, cut off by selfishness—what, but an added weight for these, the Givers, to lift?

Love is the motive force of life, and it gathers, more and more. Out of the mass emerge those races whose growing powers endue them with the greatest capacity for sacrifice, for following the ideal at all costs. However the majority of even these foremost races may fall short, however the hard-won earnings of the race are perverted by the many to personal ends, Love does make headway, slowly. All that the Givers would win for men of liberty, of knowledge, of justice, of joy, filters down unceasingly from class to class, until already some of the most precious things of life grow as common to them all as the air as we breathe.

Is not the life of the Givers well-spent? In all the long, long ages is anything else so well worth while? They lost life only to find it; and being dead, they yet speak to us. Their voices go up

> "A cry above the conquered years,"[3]

and the deepest things in us stir in answer. In such an hour we know life for what it really is—the power which comes in all its glorious fullness only to those who hold it in trust for every soul that needs.

Is there room for egotism any more, or pride—those two chief stranglers of human joy? Can one be afraid of "losing caste" by service? One lives in a world so far removed from all that—the world of fullness of life; a world wide with freedom, and rich with love, and bright with victory, however one's own small fortunes may rise or fall. For the soul has come into its own, and found its home, close to the heart of God, in the needs of humankind.

3. From Alfred Tennyson, *In Memoriam*, 1850.

Shall we fail of this wide, free life here in the South because of old prejudice, and black skins over the needs? Shall we, who were once so low, who have risen, not through decades but through centuries, risen by life poured out, reaping our gain from the sacrifice of the ages, heirs in direct spiritual succession of all foregone races of men, shall we, of all mankind, withhold our bread from the hungry, and justice from the oppressed?

We are so ready to use what we have inherited, not for service, but for pride. If humanity be like the earth, we say, we are its mountain-peaks, the Himalayas of the race.—But the seas rolled over the mountains once; and seas may roll there again. To the long look, the true look, the look to which a thousand years are but a day, mountains have risen before, and have disappeared.

> "The hills are shadows, and they flow
> From form to form, and nothing stands;
> They melt like mists, the solid lands,
> Like clouds they shape themselves, and go."[4]

The earth alone abides, mother of all mountains that ever were, or will be.

If life is not to grow dull to us, young or old, or its glamour fade; if we are one day to stand on those heights which belong to age rather than on the dull, flat barrens at their base; if life is to remain the Great Adventure, full of promise and wonder even in that last twilight before the eternal dawn, we must live it normally, through the years, despising no service that sets another heart at ease or opens a rift of opportunity to the poorest and least.

The beginnings of all great things are small. Indeed, most great things are small all the way through, made up of trifles, and great only in their accumulated results. Only the fewest people have great gifts or opportunities; and often they are not the ones who achieve the greatest things. A world filled with ordinary folk and based on justice necessitates a broad path straight from the common-places of every day up to the highest heights. And we have just that. The basal necessity is not knowledge, nor power, but love; and that is the greatest and the most freely attained of all human possession. Rich or poor or ignorant or learned, the Great Adventure shall be achieved by all who walk in love.

---

4. From Alfred Tennyson, *In Memoriam*, 1850.

Selections from Lily Hammond's
Other Publications

"Woman's Work for Woman"

Our Homes 4 (September 1895): 6–7

Some of you know of that grand chapter in the acts of the apostles, which John Paton and his followers have been writing these forty years among the cannibals of the South Seas.[1] Planted in the shadow of death, watered with tears, the good seed sprang up in that desolate soil, and brought forth fruit a hundredfold. And then what happened? When the courage of heroes and the faith of martyrs had lifted up whole peoples above their savage state, and created the wants of Christian civilization so that the tides of commerce began to flow in those regions where, at such infinite cost, the spirit of Christ had made it safe for men to go, the heathens of the United States of America stepped in to make money. If they did not precede Satan himself, they at least took him along with them, and they all landed together. It was less than a year ago, I think, that Dr. Paton, worn old man, stood before the house of Congress in Washington and besought this Christian nation to put a stop to the trade in whisky and firearms that was fast reheathenizing the people whom, through forty years, he has risked his life to save. The Senate and Congress of this country have put Christ to an open shame more than once. They did not hesitate to break up an international agreement by which all other Christian nations had bound themselves to keep liquor and firearms from the heathen of Central Africa, and it was not to be expected that they should concern themselves about Dr. Paton and the ruin of his life work. A few weeks ago I read in the daily papers of the murder of some American seaman, in revenge for grievous wrong, by some of these same reheathenized converts. The telegram added that a man-of-war was to be sent to bombard the principal town and teach the offenders a lesson: the lesson being, as I inferred

---

1. John G. Paton (1824–1907) was an Anglican missionary to the New Hebrides islands. He was well known in missionary circles through his publications. Paton was also a strong advocate of British colonization of the islands, to keep them out of the control of the French (*A Plea for the New Hebrides* [London: R. Lambert, 1885]; *The New Hebrides: Is France or Britain to Annex Them?* [Glasgow: Aird and Coghill, 1885]).

from the premises, that a converted cannibal has no rights which a heathen American is bound to respect. It is a poor dodging of the whole matter to say that we are not responsible for national sins; that is exactly what we are responsible for, and the sooner the women wake up to that fact and teach their sons the truth of the matter, the sooner we will be a Christian nation in fact rather than in fancy.

But that is only one phase of the question. Everywhere, in heathen lands, the missionaries have the same story to tell. There are some honorable exceptions, of course; but the greatest obstacles to Missions in India are said to be the lives and characters of so-called Christian Englishmen. In Japan there is the same trouble, and in China civilized heathens carry infidelity, doubt, and material wickedness from Christian countries to pull down the souls and bodies of the people as fast as the missionaries can build them up. In a recent government report on Alaska are embodied some facts as to mission work among the Alaskans, and the heavy odds against which it is carried on by reason of the conduct of traders from this and other Christian countries; facts that ought to stir to the depths any soul that has within it one spark of pity or justice.[2]

Now what are you going to do about it? Are you going to sit down satisfied with sending out a few foreign missionaries, and so neglect matters at home that after each of them Satan can send a dozen of these sleuthhounds of his own? If our Foreign Missions are to succeed as they should, they must be backed by a Christian nation at home. Nor can we afford to send a handful of heroes out of our western gates to fight God's battles in heathendom, and not lift a finger to save the debased people who pour in at our eastern gates like a flood. If we do not save them, the time is coming when they will ruin our children.

Still, it is in the main undoubtedly true that the South is as yet practically free from disturbances due to foreign immigration. Until very recently the highways

---

2. This "recent government report" is probably "In the Senate of the United States . . . Mr. Manderson presented the following statement with regard to Mr. Duncan's work among the Tsimpsheean Indians of British Columbia and Alaska" (Washington, D.C.: G.P.O., 1894). There was clearly a substantial, and probably very competitive, missionary effort in Alaska during this period. See: Mrs. Eugene S. Willard, *Kin-da-shon's Wife: An Alaskan Story* (Chicago: Student Missionary Campaign Library, 1892); Francis Barnum, *Life on the Alaska Mission, With an Account of the Foundation of the Mission and the Work Performed* ([N.p.]: Woodstock College Press, 1893); Hattie E. Genung, *A Trip to Alaska* (Boston: United Society of Christian Endeavor, 1894); Jessie W. Radcliffe, *Our Northernmost Possessions* (New York: Woman's Executive Committee of Home Missions of the Presbyterian Church, 1894); Sheldon Jackson, *Work among Natives in Alaska* (Boston: J. Stillman Smith, 1895); *The Moravian Mission in Alaska: Published to Commemorate the Completion of Its First Decade* (Bethlehem, Pa.: "The Moravian," 1895).

of the South have been closed to these toilers from over the seas. First slavery, and then poverty, barred the way; and the newcomers swept by to the ever farther West. But both these specters have vanished. The great resources of the South are becoming known, the best Southern men are awake to the need for an influx, both of labor and capital, if their magnificent state is to be developed; and statesmen and men of business are alike opening their gates to the world and pushing with well-directed energy every enterprise that is calculated to draw immigration to the South. It is bound to come; it is already coming, and bringing along with it immense possibilities both for good and for evil. If the South is simply to hold its own morally and religiously for the next ten or twenty years, an immense deal of home mission work must be done.

We can take the Cubans around Tampa, Fla., as a sample of what we may expect in the near future. There are six or seven thousands of them there, in two suburbs of Tampa, mostly cigar makers by trade. They know no English; their only idea of religion is the corrupt Romanism of Cuba, to which they are indifferent, and their ignorance of all that goes to make an intelligent citizen is simply monumental. It is idle to say that they may not become citizens.[3]

But foreigners, comparatively few as yet, are far from being the only class to whom we are debtors in the South. Miss Murfree and Joel Chandler Harris have introduced the country at large to a class of people whom we dare not neglect: the mountain whites of the South Atlantic States.[4] The homes of these people are usually built of rough-hewn logs, frequently having only one room for a large family to live, work, be born, and die in. The beds stand in corners, and when a visitor shares the home for a night, a few old bedquilts are hung from the tester of his bed, and he is invited to retire behind them—that is, if they have the quilts and the tester. If they haven't, the family adjourns to the yards while the visitor settles himself for the night, when they return, and one by one follow him to the land of dreams. I was once in one of these mountain homes which was decidedly above the average. It contained three rooms and a tiny attic, reached by a ladder. The beds (five of them, I think) stood side by side in a long, narrow room, and between them were thin wooden partitions five or six feet high, and running out from the wall as far as the foot of each bed, leaving

3. Not coincidentally, Methodist women began a concentrated mission effort in Tampa after the turn of the century: the Wolff Settlement.

4. Mary Murfree (1850–1922) wrote under the pen name Charles Egbert Craddock. Lily seems familiar with Murfree's books *In the Tennessee Mountains* (Boston and New York: Houghton, Mifflin and Co., 1884) and *The Prophet of the Great Smoky Mountains* (Boston and New York: Houghton, Mifflin and Co., 1885).

a common alleyway along the opposite wall. This family made large claims to social superiority, basing them on the fact that nearly all the girls had hats in addition to their home-woven sunbonnets, and on the possession, by the eldest girl, of a dress "with a whole dollar's worth of embroidery on it." This gorgeous garment was disinterred from the attic and displayed with solemn pride. It will be a tradition in the family.

A friend of mine spent a summer in these mountains, and went out of her way to make the acquaintance of some of the people. She found a woman twenty-five years of age, she told me, who did not know one fact of the life of Christ; and another who did not know what the Lord's Prayer was. The girls marry pitifully young, and almost before they are grown are bent under the burdens of their hard lives. Many of the men, and some of the women, are moonshiners, and the cheap and abundant whisky of the region is the cause of endless strifes, and even murders. Cunning, crafty, ignorant, suspicious, yet usually honest, according to their standard, these people wait for life and light. What they need first of all is love—human love, opening their minds and hearts to divine love; and then an elementary and industrial education. Churches of other denominations have entered this field and carried the work, in several places, to brilliant success. The girls who have been taught in these schools go away prepared to turn their hovels into Christian homes. But every school of the kind is overflowing, and only the outskirts of the region have been touched. A very fine property near Asheville, N.C., has been given for a girls' industrial school, and the funds now being raised are to provide an adequate building here, as well as at Tampa, while another school, the Sue Bennett Memorial, is to be immediately opened in the mountains of Kentucky.

Then there are the people, both natives and foreigners, in the poorer quarters of our cities; the class which, Henry George tells us, will, if let alone, furnish the barbarians to wreck our civilization, as the Goths and Vandals wrecked that of Rome; the out-of-works and tramps, the criminal and dangerous classes, the outcast women, and that large class which lives always on the edge of want, and which is the recruiting ground for criminals of every degree: the unchurched masses, as they are called, including also the large body of more or less comfortable working people, who have become estranged from the Christian religion as it seems to them represented in the Churches.

Now I do not speak of your duty, or mine, in regard to these people. Duty, at best, makes stepping stones for us through the miry clay of selfishness, that we may reach the firm, high land beyond, where the love of Christ constrains us, and where our love for him turns every task, however small or repulsive, into a splendid opportunity, a glorious privilege. Those of us who have children know what a pleasure it is to have the little things do some service for us, however trifling, just because they love us and want to help us in our work; there is scarcely a job in life equal to that with which we recognize the love, even if the service itself be bungling; and we know, perhaps, the sharp pain that comes when we have made a way for the child to serve us, a chance for it to show its love, and the little creature, absorbed in its own amusements and toys, turns indifferently away and lets the opportunity slip through its careless fingers. Nothing hurts much worse than that: to have love met with indifference, and the opportunity that love prepared flung carelessly away. And I don't think anything hurts our Heavenly Father more than that: for his little children, through idleness or selfishness or thoughtlessness, to turn their backs on the good works which his loving, patient thought prepared beforehand expressly for them, that they should walk in them. Then newspapers are full of crimes; fresh crimes with every day: murders, lynchings, thefts, dishonor, drunkenness, debauchery; the world groans under the awful load. But after all none of these are the thing that damns men's souls; if that were so, most people would be safe. When the Israelites of old committed all these sins, and added open idolatry to the horrid list, God brought just one charge against them: "Israel doth not know," he said, "my people doth not consider." Not what they did, though that was bad enough; it was what they did not: they would not think God's thoughts nor see God's will. And when Christ drew that great picture of the last judgment, he did not condemn a single soul because of any outward sin; they were driven out not because of anything that they had done, but because of what they did not: because they had neglected their opportunities.

Only infinite love could bear with this world at all; could give out each new day fresh from the heart of God, crowded with opportunities for loving hearts to broaden out into, and fill with the incense of happy service; and then, night after night receive back from his children's heedless hands those same days after they had worked out not his will, but theirs in them; distorted, ruined days, full of great gaps and blanks, and yet puffed up with blind pride and selfishness. St. James says of certain men of this day that their silver and gold were cankered, and that the rust of them would witness against them at the last day. I think that is the most awful witness which any soul will have to face in that great day: the witness of the dull, heavy capabilities that might have been polished by loving service until they shone even amid the splendors of God's throne; the hidden .

talent, a little one, perhaps, and scorned because it was not great; the little rusted talent that might have been polished against God's opportunities till it glittered like a jewel in his hand at last; to see the life we might have lived stand up before us, tall and fair, its shining treasures heaped at its feet: the little things done in a great way, done out of a great love; and then to turn to reality: the shriveled, withered, undeveloped life, its rusted riches shaking in its palsied hand. May God's grace save us from that sight!

I think we get things twisted so that we lose their due perspective and their right proportion. A bit of gold, beautiful and useful in its place, can be held so close to the eye that its little disk can shut out the light of moon and stars and all the glories of the illimitable skies; and I think this present beautiful life is so close to us, these things that are seen are so near and real, that the eternal things seem shadowy and far away; we shrink and shudder at the great gateway that leads to them, and our name for more abundant life is death. I think we need to take death for our friend and let him deepen and enrich and beautify our lives. If the great hope of the whole Church militant is the second coming of the Christ

> To take away transgression
> And rule in equity,[5]

the great hope of the individual soul is surely the time when, having finished the course and kept the faith, it is freed forever from error and weariness and pain, and enters into the presence of Christ to see him as he is, while out before it stretches an endless vista of ever increasing knowledge and service and joy.

To live in the presence of that hope does not sadden life; it fills and enriches it not only with a wiser patience in its puzzling trials, but with a greater joy in all its happiness, and with a deeper longing to fill up every waiting cup of opportunity with loving service of Him whose love has prepared for us not only the beauty of these seen and temporal things, but the glory of the unseen eternity beyond. I think that we would grow to love him more, and to walk more closely with him. I think that the little things which now seem so big—the struggle for place and power and riches, the envyings and strife—would shrivel up and blow away before this clear, fresh wind of promise from beyond the gates. I think that in the bright sunlight of this glorious hope our dim sight would grow stronger, and the unseen things would be nearer and great and beautiful. I think that a

---

5. From the hymn "Hail to the Lord's Anointed" by James Montgomery.

great love and pity for the world that lieth in darkness without this hope would begin to fill our eyes, and that it would be not the duty, but the joy and privilege, of our lives to lead their halting steps into the shining way of peace wherein our own feet walk.

I do not think it is an idle dream that this great country may shelter a righteous people. I believe that God's children, backed by God's power, are strong enough, if they will have it so, to rule this country and to put down wickedness in high places; but they can only do it by flooding the low places with love and light, by opening the blind eyes, by loosing the prisoners from captivity, by letting the oppressed go free, by giving every darkened and degraded soul within our borders the opportunity its Maker intended it to have: of knowing and loving Jesus Christ and growing up into him in all things.

"A Southern View of the Negro"

Outlook 73 (March 14, 1903): 619–23

The author of the following article is a daughter of Southern parents—both slaveholders and both the children of slaveholders. Twenty-eight of the forty-three years of her life have been passed in the South. Her husband is the son of a slaveholder, and some years of active work with the Woman's Home Mission Board of the Methodist Episcopal Church, South, have given her exceptional opportunities for getting at an understanding of the point of view of thoughtful and philanthropic people throughout most of the Southern States regarding the Race Question. The Outlook *believes that the Race Problem is one of the two most important National problems which the people of the United States have to meet and solve. It also believes that no civilized people have made in so short a time over such difficult obstacles so great an amount of industrial, educational, and social progress as the Southern people have made in the forty years since the Civil War. Believing this, and believing that the Race Question must, in its last analysis, be solved by the South itself, it sees, in spite of some manifestation, both North and South, of conflict, irritation, and misunderstanding, every promise that a solution will finally be reached. But it can be reached only by dealing with it, on the part both of the Northerner and the Southerner, in the spirit to which the following article by a Southern woman gives expression. — The Editors.*

Whatever antagonism exists between the Southern whites and the negroes is pretty well known in all its phases to the country at large; but the more hopeful aspects of their mutual relations seem little understood beyond our own borders. It is known, for instance, that many Southern people hope for no solution of the negro problem which will allow the negro to remain in the South on friendly terms with his white neighbor. Colonization, voluntary or enforced, is their expedient. There are also those who prophesy the extinction of the negro as a natural result of a higher civilization acting upon a lower race. But side by side with these impatient or despondent people is a large and growing class of Southern whites whose point of view is less well known abroad. They agree with the other class with regard to the facts of the negro's needs and deficiencies—

these are too near at hand and too clamorous to be overlooked or mistaken. But, while assenting to the general conditions, they note the increasingly numerous exceptions to the rule, and draw from the acknowledged facts more hopeful conclusions than do their neighbors. It is for this class that I wish to speak.

There is among us so strong a disapproval of some aspects of negro education that we are sometimes thought of as opposed to their education altogether. One fact should end this misapprehension. The Southern whites, though still paying ninety-two per cent. of all money for school purposes, spent, in the twenty-five years following the war, $120,000,000 on schools for the negroes. In relation to the need it was a small sum, but it was great in relation to the poverty from which it came.

The feeling against college training for negroes is certainly strong, but the cause for it is not hard to understand. It is always both an easy and a dangerous thing to develop the minds of ignorant people faster than their moral natures; and many of the negroes have been thrust into a new world to which they are imperfectly related mentally, and not at all related morally. Such negroes despise the old life of manual labor, though incapable of making an honest living in any other way, while their wants and ambitions have been multiplied. Whatever their color, people like that are a menace to any community; and the Southern people have suffered enough from the mistaken beginnings of negro education to be pardoned if they are oversensitive at this point. But they do not deny the negro's right to a college education. The Southern Methodist Church—as a member of that Church I can speak more definitely of it than of any other—has long been committed to the higher education of the negro at Paine Institute at Augusta, Ga. This institution is the joint property of the Colored Methodist Episcopal Church—a negro organization—and of the Methodist Episcopal Church, South, and has the official indorsement [sic] of the General Conference as well as of the several Annual Conferences. Its President is a member of an old South Carolina family, and its faculty is made up of Southern white and negro teachers. For years this school has been sending out men and women of good scholarship and fine character to become leaders of their race as teachers, preachers, and citizens.

In regard to social equality, the better class of negroes do not want it. Certainly they will never get it, South or North, for at least as far in the future as the mind of the white man can project itself; but this fact does not prevent mutual kindliness nor respect. In the best stores of our Southern cities white women can be seen to wait while the clerk attends to the colored customer who preceded them, and not one of them apparently gives it a thought. In the banks negro men take their place in line, and white men wait their turn behind them. Down on our public square, where the street is being repaved, white men and negroes work side by side as they did to build the house in which I live. If antipathy exists, a friendly spirit is still more evident. No honorable negro lacks the respect of his white neighbors. This respect does not take the form of social intercourse, which such negroes desire as little as we; but it is none the less expressed and understood.

It is difficult for the people of the North to understand either the pressure of the whole great race problem upon us as a people, or its endless ramifications into the smallest details of our individual daily lives. The sharpest criticism of the negro we ever hear comes from the Northerners who come to live among us, and who find the dirt, shiftlessness, and dishonesty of the colored laborers, men and women, quite beyond endurance. They cannot understand why we "put up" with it all, and look askance at us, as lazy and shiftless ourselves—an opinion, be it observed, from which we radically dissent! After years of painful discipline—if they do not give up the struggle first, and return to the land of cleanliness and trained workers—they come to one of two conclusions. Either they do their work themselves, and are looked upon by the darkies as "po' white trash;" or they adopt the attitude of their Southern neighbors, endure the pilfering and the slipshod work, and do what they can to awaken in these childish and undeveloped creatures some idea of trustworthiness and honor. It is not an attractive task. The long procession of incompetents tramp through our homes and business houses, never content long enough anywhere for the kindest or wisest of us to make much of an impression on them.

It is the more difficult to make any lasting impression upon them for the reason that, as a race, they are grateful only superficially, and in the immediate presence of expected benefits. But those of us who are discouraged by this patent and ubiquitous fact forget that gratitude is not a primal instinct; it is a late development in the progress of any race from barbarism, as in the growth of the normal civilized child. An illustration such as any housekeeper can furnish is found in a girl whom I tried hard to help during the year in which she cooked for me, and who left me at a moment's notice one morning when told that, on account of usual rain and mud, the porch needed an extra scrubbing. I was ill and without other help, but that troubled her not a whit. Two weeks later the "collector," finding that she had left me and thinking her unprotected, tried to take away the furniture she had nearly paid for on the installment plan. She came to me with the untroubled confidence of a child, and of course received help as freely as she asked it. Embarrassment was of another world. Such matters are refreshing from their comical side, and should burden nobody with a sense of the negro's depravity. They spring from an undeveloped mental and moral consciousness. A few generations of reasonable patience and the negro will have passed this trying point.

But there is a darker side. It would be difficult to exaggerate the lack of morals among the mass of the negroes. Yet the whole human race has come up from the depths in this respect; and, remembering how recently their forefathers were savages, the situation is not without encouragement. Whatever the height of our own moral superiority, it must, in God's eyes, just measure the depth of our debt to the weaker race. The difference pledges us, not to condemnation, but to service.

But there are chaste negroes and honest ones. I know many personally, and I cannot think my own experience very exceptional. A woman who was in my house thirteen years—a girl grown up since the war—is a fair specimen of this class. I believe in her virtue entirely, and would trust her with anything I possess, while her long and faithful service compels my genuine affection; and I am but one of thousands who could bear a like testimony.

It is in these exceptional negroes, and in their constantly, if slowly, increasingly numbers, that we find a visible warrant for our faith in the future of their race, as well as for our faith in the providence which has bound up their future with that of our whole country.

Southern white women are sometimes said to be indifferent to the needs of the colored people. The charge is not without foundation; yet very many of the negro's best friends and most sympathetic helpers are to be found among the women who have inherited this attitude toward them from their mothers and grandmothers. In their painful progress from barbarism the negroes owe much to the Christian Southern women of the past, and more than is known to those of the present.

The new industrial school at Paine Institute is a sign, small but significant, of a growing desire among Southern women to help their darker neighbors through organized effort. It is also an indication of the growing belief that a final solution of the whole difficult problem will be reached for the mass of the race along the lines laid down at Hampton and Tuskegee. This school has been enterprised [sic] by the Woman's Board of Home Missions of the Methodist Episcopal Church, South, which is composed of women from every Southern

State. A young colored woman, a graduate of Hampton, was placed at Paine this fall as instructress, and Dr. Walker writes that she is doing fine work notwithstanding the temporary lack of suitable accommodations. We have just let the contract for two industrial cottages, to be erected at once. We offered the work to a negro contractor living in Atlanta, an ex-slave; but, to his regret and ours, his time and resources for months ahead were already pledged in contracts with white people living in that city, and he could not undertake it.

It is chiefly industrial education, with its already notable good results, that is changing the attitude of many of the thinking men of the South to one of unmistakable hopefulness. Dr. J.J. Tigert, the editor of the "Southern Methodist Review," and one of the acknowledged leaders of his denomination, says in a recent editorial:

> We confess, for our own part, that we no longer share the pessimism with respect to the insolubility of the problem which has seemed to dominate much of Southern thought and sentiment. There are too many indications of the steady improvement of the negro in his Southern habitat. Commercially, educationally, religiously, the colored man is on the up grade. Many of his race are earning the cordial respect of the white people of the South by good conduct alike on the farm and in the shop, in the school and in the church. Social and moral distinctions, which are recognized by the negroes themselves, are rapidly developing among them. He who looks upon the race as a common mass of uniform quality is vastly mistaken. The worthless elements are no doubt still present in large proportions; but the worthy elements are visible and growing to him who has eyes to see. Time and patience will be needed for a permanent solution of all the difficulties of the situation; but the practical demands of business life, and various influences, both emancipating and conservative, which grow out of daily association and common interests, will make their scarcely perceptible contributions until, in ways whose operation is not measurable, but whose results are determinative, the vast and complex problem of the two races living side by side in concord and amity will be solved.

To some at the North these words may seem over-sanguine in view of the recent wholesale disfranchisement of the negroes in several of the Southern States. The charge which is brought against these States is not that negroes unfit to vote are excluded from the ballot, but that white men equally ignorant are not excluded also. But whenever the great majority of intelligent citizens in any State do a thing which to those at a distance appears unjust, it is safe to conclude that the action cannot be explained by the assumption that the intelligent majority has either laid aside its intelligence or has acted from unworthy motives. Explanations like that do not explain, North or South. Mistakes may be made, the correcting of which will be costly enough; but in every State in the Union there is enough of the spirit of patriotism and fair play to prevent the securing of any great majority for an act of selfish tyranny. As a matter of fact, the ignorant white vote at the South has never been, as at the North, a menace to good government. Such voters have not been gathered into towns, but scattered through the country, and coming into frequent and friendly touch with the educated classes both in the country and in the towns where they go to do their trading. They have stood entirely apart from the questions of municipal government, and have been overwhelmingly on the side of law and order in the country communities. The dangers of our political life have come from the manipulation of the ignorant colored vote by a few unscrupulous whites. It is impossible for the North to realize or the South to forget the horror of the days when that vote ruled the South. In the interest of both races, for the sake of justice and decency, it must never rule again. The States which have barred the ignorant black vote but not the ignorant white vote have drawn, not a color line, but what they believe to be a danger line. All this is said, not in defense of an abstract principle, but in explanation of a concrete fact.

There are many men in the South who do not favor the retention of the ignorant white vote. The majority of them, as might be expected, are found in those States where the ignorant black vote is less overwhelming or the ignorant white vote more significant than elsewhere—that is, where the conditions tend to approximate those of the North.

It should be remembered that those States which have disfranchised these ignorant voters are taxing every resource equally with the other States to educate the negroes and fit them for citizenship. There is neither the intention nor the wish to keep them disqualified, nor to bar them out when disqualified. They are admitted as voters, and will be for years to come, on a lower level than would admit them to suffrage in one of the wisest Northern States. A mistake may have been made, but it was in the sincere belief that it was best for all classes, and with no desire to oppress the helpless or to shirk the duty laid upon the South of solving the negro problem in justice and honor.

To those of us who believe most thoroughly in a restricted suffrage the country over, there is a danger in the future which is as yet unknown among us. The rapid growth of our manufacturers is drawing the scattered country population into our cities and laying the foundations of the Southern slum. The conditions which have hitherto safeguarded the ignorant white vote are rapidly changing, and the seeds of a new peril to clean municipal government are being sown. Unless the school term can be lengthened and compulsory education laws passed throughout the South, our children will find that the color line and the danger line no longer coincide. The ignorant white voter of to-day will give no trouble; but what of to-day's mill children, controlled a few years hence by the political boss? The spectacle so long familiar at the North may yet be seen at the South— the intelligent white vote arrayed against the ignorant white vote, and fighting it in the interest of good government.

But it is a tremendous task which is laid upon the Southern whites, both in behalf of the negroes and to hold fast by patience and hopefulness within their own hearts. It is for the North, free from the daily burdens and conflicts which that task involves, to give us more of generous and brotherly understanding. With all her heroic effort, the white children of the South in many places are still inadequately provided for; to meet even in a small measure the needs of the colored population often seems to involve the sacrifice of needed provision for the whites. There is nothing comparable to it in all the North or West. But, whatever the South may lack, she has never yet turned her back upon the difficulties nor failed in the power of sacrifice for her ideal of duty. As much as in us is, we are debtors to the whites and to the negroes also. Southern statesmanship and Southern Christianity have long since owned the debt, and by the grace of God they will yet pay it in full.

"A Black-and-White Christmas"

Christian Advocate 76 (January 15, 1915): 26–27

All over Southern Methodism has swept the Christmas fever of brightening the lives of the poor with a few of those comforts and luxuries which are everyday affairs to the well-to-do. Thousands of Christmas baskets have been sent out to those whose Christmas dinners would otherwise have been either entirely lacking or devoid of Christmas cheer; thousands upon thousands of Christmas stockings have been filled which but for this Christmas spirit of love would never have been hung at all. Toys, goodies, substantial food, clothing, fuel, and smiles of Christmas cheer—we have given them all, tons of them, this Christmas to— the poor? Well, to some of the poor, to the poor who have white skins or who would have white skins if they were clean. No dirt stops us, no degradation, no poverty, if only they belong to white folks. We drop our silver and an occasional greenback into the Salvation Army pots with a comfortable sense that the poorest, lowest, dirtiest folks in town, even the "bums" and tramps, will get their bit of Christmas too.

I am fifty-five years old, and, except for a few years of illness, I have been every Christmas since I was twelve with some group of Church people who were working to provide a happy Christmas for the poor. But I have never in all those years heard or seen anything to suggest that there were any poor in the community except the white poor. Of course this statement applies to myself as well as to the rest, and for many years it did not strike me as peculiar. Doubtless many individual Christians did what I often did myself—sent something to some negro woman they happened to know of personally. But so far as my experience goes, white Christians do not at all consider it a part of Church privilege or Church obligation to do anything whatever for poor folks at Christmas unless they have white skins. We hunt up the poor white folks, stepping over suffering colored ones by the dozen to find them; and when they are pretty well rounded up, we say the poor are all provided for. The black poor do not exist to our consciousness.

So I want to chronicle some recent Christmas happenings in Augusta. The first is the new departure of some of our young people at St. John's Church. The young people's mission study class filled nearly fifty Christmas stockings for the poor and sent half of them to poor white children and the other half to our Bethlehem House for the children of the negro poor. So far as I know, this is the first instance of an organized body in a Southern white Church recognizing the Christmas claims of just the poor—not the white poor nor black poor, but just the poor. It will not be the last instance. It is too closely akin to the spirit of Christ not to spread contagion among those who love him.

That was the beginning of our black-and-white Christmas. The next thing was the resolve of a few older white folks, also members of St. John's, to put a certain colored orphanage on their Christmas list. Twenty-three little starveling negroes, gathered in off the streets and out of the juvenile court by a black man and his wife who do not possess half enough to keep themselves in any adequate comfort. Yet they share their little all with these waifs and strays, with nobody, black nor white, to stand behind them; wearing such clothes as they can get, eating when they can, and going hungry when they must. In white folks we would call it heroic, but somehow a black skin renders heroism invisible to the naked eye.

So these white folks decided to put the orphanage on their list; and when the black students at Paine College found out about it, they wanted to help. And the black poor at the Bethlehem House wanted to help too. There were twenty-three pairs of brand-new stockings, and the Paine students filled one of each pair with good things to eat until they bulged in the most approved Christmas style. They made a noble pile. And some of the white folks provided material, and the girls in the Bethlehem House sewing classes made it into shirt waists— O no, not enough to go round, but enough to put Christmas joy into the hearts of the little black sewing class and the warmth of Christmas love into that poor orphanage. And there were a few things more prosaic—sacks of meal, potatoes, and cabbages—and one big-hearted member of St. John's, who has a hand in no end of Christmas doings, topped the load with a great bunch of bananas and a bucket of candy so big that I'll be afraid to make any inquiry about those children for the next two weeks, only I do know a first-class negro doctor who will physic them free of charge.

And Christmas Eve Paine College had its Christmas tree—a great big beauty of a tree, the loveliest I ever saw. For not only was it beautiful as a tree, but, evergreen thought it was, it was a black-and-white tree—no, an "all-ye-are-brethren" tree. For it came from St. John's Sunday School, where it gladdened the hearts of white children before it delighted their darker brothers and sisters at Paine.

And out of a running-over happy heart I say: "Thank God for a black-and-white Christmas!" It's one of the greatest joy producers on record. Try it next Christmas and see.

Southern Women and
Racial Adjustment

1917

Note.

In this paper Mrs. Hammond has told what the white women of the South have done and are doing for the unprivileged black women. It is a splendid story of gallant service. Its sanity and patriotism make their own high appeal.

James H. Dillard
Charlottesville, Va.
October 15, 1917

Note by the Author.

For the opinions expressed and the conclusions drawn in the following pages the writer alone is responsible; but she wishes to acknowledge her indebtedness to the following women, without whose kindly aid in gathering the facts set forth this paper could scarcely have been written:

Mrs. Percy V. Pennybacker, president of the National Federation of Women's Clubs during the last biennial period; Mrs. Edward McGehee, Mrs. John I. Moore, Mrs. W.S. Jennings, Miss Helen Norris Cummings, Mrs. Court F. Wood, presidents respectively of the State Federations of Mississippi, Arkansas, Florida, Virginia, and the District of Columbia; Mrs. Z.I. Fitzpatrick, late president, and director-for-life of the Georgia State Federation; Mrs. C.P. Orr, formerly president of the Alabama State Federation; Miss Elizabeth Gilman, chairman of the Advisory Committee on Work for Colored People, Baltimore Civic League; Mrs. Gordon Green, president City Federation, Jackson, Miss.; Mrs. John Love, president of City Federation of Clubs and of City Federation of Missionary Societies, Meridian, Miss.; Mrs. W.L. Murdoch, formerly vice-president of the Southern Sociological Congress; Mrs. Lella A. Dillard, State president Georgia W.C.T.U.; Mrs. Elizabeth Preston Allan, chairman of the Committee for Colored Work, Y.W.C.A.; Mrs. W.C. Winsborough, secretary Woman's Home Mission Board, Southern Presbyterian Church; Mrs. B.W. Lipscomb, Home Base secretary Woman's Missionary Council, M.E.

Church, South; Mrs. L.S. Arrington and Mrs. W.D. Haas, superintendents Social Service, North Georgia and Louisiana Conferences, Woman's Missionary Council; Mrs. H.M. Wharton, chairman Personal Service Committee, Southern Baptist Woman's Home Mission Board; Mrs. Wm. McGarity, secretary Texas Baptist Home Mission Society; Mrs. Bolton K. Smith, president of the Bishop's Guild, State of Tennessee.

The writer also wishes to thank the following colored women for their kindness in furnishing facts in regard to colored women's organization and work:

Mrs. Booker T. Washington, editor *National Association Notes*; Mrs. E.E. Peterson, national organizer for colored women, W.C.T.U.; Mrs. H.L. McCrory, president of the Colored Branch, Associated Charities, Charlotte, N.C.; Mrs. Sarah Collins Fernandis, executive secretary of the Advisory Committee, Civic League, Baltimore.

She would also thank Bishop Lloyd, president of the General Board of Missions of the Episcopal Church, for many courtesies; Bishop Guerry, of South Carolina; and Professor Imes, of Tuskegee Institute.

L. H. Hammond

Dalton, Ga.

October 1, 1917

And here to us the eternal charge is given
To rise and make our low world touch God's high.
—Alfred Noyes: *"In Time of War"*

Southern Women and Racial Adjustment

The manners and morals of every community reflect the standards sanctioned or permitted by its privileged women. Individuals stand above this common level, blazing ethical trails into the unmoral wilderness of our wider human associations, and draw after them, here and there, adventurous groups; but there can be no mass advance until the individual impulse toward righteousness, which is justice in its finest sense, is reinforced by a common standard embodying a force greater than the individual.

These common standards are furnished, actively or passively, by the privileged women, from whose homes they spread into the community. Racial adjustment, like many other moral issues, waits on the leadership of these women. Their attitude toward it is thus of both sectional and national importance; and their increasing development of broad humanitarian standards in racial relations is worthy of note.

New Thoughts for New Times.

One great obstacle to better racial adjustment has been the retention by many of us of the viewpoint of a day that is past: our ideal of a good free Negro has been too much like the one that fitted a good slave. Every misfit action has a misfit ideal at its root; and our anomalous crop of racial relations, with its fruitage of lynchings and migrations, is the result of trying to grow the Negro's life to-day on past ideals. Usefulness to his master is a slave's chief virtue; that of a freeman is his usefulness to the human race. However undeveloped or ignorant he may be, the standard of value is shifted at once from an economic to a moral base; and the foundation of all morality is the home. Material progress waits on moral progress; and the full prosperity of Southern industry and commerce waits in a most vital sense upon the moral status of the Negro home. It is the privileged white women who alone can fix this status for the entire community, building it up in white respect, and helping the better class of colored women to build it up in colored life.

The purpose of this pamphlet is to show our women's entrance upon this great humanitarian and patriotic service. To perform it they are adventuring into the unknown, discovering their cooks and washerwomen as women beset by womanhood's clamorous demands and utterly unable to meet them without help and sympathy. It is out of this thought of privileged white women for these handicapped mothers, children, and homes that the eventual adjustment of our bi-racial Southern life will come.

Beginnings.

All women's modern activities began in individualistic religious service. The old Dorcas and missionary societies first widened their horizon to include conditions beyond their homes, and taught them teamwork; which overflowed, in time, into the Woman's Christian Temperance Union, the early cultural clubs, and the Federation. The interest of Southern women in the welfare of "free people of color" follows this line of development.

Their first service to the freed Negroes was purely religious and individual. In a number of states colored Sunday schools were taught here and there by women of the first families. The Episcopal Bishop of South Carolina reports plantation Sunday schools conducted by such women which run back from forty to sixty years without a break. In the darkest days of the last century these scattered schools kept alive a sense of the responsibility of the privileged woman to the unprivileged.

The Woman's Christian Temperance Union.

Through this body Southern women took their first steps in organized service. Work among Negroes was decided on at a meeting in Chattanooga in 1871. A prominent South Carolinian, as superintendent of Colored Work, spoke to and for the Negroes throughout the South. From that time the policy of the Southern state organizations has been to promote temperance work among Negroes as part of each local union's duty. Although this has never been thoroughly carried out, and many women are indifferent, in this as in every group, to Negro welfare and to the interdependence of their good and ours, yet few could be found who would oppose the policy. Some of the Union's most noted speakers are Southern women, and in the South they never speak without some strong word for the Negro, and especially for the Negro woman. A place for colored people is almost invariably reserved at the white meetings; and, when time permits, the speakers address colored gatherings, to which they are accompanied by local white leaders.

When Atlanta went dry in 1885 the white women held prayer-meetings with the colored women throughout the city; and it was publicly acknowledged that the colored women, backed by their pastors, had contributed largely to the victory. In the worst days of our convict camps the Georgia Union led and won a fight for the segregation and protection of the women prisoners. The treatment of the colored women in the camps was the avowed cause of this campaign.

The attitude of the Unions has had far-reaching effects. Their viewpoint has been more humanitarian than racial, and almost unconsciously they have carried into thousands of communities a latent thought of the common human needs of white and black. This thought, in the last fifteen years, is growing in the organized church work of Southern women, and has been carried by the church women into the wider associations of their Federation community work.

Southern Methodist Women.

The first organized body of church women to take up work for colored people was the Southern Methodist Home Mission Society, now merged with the Foreign Society in[to] the Women's Missionary Council of that church. In 1900 they decided to open an industrial department for girls in the school at Augusta, Ga., maintained by their church for the training of colored ministers and teachers. The work met with strong opposition at first, but has won its way to general respect and support, as is evidenced by its increasing development. The Council now operates, in addition to this industrial work, two settlements, one at Augusta, the other at Nashville, Tenn. In both places the Board of Directors is made up of locally prominent men and women of both races. The aim is community betterment, and care is taken to interest the better class of colored people without regard to denominational lines. The older students of the colored normal schools and colleges assist regularly in the club and class work, gaining a measure of training in community work which will bear fruit in their home communities.

The Nashville enterprise has taken on unusual significance, having interested people of both races of all denominations, the Southern white schools, and the colleges for Negroes maintained by Northern people. Courses in Social Service are offered at Fisk University, the field work being done at the settlement under the direction of Southern white women. The National League on Urban Conditions Among Colored People coöperates by maintaining scholarships for these courses at Fisk, which are open to graduates of all colored schools of a certain grade in the South. Vanderbilt University not only furnishes lecturers to these students from its faculty, but students enrolled in the Vanderbilt School of Religion and Philanthropy help in the work of the settlement, thus learning the needs of the colored poor. These initial steps in establishing contact and understanding have already had good results. A Public Welfare League, composed of men and women of both races, is in operation. Its program includes the promotion of a better understanding between the races, the improvement of housing and working conditions for Negroes, and the training of students in methods of community betterment and of race coöperation. This last item is of especial importance, Nashville being to an unusual extent a school center for both races. Among the things already achieved by the Public Welfare League are a public library for Negroes, the organization of probation work for colored juvenile offenders, and two playgrounds for colored children, the city furnishing equipment and salaries, and students trained at Fisk and in the settlement acting as supervisors. A further development of this coöperative spirit was seen after the great fire of 1916, when the white Commercial Club and the Negro Board of Trade worked together in relieving some 1,500 colored fire sufferers.

Local Work of Southern Methodist Women.

The undertakings above described are under the immediate care of the women's central missionary organization; but additional work for the 4,700 local auxiliaries has been outlined by the Council. It includes service in colored Sunday schools, promotion of colored missionary societies, school betterment, recreational facilities, and especially the formation of and coöperation with colored women's Community Clubs for betterment along all lines. In the fall of 1915 over 200 auxiliaries were regularly reporting such work. Its effect on public opinion is illustrated by the experience of the superintendent of Social Service for the Louisiana Conference.

"I have changed my views about the Negroes greatly in the last few years," she said recently. "Our Council has educated me; and I think many others feel the same way. A number of our Louisiana societies are working for colored people."

An initial point of contact established, growth in sympathy is certain. Handicapped motherhood and childhood of any race make to privileged women an appeal which is irresistible once it is understood. The women of the North Georgia Conference recently illustrated this fact.

This body has shown by conference action from time to time a broadening sense of obligation to the Negroes; but at the 1917 meeting their growing insight was focused on a wrong which stirs women for women everywhere.

The perennial petition to the next legislature to raise the age of consent from ten to eighteen years was up for its annual endorsement here, as at every gathering of women in the State. This year the W.C.T.U. was leading the fight. In their communication to the Methodist women they referred to the fact that certain legislators had openly objected to the protection the bill would afford colored girls. The W.C.T.U. and the Methodist women unanimously adopted a resolution calling for "the protection of the childhood and womanhood of Georgia without regard to race." Other bodies of women took the same stand and will keep it until the bill is passed.

Southern Presbyterian Women.

These women lead the South in Sunday-school work among Negroes. Some of them have been teaching in colored Sunday schools ever since the war, and of late years the work is spreading. The first wife of President Wilson told the writer that when, as a young girl, she went to New York to study art she sought out a colored Sunday school and taught a class there the two years she was in the city. She said that if she had come from any section but the South she would have taken some other form of church work; but, being a Southern girl, the daughter and descendant of slave owners, she felt that service to colored people was her especial obligation; and, true to Presbyterian type, she sought a Sunday-school class.

Of late years, however, these women are leading interdenominational organizations of church women in several cities for this and other purposes. The Federation of City Missionary Societies at Meridian, Miss., is typical.

The Presbyterian women led in forming the Federation, which organized an interdenominational Bible Teachers' Training Class from the various colored Sunday schools. It meets weekly in the colored public library with the best white teachers of the city in charge. Then came a Story Tellers' League of the colored teachers. It, too, meets weekly at the library, a white woman telling a story to be repeated by the members at the colored schools. The monthly stereopticon lectures of the Missionary Education Movement are repeated before the colored people; and on one night of Christmas week the Negroes hold a musical service around the municipal Christmas tree.

In Uniontown, Ala., the women of a Presbyterian Bible Class decided to set apart a definite hour each week when each of them would teach the servants in her home the Sunday-school lesson for the next week. This was ten years ago. The basal need in racial adjustment—a human as distinguished from an economic point of contact—thus being met, vision and a broadening service have followed. An interdenominational Bible Class for colored women was formed, officered by colored women and taught by white. Class committees were formed to read the Bible to the colored sick and aged. This brought forward various problems of poverty, and led to relief work guided by the white women and done by the Negro. The children of these homes came into view, and a white teacher maintains for them a weekly story hour.

Institute for Colored Women.

A significant development from this widely scattered local work is the inauguration, a year or two ago, of a yearly Institute for Colored Women by the Southern Presbyterian Women's Home Mission Board. It is held at Stillman Institute, Tuscaloosa, Ala., the church training school for colored Presbyterian ministers. In 1916 there were 155 women in attendance from six states. Leading white women were present from the Boards, as well as from Alabama and other states. The courses were given in part by them and in part by colored women. They included Bible study, and lectures on moral training in the home, the home and the school, practical homemaking, care of babies, common diseases, sanitation, preservation of food, etc.

A combination of the Methodist Community Clubs conducted by local auxiliaries with a multiplication of such yearly institutes by the general organizations seems an ideal plan for missionary societies to adopt. Both forms of service are closely fitted to the needs of both races; for the rendering of service by those who can give it is as vital to moral health as is the receiving of it by those who need.

Southern Baptist Women.

The Baptist Women's Board has no specific enterprise for colored people. They definitely teach, however, through their literature, the duty of local Christian service. This chiefly takes the form of helping the colored Baptist women to form and conduct missionary societies. This practice is widespread. The Home Mission Board has a Department of Personal Service which officially includes work for Negroes; and in several places the coöperation in missionary work above referred to is leading out into the field of social service, especially in those interdenominational missionary federations which are appearing in many of our cities.

A fine instance of local social service was found in Baltimore, where the

Baptist women for years carried on a number of industrial schools for colored children. Through the children the mothers were reached, and a strong colored leadership was eventually developed which warranted turning over the work to these women, who have since conducted it.

In Texas, a number of auxiliaries are doing work among colored people. In Belton the white college girls, enlisted by the Baptist women, gave a fine missionary program recently in one of the colored churches. In the annual State meetings of the white societies the officers of colored Baptist schools regularly present their work, and a collection is taken for them. In Austin courses in Bible study are given for colored women.

A remarkably successful coöperative work is carried on in Birmingham, Ala., under the leadership of two white missionaries of the Northern Baptists Women's Board. These women have not only a present enrollment of over 700 colored women in their four-year Bible course, but they have enlisted the white women of the city as teachers of these classes. Every denomination is represented, and the teachers have the backing of their local missionary organizations.

Episcopal Women.

The work of the women of the Episcopal Church is on a different basis from that of all other churches. It is purely auxiliary to the General Board of Missions, which determines the activities of the women, appropriates the funds raised by them, and is composed entirely of men. This explains their lack of initiative in church work—a lack not found in their Y.W.C.A. or their club work. As church members, however, their directed activities include the work for Negroes maintained by the General Board. This work is larger and better supported by the Southern dioceses than the work for Negroes of any other Southern church, and in this the women have their share. They also share in the local work of the parishes for Negroes, which is chiefly the maintenance of parish schools; and where, as in the diocese of South Georgia, the church employs a trained colored woman for work among her people they give both interest and money to the work. In Tennessee the Bishop has organized a Bishop's Guild among the women for the sole purpose of promoting the educational work of the diocese for Negroes.

The colored women of the diocese are organized, like the white women, into auxiliaries of the Board of Missions; and the diocesan officers of the white organizations not only attend the annual meetings of the colored women, but assist them throughout the year in their work. In the main, however, the social service activities of these women, as of the women of other denominations, find their largest expression outside of their church organization.

Y.W.C.A. Work Among Colored Women.

It seems well to consider this phase of the subject in connection with church work, though it is more recently begun than the club work. For years the only Y.W.C.A. work among Negroes was done from the New York headquarters by a colored secretary in charge of the colored schools. There are now 51 associations in as many schools, and interest is aroused in 50 more. The feeling, however, has been growing among Southern workers that the time has come for coöperative work, and in the fall of 1915 it was decided on at a conference held in Louisville in which women of both races and of both sections took part. A joint committee of Southern white and colored women was formed both to promote the interests of the college associations and to encourage the formation of city associations, independent, and yet linked as "branch associations" to the central white organization of their respective cities, to which they could look for guidance and coöperation, after the plan was found successful in the work for immigrant races in the North. Associations are already in operation in Richmond, Charlotte, and St. Louis, and a number of cities have made application for organization, a necessary feature of the application being the endorsement of the local white association. Jacksonville, Fla., Winston-Salem and Wilmington, N.C., and Lynchburg, Va., are among the cities applying for organization.

Colored student conferences are now held annually in the South, attended by Southern white women. The most promising students are given six weeks' intensive training in the summer at New York headquarters to prepare them for future secretarial work among their people. Conferences are also held on city work, and here both races and both sections are brought together, and a broader basis is being laid for mutual understanding.

Southern Club Women.

The facts already recited show Southern women shifting the race problem from a sectional to a human basis, and broadening their adjustment to those Christian standards which fit the whole Race of Man. They are opening the doors of our sectional life to the free winds of world-thought by opening our hearts to the needs of all human life. When one's heart is open to human needs the life of the world flows into it. The smallest, most secluded dwelling place, the daily round of pettiest tasks, is then filled with the throb of a common aspiration, the love of a common justice, the thrill of a universal hope. This liberty of soul our women are achieving for us. Like all the priceless things of life, it lies close to everybody's hand, inextricably tangled in our everyday relations and living. What we need are eyes to see it—a standard of values made visible from the unseen. And this it is the office of women to give.

Their initial inspiration has come from the churches and church teaching, but it is working out, in the main, through organizations outside the church. The beginnings of fifty years ago gathered strength in the W.C.T.U., the first association of women in the South for bettering home conditions. In like manner the social service development of recent years germinated in the church, and there passed its first critical stage; but its flowering is outside the church, as its fullest fruition will be. The church women have created outside of their churches a free, flexible organization to which nothing that concerns human life is alien, and where denominational and class lines do not exist. And here, with the Christian inspiration drawn from their churches, they are, half unconsciously as yet, approaching our old sectional problems from the human, or world, standpoint. The results are already impressive; their implications are greater still.

The Democracy of the Microbe.

Any one who will follow common sense far enough will land up to their eyes in Christianity; the two refuse to accept divorcement. The club women came upon Christian principles of racial adjustment without realizing that they were dealing with racial problems at all. They simply started out with common sense as their guide and cleanliness as their goal.

Their clean-up campaigns, confined at first to the white part of town, were pronounced by common sense to be only fifty per cent efficient; so the coöperation of colored women was sought. The club of Charlotte, N.C., was one of the pioneers—and less than a decade ago. They invited the women of the colored missionary societies to a meeting at which the mayor, the health officer, the white and the colored women all spoke; and the result, attested to by the club president, was that the white women were put on their mettle to keep up with the colored ones in the cleaning that followed. The city's health record and the babies flourished in consequence.

In this way, in several pioneer towns, a common meeting ground was discovered for the women of the two races—the need of human homes for cleanliness and health. The meeting of human needs never endangers the preservation of true racial lines; this the women clearly sensed, and went to their new work joyously. Common sense, prodded by the microbe, had prompted the first step; but some of the women glimpsed a background of religious teaching and motive with which the experiment fitted in, and from which it drew high sanction.

In a few years this coöperation for community health has spread throughout the South, leavening popular thought with a consciousness of a common need, which must be met for both races or for neither. And while that leaven works the women have been making further discoveries.

The Negro Home.

In a Georgia city a clean-up committee, going to their work-section, passed through a section in charge of colored women. There had been heavy rains, and the committee beheld several blocks of colored houses standing in a great pool of stagnant and slimy water. Inquiry showed that the city Board of Health had long since reported the need of a sewer there, and the Council had voted to put it in "as soon as funds were available." The cost would run into the thousands, and the city needed many things.

But to the club women a new thought came as they watched the colored children playing in that filth, and the mothers plodding in the marsh of their little yards—a thought, not of Negro houses, but of Negro homes. It is a big club, with wealth and prestige, and when it reinforced the request of the Board of Health, as it promptly did, the sewer went in, and a rankling bitterness went out of a number of Negro hearts.

Again, some club women, two or three years ago, as a result of one of these clean-up campaigns, began to visit occasionally a colored Mothers' Club to talk about some of the problems common to all mothers. Thus they learned that in the hitherto respectable section in which most of these women lived three houses of vice had been opened, all owned by white men, though one was run by a colored woman. They had made short work of her case after a fashion of their own: she had simply developed an insuperable objection to the neighborhood, and had forced her employer to let her move. But against the white [men] they were helpless. An appeal to the police would have closed the houses in that city, but they feared the vengeance of the proprietors and their women—a thing the police could take no cognizance of until it became an accomplished fact. Most of them owned, or were buying, their own homes; they could not leave, or risk being burned out.

The club's Department of Civics took the matter up at once, and without involving the colored women. The houses were closed, and the sense of the common needs of human homes was broadened in that community.

The same result, in another city, came through the failure of a similar effort. A club committee on housing inspected a district including some colored homes. They ran across a colored woman of the finest type who was leading a little group of her friends in some home mission work among these Negro poor. She was handicapped by a vice resort owned by a white man and kept by a Negro woman who preyed upon the girls of the neighborhood.

The bond of a common womanhood, deeper than all racial separateness, asserted itself, as it will when such an emergency is understood. The club women declared war on that house for the sake of colored mothers and homes. The man, however, had brains, money, and power; he still holds nine points of the law. But he has taught those women some truths about the needs of colored homes which will bear fruit in that community long after he is forgotten. He has also prolonged from acquaintance into friendship the contact between educated women of the two races who made common cause against a common foe.

The Educated Colored Woman.

This discovery of the educated colored woman is of deep significance. It is she who must lift her people, but she can do so little without our help! The experience of one club woman is typical here. She seized upon a friend in the street one day to share her recent discovery.

"You know I'm on the committee to meet the colored teachers in the clean-up campaign," she began. "——— is the chairman of their committee"—naming the head of a local school. "You know she's a college graduate; I've heard about her for years. I thought she'd be a sort of spoiled cook, you know—forward, and all that. Well, she's perfectly *fine*! I didn't know there were any Negroes like that. That committee will work like it was greased. It means everything to the Negroes—and a lot to us, too—to have a woman like that at work among all these colored people here."

Her face was alight with the interest of her discovery—a feeling a number of women are coming to understand as they make similar discoveries in their own communities. Said the president of a city federation in Mississippi lately:

"I had such a sense of adventure when I first began to get acquainted with those women here. You know we couldn't even get the poorer Negroes to clean up except through these educated ones. The first I went to talk to them about it you can't think how rattled I was. I'd been speaking in public for years, and never thought about being embarrassed. But they looked so different from any Negroes I'd known. I didn't know what their thoughts were like, or how to get at them. I've done some mental gymnastics since, and I trust I'm a broader woman for it."

The outstanding feature of her experience, however, and that of many others, was the finding, in these uncharted regions, the same old landmarks of human need. They are common to all races and all time, and a realization of this fact is one of the things which is helping us to broaden out of a sectional into a world life.

White and Black in Baltimore.

So far as the writer can learn, coöperation in Baltimore has developed further than in any other city. For this reason a somewhat detailed account seems advisable.

In 1911 the Women's Civic League appointed an Advisory Committee on Work for Colored People. A fund of $1,000 was raised, and a trained colored woman secured who was a graduate of Hampton and a student at the New York School of Philanthropy. She was made "executive secretary" for the white Advisory Committee, and under its direction organized the colored women into the "Coöperative Civic League," of which she became president, while remaining as executive secretary of the Advisory Committee.

The work was opened in a house the colored women undertook to buy, the white women paying the worker's salary and other expenses. A day nursery was opened which the latest report shows still in successful operation. The mothers, all of whom work away from home, pay a small fee which covers the cost of food. Investigations by the colored worker showed many mothers of school children in the neighborhood who had "to lock their doors in the morning only to reopen them at night." The Advisory Committee secured permission from the Board of Education to have lunches served in the schools. This is done at a charge of two cents per child per day, the Committee meeting the deficit.

The following activities are regularly maintained: settlement work, with clubs, classes, etc.; back-yard and vacant-lot gardening; flower market; distribution of seed; "a series of meetings annually, spreading the gospel of civic betterment; the organization of the school children into Clean City Clubs; and, withal, a wholesome spirit of mutual helpfulness."

The agencies coöperating with this movement to meet the human needs of the community without distinction of race make an impressive list: the Federated Charities, Children's Aid, Visiting Nurses, Johns Hopkins Hospital, Juvenile Court, Parole Board, Board of Health, Babies' Milk Fund, and the Associations for Summer Outings and on School Attendance. The Civic League has also taken an active interest in the movement for better housing for colored people, in which city officials and leading citizens are now interested. A club member is on the city committee now formulating plans for sanitary houses in the poorer Negro quarters, and another member has erected in one of these sections a small group of sanitary houses as an investment, and also as a demonstration.

A member of the Civic League's Advisory Committee writes:

"The day nursery is for us just the opening point of contact with the colored women, who had the idea for a long time of having such an institution. They are primarily responsible for the nursery and its upkeep, while the Advisory Board is responsible for the more general social work. The committee of white women meets first separately, and then with the committee of colored women, and our general work has been without friction. . . . We have felt that there should be a guiding hand with them, and I think the colored women realize that we are very deeply interested in the welfare of their race."

The white committee raises $1,100 annually for the work. Among the activities promoted are a class of forty-one organized "for the study and practice of social service"; a playground; an athletic league; and work for better health conditions among colored people, done in coöperation with the medical faculty of Johns Hopkins. The Committee also acts, by request, in an advisory capacity to the Home for Friendless Colored Children, and has been before the State legislature to secure suitable appropriations for it.

The response of the colored women to the club women is noteworthy. The colored teachers are active in the school-lunch work. Fifteen volunteer colored workers teach the classes in industries. An independent colored club in another part of the city is developing similar work and coöperates with the Advisory Committee.

Club Work in Many States.

The briefest summary of Southern club work for Negroes is impressive. Even though in some states little is yet done, the trend is unmistakable. Clean-up coöperation spreads everywhere. In many cities Baby Week includes days for colored folk. In Florida and Mississippi fine health work is being done. The president of the Mississippi Federation writes:

"The Federated Club women of Mississippi are organizing the Negro women in Civic Clubs and are passing on their literature and helps to them. They are of the greatest help in the City Beautiful campaigns. . . . Frequently the club women go to the Negro schools and give health talks. The Negro is helping us, through the Civic Clubs, to fight tuberculosis, typhoid, etc. We find in every community an intelligent Negro woman to act as a leader for her people. One club, in its paper, gives space to the activities of its colored Civic League. We have found wherever we have a Negro club there is uplift and a reaching out for more knowledge in sanitation and health."

This State Federation conducts yearly a State-wide "cleanest town" contest in coöperation with the State Board of Health, and the women make special mention of the help given by the colored clubs. The extension of this coöperative health work to the rural districts is planned by this vigorous Federation for the immediate future.

In Arkansas the State president reports the club women active in the organization and promotion of colored clubs. Coöperation in sanitation is general, and health conditions among colored people are improving. The State Federation supports a colored farm demonstrator and a colored woman to organize canning clubs. These two have general supervision in ten "black" counties, the local white club women finding in each county a colored woman to coöperate with these supervisors. The leading women of the Federation speak to colored audiences, and as an organization they are helping the Negroes of Arkansas to better health and living conditions.

The State president of Georgia reported at the last biennial that the moonlight schools, encouraged by the club women, hoped to eradicate illiteracy among both races by 1920. Baby Week is commonly observed for both races. This Federation maintains an organizer to form Junior Civic Leagues in the public schools. She goes to schools of both races, and over 2,000 colored children were enrolled at the last biennial. The children's pledge covers clean speech, loyalty to country, personal and neighborhood cleanliness, kindness, and respect for the rights of others. Instruction in sanitation and hygiene is given.

In Virginia the Civics and Health Departments of the clubs are giving much attention to health and civic improvement work among colored people. They are also stressing the need for a medical inspection of schools to include those for colored children. Here, as in all the states, it grows more common to include the colored people in the prizes offered for the best gardens and back yards. The probation work in Virginia is not, so far as I can learn, connected with the clubs; but club women are members of the probation associations in various towns; and the State Board of Charities and Correction reports coöperative work in a number of cities where colored volunteer probation officers look after delinquent colored children. Individual white club women, too, have contributed generously to the reformatory for colored girls enterprised by the colored women's State Association and jointly supported by them and by the State. The Board of Trust of this institution is composed of men and women of both races, these club women among them.

The Federation of the District of Columbia promotes health work for both races, a colored doctor being asked to serve with the Baby Week campaign committee.

Florida is active in health work for colored people. In Jacksonville they have secured two public colored nurses for them, and also two district nurses. Prizes for improvement, home gardens, etc., are given by several clubs; Baby Week is widely observed for both races; and an effort is being made to open in Jacksonville, with State Federation backing, a domestic science school for colored women.

The broadening interest of the Alabama club women began in an investigation made some years ago by the then president of the State Federation into the criminal statistics of the State. This investigation was undertaken at the request of a State officer, and was a revelation to her in regard to Negro criminality. She had never been especially interested in colored people before, she said, except in those individuals known to her; but she saw, from these records, that something was radically wrong in Negro life, and set herself to find out what it was. She first investigated the schools, which, she felt, explained much; and from them she was led, step by step, into a further study of colored life. Her outspoken sympathy, her understanding, and her service have had, and are still having, wide results.

Some Work of Local Clubs.

A few typical instances of work done by local clubs must suffice.

Last year the Atlanta club women conducted a cooking school for colored women and girls which had an attendance of 800. They announced it as intended primarily for colored home-makers, and not for the purpose of furnishing cooks for white homes.

In Augusta the Social Service Department of the city Federation secured the improvement of the county reformatory, occupied almost entirely by colored children, and has taken up the cause of the youthful delinquent regardless of race. This club is working for municipal playgrounds for both races; and in clean-up and temperance campaigns, as well as in welfare work after the great fire of 1916, they have shown a broad grasp of the underlying needs common to all classes and races.

Louisville clubs maintain penny lunches at five white schools and one colored school.

The club women of Birmingham eight years ago investigated the worst colored slum of the city, and so roused the people in regard to conditions, and the consequent terrible human waste, that a $60,000 industrial school was erected there, which has, according to the city superintendent of schools, transformed the entire neighborhood. The club women are in touch with the head of this school, who serves as a medium of communication between the best people of both races. The club women arrange for talks in the school by doctors and nurses on the care of children, sanitation, etc.

In Jackson, Miss., coöperation has spread from clean-up campaigns into Baby Week, prize garden contests, etc. The colored Civic League, led, according to the testimony of white club women, by a colored woman of exceptionally fine type, coöperates with the white club in all matters of health and civic betterment. The white club employs a white visiting nurse, who serves the homes of both races. When a cyclone destroyed a Negro section of the city this nurse was established in a tent among the stricken people, and gave her entire time to them until their suffering was remedied.

In Memphis prominent club women are on the Advisory board of a colored Industrial Settlement Home enterprised by a big-hearted colored woman for the poor of her people. To assist in raising the funds needed they arranged a concert by the Fisk Jubilee singers at a colored auditorium, advertised for white patronage, and announced their own intention of being present. A large audience of both races resulted, as well as wide publicity for the excellent work of the settlement.

Work of Colored Club Women.

The above instances are sufficient to indicate the importance of organized white women as a factor in racial adjustment; but what of organized colored women, the other factor necessary for success?

Over 50,000 of them are enrolled in their National Association. They have organizations in thirty states, including all those of the South; and at one of their biennials the writer heard two addresses which for clearness, restrained and forceful speech, and a moral passion rising to heights of genuine eloquence, would have done credit to speakers of any race. The Association publishes a small monthly magazine, edited from Tuskegee by Mrs. Booker T. Washington. It shows these women taking their part in women's world-wide fight against vice, disease, and injustice; struggling for better health conditions, for home and school improvement, care of children, and all the fundamental interests of women, to whatever race they may belong.

These clubs maintain homes for orphans, old folks, outcast women, working girls; and friendly shelters, day nurseries, and missions. The Teachers' Leagues maintain mothers' clubs, and classes in sewing and domestic science. Work is done for colored hospitals. In Virginia and Missouri the State Associations have secured reform schools for colored girls. In Virginia the organization bought the farm for the school, paying $5,000 cash, and pays about one-third of the yearly expense. The State, with generous assistance from individual white club women, erected the buildings, and pays two-thirds of the running expenses.

The Kentucky State Association has raised in two years $3,000 for improving schoolhouses and helping poor children. South Carolina clubs have in the same time given $1,100 for the same purposes, and over $3,000 for civic and uplift work.

The National Association has a Department of Rural work, with headquarters at Frankfort, Ky. The chairman has enrolled in her own State, in the last two years, 6,000 women in 670 rural clubs and 362 school leagues. These country women have in that time raised $2,000 for their club work. Yet only 15 of these 670 clubs have joined the national organization.

An Opportunity.

This last fact reveals one of the greatest opportunities of our white clubs for a social service to which our whole nation would be indebted—the opportunity to help these struggling, scattered, handicapped women in their efforts to lift the standards of their people's homes.

Few of the colored clubs can afford affiliation with their national or state organizations. Many of them, doubtless, do not yet see the need for wider association; they simply try to minister, in a more or less haphazard fashion, to local needs for which their slender resources are pitifully inadequate. But undoubtedly delegates' expenses and dues to the larger associations are beyond the means of most of them, and so they not only miss the direction and inspiration of contact with their best women, but, missing it, work blindly, their spirit of service often misdirected to ineffectual ends. When their race so suffers for service, this waste is genuinely tragic.

For most of these mothers, and the children in their homes, our white women are the only chance for better things. This is also true in the North, where, especially since the exodus, white women have now a chance for this Christian and patriotic service. But we of the South have the right of leadership in this matter, and the signs that it will be exercised are not wanting. The women of Arkansas, of Mississippi, of Baltimore, the women of the various home mission bodies, of the W.C.T.U., and the Y.W.C.A, and of local clubs and societies in every state, are opening doors of service to these isolated unprivileged women, and guiding them in ways they need to learn.

In a Tennessee town, where one of the officers of the National Association spoke, a number of the white teachers went to hear her to learn what the colored women were doing, that they might help them.

A Texas judge said recently to the writer that one of the greatest needs in race adjustment was for white teachers to go to colored teachers' meetings and help to strengthen their interest in the moral, hygienic, and industrial development of their pupils, both in school and in home life. The Southern Teachers' Association, a few years ago, went on record as believing in the necessity for Southern white teachers in colored normal schools. For fifty years the Southern Methodist Church, at its General Conferences, has officially received fraternal delegates from colored Methodism, and has appointed its delegates to visit them in return. Colored men and women are introduced and speak at many of the official gatherings of Southern Presbyterian and Southern Methodist missionary women, and white women of the churches and of the clubs speak in colored women's meetings when asked.

Would it not be well for the club organizations to recognize officially the need for these points of communication between the women of the two races? At a meeting of the Arkansas Federation seats were reserved in a gallery for colored club women, who not only came and were helped, but whose interested stimulated the white women to helpful coöperation in many places. The policy of the Baltimore Civic League toward the Coöperative Civic League might be equally useful in other places, and in the state organizations also.

Coöperation in War Times.

The war is accelerating the trend toward coöperation. The need for food conservation, for the multiplied services of women, is widening the human platform on which the races can meet. The war work of the president of the last National

Biennial, one of the most distinguished women of the South, is typical of what thousands of women are doing on a smaller scale. In response to a call from the State of Texas she gave her entire time, for many weeks, to a State-wide campaign for food production and conservation, speaking several times a day to large audiences of white and colored people. She told the writer that in every place she impressed upon the women who took charge of the local work the necessity for carrying it on, in all its phases, among both races.

The Red Cross is being organized among the colored people throughout the South, the leaders in the work being the white club women. In Atlanta, where preparations for a great base hospital go forward, the club women set a day for a linen shower for it; and, under the guidance of the president of the State Federation, the colored women were asked to observe the day, which they did, taking a generous part in the common service.

This has been the theory of the women in every state, in almost every county; and though frequently but imperfectly carried out, the main effort being to enlist and educate white women, yet the fact remains that the Great War is bringing to all our women what before was given to only a few—a consciousness of spheres of action and responsibility in which the bond of a common humanity takes precedence of the bond of race.

Not that race consciousness is weakened; that would mean disaster to white and to black. What the war is bringing us is a realization of the inseparableness of the interests of the two races in economic life and in all that makes for the moral and physical health of our communities. This understanding, not by the few, but by the masses, is a necessary part of the process by which the mists of prejudice will be lifted and the true lines of racial demarcation will stand clear and immovable in the light of conscience and common sense.

A Question of Womanhood.

The facts herein given, the trend of the movements recorded, tend toward one end: the recognition of womanhood as a thing deeper even than race, a thing for all women to protect. The full recognition of this truth will do more to settle "the race question" than all other things combined, for all other things needed will come out of it—full racial justice, true racial separateness, full human coöperation and respect. The status of the Negro woman and the Negro home in the minds of the privileged white women will determine the status of the race. Among all races, in all times, it has been the lot of the women to bear the unbearable things. As they have won respect and protection the race has climbed toward freedom and self-control. There is no way to raise the Negroes except by this world-old process, and no one can set it in motion as can our Southern white women.

It is time for us to take stock of our responsibilities. Not long ago the writer heard a trivial, yet most serious, aspect of the matter put by a Southern Methodist presiding elder.

"You white women," he said, "are the main obstacle to Negro morality. You teach us men, and your children—your sons—that morality in a Negro woman is beneath a white person's notice."

"What do you mean?" a hearer demanded indignantly.

"This: Social distinctions, which we all know are established forever, like the mountains—know it so well that it is a waste of breath ever to say it—are forever being confused in your thoughts with distinctions in justice and in law. This class of distinctions must be abolished, for the sake of our own civilization, if for nothing else. For instance: You refuse to give a Negro wife her legal title of 'Mrs.' It's not a social matter, as so many think; it's a legal right, defining a legal status fundamentally necessary to civilization. But you Christian women refuse it to women sufficiently handicapped, heaven knows, without this added difficulty. I'm not talking about your cooks; in the kitchen a woman of no race would expect the use of her legal title; but you refuse it to the race. You make no distinction between the Christian wife and the mother of half-a-dozen haphazard mulattoes; they're all 'Sally' to you. You say, in effect, that morality in a Negro doesn't count. You teach your sons that from babyhood. The Negro women pay for it; but by God's law your sons pay, too—pay a debt more yours than theirs. And the daughters they marry pay, too."

A few years ago Dr. John R. Mott called in Atlanta a Christian Student Conference for colored students. Five hundred of them came, from eighteen states. Seventy white people, men and women, mostly Southern, were also present—bishops, missionary secretaries, Y.M. and Y.W.C.A. folk, college presidents, teachers, and people interested in Christian work. Among the addresses was one by A.M. Trawick, a Southern man and a secretary of the International Y.M.C.A., on the rights of the Negro woman and the Negro home. In an informal after-meeting for women a colored woman spoke. She was known to some of the white women present for her service to her people, and especially for her efforts to shield the girls of her race. She confessed her long hatred of white men; and, beyond them, her hate and bitterness toward white women for their indifference toward a matter so tragically vital to the welfare and honor of both races. Her sense of wrong, her anguish and shame, her fierce contempt for white religion scorched her white hearers like flame.

"And to-day," she said, controlling with great effort her shaken voice, "there was a miracle! A white man—*a white man!*—stood up, not just before Negroes, but before white people, *before white women*, and said that colored women should have protection and respect. It didn't seem possible. That I should have lived to ———" Tears choked her. She stood shaking with emotion, tears pouring down her face, her drenched eyes fixed on the little group of Southern white women, from whom she apparently asked nothing, and expected less.

Is it not time for the increasing body of our women who care for the womanhood of all races to make their attitude known? To stand openly, and together, for the protection of these women and their homes?

"The Forward Look."

One of the first steps necessary in this protection is to bury the Old Black Mammy. She may still be loved and honored. Her being dead is no bar to affection; but it certainly should bar a daily association with her corpse which threatens the corruption of sentiment into sentimentality. Wrenched from a past environment to which alone she belonged, and set up, fetish-like, in a life in which she can have no rightful place, she expresses an attitude of the white mind which is at once ludicrous, tragic, and fraught with future peril.

We must face the future, not the past. Yet scores of thousands of Southern folk, seriously and kindly considering the Negro problem, will insist upon the South's friendliness to the Negroes, and offer as proof, not efforts being made to meet their present needs, but the touching and universal cult of the Old Black Mammy!

She deserves a funeral, bless her; and she certainly needs one—a competent, permanent funeral that will not have to be done over again every few days. Her removal will clear the atmosphere and enable us to see the old soul's granddaughters, to whom we must in justice pay something of the debt we so freely acknowledge to her. We must lay aside the mental attitude of the past—the attitude of a people toward a slave race—and face the present with a forward look. To accomplish this is the task of women, and by all the tokens they are accepting it as theirs. They have begun in this territory, as here shown, that spiritual pioneering which is their chief, though by no means their only, public function. And in exploring these untried paths in a changed world they are once again discovering that immemorial country in which, through all the ages, human souls have been working out, in finer ideals of righteousness and of service, a better justice for the Race of Man.

Index

The Publications of the Southern Texts Society

Books published by the University of Georgia Press

A DuBose Heyward Reader
Edited and with an Introduction by James M. Hutchisson

To Find My Own Peace: Grace King in Her Journals, 1886–1910
Edited by Melissa Walker Heidari

*The Correspondence of Sarah Morgan and Francis
Warrington Dawson, with Selected Editorials Written by
Sarah Morgan for the Charleston News and Courier*
Edited by Giselle Roberts

*Shared Histories: Transatlantic Letters between Virginia Dickinson
Reynolds and Her Daughter, Virginia Potter, 1929–1966*
Edited by Angela Potter

Princes of Cotton: Four Diaries of Young Men in the South, 1848–1860
Edited by Stephen Berry

Mary Telfair to Mary Few: Selected Letters, 1802–1844
Edited by Betty Wood

In Black and White: An Interpretation of the South
Lily Hardy Hammond, edited by Elna C. Green